Contributors to *The Bar on Trial*

Robert Hazell (editor) was called to the Bar in 1973, but has now left practice in order to work in the public sector. He is a magistrate and the author of *Conspiracy and Civil Liberties* (1974).

Jonathan Caplan has a general common law practice. He is joint author of *The Confait Confessions* (1977), and contributed to Ivan Illich's *The Disabling Professions*, as well as writing occasional articles for *The Times*, the *Sunday Times* and the *Observer*.

Helena Kennedy has a predominantly criminal practice. An executive member of the Haldane Society, she is an occasional contributor to the *Morning Star*.

Alex Layton read law at Oxford and then in Munich, and now practises in general common law.

James Munby was a Harmsworth Scholar at the Middle Temple, and has been at the Chancery Bar since 1971.

William Rees qualified as a barrister in 1973; he is now a university law lecturer, and a regular contributor to law journals.

Richard Tyson worked in an advertising agency before joining the common law Bar. He is now a member of the Young Barristers' Committee and of the Bar's Sub-Committee on Social Welfare Law.

Nicholas Warren is a Chancery barrister. Also a Harmsworth Scholar, he is the joint author of *Settlements, Wills and Capital Transfer Tax* (1978).

Also by Robert Hazell
CONSPIRACY AND CIVIL LIBERTIES

THE BAR ON TRIAL

Edited by Robert Hazell

QUARTET BOOKS
LONDON MELBOURNE NEW YORK

First published by Quartet Books Limited 1978
A member of the Namara Group
27 Goodge Street, London W1P 1FD

Preface and Chapters 1, 4, 5, 8, copyright © 1978 by Robert Hazell
All other chapters copyright by the individual authors, 1978

ISBN Hardcover 0 7043 2106 8
      Paperback 0 7043 3217 5

Printed in Great Britain by offset lithography by
Billing & Sons Ltd, Guildford, London and Worcester

Distribution in the USA by
Horizon Press, 156 Fifth Avenue,
New York, NY10010

CONTENTS

PREFACE	9
ACKNOWLEDGEMENTS	15
1. INTRODUCTION TO THE BAR *Robert Hazell*	17
Barristers and solicitors: the divided profession	17
The steps in a barrister's career	20
(1) Admission to an Inn of Court	20
(2) Pupillage and a seat in chambers	20
(3) Silk	23
(4) The Bench	24
The organization of a set of chambers	26
A cloistered profession	28
The government of the Bar	32
Recruitment and accommodation	35
2. THE INNS OF COURT *Nicholas Warren*	38
The importance of the Inns	38
The history of the Inns	39
Serjeants' Inn	42
The legal relationship between the Inns and their members	44
The Inns and their students	47
(1) Admission fees	48
(2) Dining	49
The Inns' finances	52
The Inns as landlords	56
Democracy in the Inns	59
The future of the Inns	65

3. LEGAL EDUCATION *Alex Layton, Richard Tyson and William Rees* 68
    The Bar's attitude to legal education 68
    The Ormrod Report 69
    The Bar exams examined 70
    The Council of Legal Education 71
    Practical Exercises 72
    The social and educational background of Bar students 73
    Overseas students 74
    Finance 75
    The role of the universities 76
    The content of university law courses 78
    Conclusions 79

4. PUPILLAGE *Robert Hazell* 82
    Finding pupillage 82
    The quality of the training 87
    Training outside the Bar 88
    The cost of being a pupil 90
    Finding a tenancy 95

5. CLERKS AND FEES *Robert Hazell* 99
    What do barristers earn? 99
    The role of the clerk 104
    Useful functions of the clerk 106
    Other functions performed by the clerk 108
    The determination of fees 109
    Clerk's fees 114
    Chambers efficiency 116
    Late payment of fees 118
    Returns 119
    Are clerks necessary? 122
    Partnerships 123

6. THE CRIMINAL BAR *Jonathan Caplan* 130
    The cost of criminal legal aid 131
    The cab-rank rule 133
    Prosecuting counsel 134
    The polarization of the criminal Bar 136
    The conduct of the defence 138
    Plea bargaining 141

The attitude of detachment	142
Standing up to the judge	143
Miscarriages of justice	145
Conclusions	146

7. WOMEN AT THE BAR *Helena Kennedy* — 148
- The struggle for admission — 148
- The position of women at the Bar today — 148
- Barriers to entry — 150
- The kind of work women do — 153
- The effect of prejudice on the morale of women barristers — 156
- The effect of prejudice on the law — 157
- The Bar Council's Special Committee — 158
- Dress — 159
- Conclusions — 160

8. INDEPENDENCE AND FUSION *Robert Hazell* — 163
- The Bar's growing dependence on public funds — 163
- The independence of the Bar — 167
- The spectre of fusion — 169
- Fusion dissected — 171
  - (1) Audience rights — 171
  - (2) Direct briefing — 172
  - (3) Partnership between barristers and solicitors — 173
  - (4) General practitioners and specialists — 174
- Fusion defused — 175

9. A LOOK INTO THE FUTURE *James Munby* — 179
- The effect of law reform — 179
- Changes in the legal system — 183
- The effect of the economy — 184
- The shift from civil to criminal work — 185
- The decentralization of the English legal system — 187
- The shape of things to come — 189

NOTES — 193

BIBLIOGRAPHY — 213

INDEX — 217

THE BAR ON TRIAL

PREFACE

This book is written by eight young barristers who are deeply concerned about the future of the English Bar. It is the first to break what has been a notable silence about the Bar's activities. The restrictive practices of the Bar have been well documented by academic writers (notably Professor Michael Zander and Professors Brian Abel-Smith and Robert Stevens), but from inside the profession critical comment has been confined to a couple of little-known memoirs. * The difference about this book is that it is the first systematic study criticizing the Bar, written by members of the Bar. Its purpose is to try to change the Bar, to make it more useful to society, and to make it more satisfying for barristers to work in.

The book contains a detailed account of the education and training of barristers in England, of their business and professional organization, and of the quality of service they provide to the public. It may be seen by some as an attack on the Bar and everything it stands for. This would however be a misunderstanding of our purpose; for the book is designed not to pay homage to the Bar's good qualities, but to try to do something about its bad ones. This does not mean that we fail to recognize the good qualities; the undoubted integrity of English barristers, their sense of dedication to their clients and their generally high level of professional competence have all contributed enormously to the quality of justice administered in the English courts. We would not seek to

* C. P. Harvey: *The Advocate's Devil* (1958), and J. Parris: *Under My Wig* (1961)

belittle any of these achievements; but we feel that they are sufficiently well known not to require any further emphasis from us.

The Bar has never lacked advocates to praise its virtues; what has been far less common is any mention of its shortcomings, particularly from barristers themselves. Our purpose is to redress this balance; in so doing we may appear negative, but our purpose is positive. We have tried throughout to avoid making purely negative criticisms, for we fully accept the responsibility which lies on the critic to suggest alternatives; and wherever we have criticized existing arrangements we have taken care to explain how we think they should be reformed.

Reform is a matter of urgent necessity. The Bar is a deeply conservative profession, which has always been reluctant to espouse any kind of change. This resistance to change has now reached the point where we feel that it seriously threatens the profession's future. It will of course survive in some form, but whether it will be of any use or significance in our society depends upon its ability to adapt. The present organization of the Bar prevents barristers from providing the public with the efficient and sympathetic service they are entitled to expect. As a result it is slowly, graciously but perceptibly losing its former influence and power.

Our concern at this state of affairs arises partly from reasons of self-interest; we want our profession not only to survive but to flourish. More important however is our conviction that the Bar can offer so much that is of value, but that under present arrangements it is prevented from doing so. This is the spirit which led us to write this book, which is not one of hostility to the Bar, but of genuine concern that unless some of the reforms we advocate are adopted it will continue inexorably to decline.

When we started work on the book early in 1974, although reform of the Bar was our grand design, the best we could realistically hope for was to start a debate on the subject. At that time there was very little exposure given in the media to the activities of lawyers, and in the public mind the old chestnut lived on that because English law was the best in the world the English legal system must be too. Within the legal profession the mood was still one of complacency, and our intention was to try to shake the Bar out of its inertia and to call it to account before the public, by challenging some of its time-honoured restrictions and monopolies, and by stating the case for a public inquiry to investigate whether these practices were truly in the public interest.

Since then there has been a revolution in attitudes. It is difficult to put one's finger on any single cause, but the parliamentary campaign by Jack Ashley M.P. and Christopher Price M.P. for an investigation into the legal profession could never have succeeded without the support of the Press and the research work of people like Michael Zander. Not only did the Press generally welcome the establishment of the Royal Commission into the legal profession announced by the Prime Minister in February 1976, but newspapers like the *Sunday Times* can justly claim credit for their share in having brought it about, by publicizing certain flagrant injustices (such as the thalidomide case), and by drawing attention to the high cost of going to law and the high fees earned by lawyers – fees which nowadays fall more and more to be paid by the state.

With the establishment of the Royal Commission the complacency of the legal profession has been shattered. No longer can the old *non sequitur* that English law is wonderful, therefore so are our lawyers, be propounded with the same confidence that the public will be taken in; the profession is now exposed to a much more searching kind of scrutiny than any experienced before, and for the first time it has been forced to reconsider habits and assumptions which have been taken for granted by lawyers for generations. Even the Senate of the Inns of Court and the Bar, under the leadership of Peter Webster Q.C. (a very different Chairman from his predecessor, Sir Peter Rawlinson) announced that it intended to embark on a radical re-appraisal of every aspect of the Bar's activities. Alas! Peter Webster's good intentions were soon swept aside by his colleagues, for the Senate's evidence consists in the main of a reiteration of the defiant defences of the *status quo* so often made by the Bar Council in the past. Separation of the profession into barristers and solicitors is declared to be in the best interests of the public; any extension of audience rights to solicitors in the higher courts would (the Senate asserts) serve to limit, not widen, the choice of advocate available to the client; partnerships of barristers, or between barristers and solicitors, are held to be undesirable; barristers' clerks should continue to function much as before; and the two-tier structure of Q.C.s and junior barristers should be retained.

These propositions are examined in detail in the chapters which follow. The book is not, however, a critique of the Senate's evidence; it was conceived in 1973, long before the Royal Commission (or indeed the Senate) came into existence. Most of it was written in 1975 and the rest in 1976. This long gestation period has not been without its difficulties, as chapter after chapter has required revision in the light of some new development or fresh piece of information; but one good result has been that the book is now far more informative and up-to-date than it would have been if published (as originally intended) three years ago. Wherever possible it has been updated to reflect the state of affairs prevailing in June 1977, and in a few places it has been further updated to March 1978.

Nor has the long delay made the book any less timely. Apart from the immediate interest generated by the Royal Commission there are a number of other factors which make a study of the Bar particularly topical at the present time. In the first place, it appears at a time when the monopoly of wisdom claimed by the professions in their chosen fields is being called increasingly into question. Not only has the Government as paymaster begun to take a much keener interest in professional restrictive practices; but there is a growing reluctance across a wide range of professional responsibilities (education, for example, or medicine) to accept that the professions know what is best for the public they claim to serve. A greater degree of public control and accountability are necessary, but as yet no one has devised a satisfactory machinery for achieving this; complete state control is clearly undesirable, but so also is complete *laissez-faire*.

The second respect in which this book is timely is that it appears in an age of rapidly diminishing respect for the law and for our legal system. Ordinary people increasingly express their alienation from the law and the courts by contempt and defiance of judges, lawyers and the law's institutions. Barristers invariably put the blame for this state of affairs on the public; but the fact that people are so alienated suggests that at least part of **the blame** must lie with the lawyers. In order to restore respect **for our** law we need lawyers who speak the idiom of the people, and who can command their respect because they command their understanding. Yet barristers in particular always give the impression of trying to be as different as possible from ordinary people; in their dress, their habits of speech and their self-imposed isolation they like to inhabit another world. This book represents an attempt to draw the legal world and the real world closer together, by revealing to the layman some of the mysteries of the barrister's calling, but also by seeking to persuade barristers to abandon those mysteries which no longer have any justification.

In the face of the Royal Commission the leaders of the Bar are anxious that the profession should close ranks in order to present a united front displaying the sign *No Change*. It will be a great pity if the Senate succeeds in holding this line, because the Commission represents the first real opportunity to all those barristers who are concerned about the inefficiencies and injustices of the Bar to do something about it. If this book has a single common theme it is to expose and destroy inefficiency and unfairness; they go directly against the interests of our clients, and in the long run they must be contrary to the self-interest of the Bar. The number of barristers who are beginning to realize this and to worry about it is greater than one might suppose. Hitherto they have been fearful of speaking out, and had little incentive to do so because it was so unlikely that anything could ever be done.

Now there is a real possibility that a great deal can be done; but even the Royal Commission can only sketch in the broad outlines of reform. It cannot legislate in every detail, and a very substantial amount will still remain to be done by the profession itself. Once the Royal Commission has started the process of reform there will be a great need to keep up the momentum, and to ensure that the Bar plays its part in implementing not only the letter but also the spirit of the Commission's proposals. If this book, having indicated the lines along which we think the profession should be reformed, inspires those barristers who have hitherto remained silent to join in the struggle to achieve those reforms, then it will have fulfilled its purpose.

A word about the contributors, and about the way this book has been written. It does not contain a homogeneous blueprint for reform; we divided up the subject-matter and then worked on our own chapters independently. It follows that no participant should be presumed to agree with all of the views expressed by his colleagues; each contributor is responsible only for the contents of his or her own chapter.

Most of us have been at the Bar for about five years; one is still in pupillage, two have just started taking pupils. We include representatives from the Chancery Bar, the criminal Bar, and from practice in general common law. Two of us have left the Bar; one is a university lecturer, the other is myself. Lest my motives for doing so be misunderstood, it should perhaps be said that my reasons for leaving had nothing to do with this book, nor with any lack of openings had I wished to remain, but consisted simply of a desire to work more directly in the field of social policy. Nothing in this book should of course be taken to reflect the views of my present employers; and indeed most of the chapters which I contributed were written while still at the Bar.

18 Roden Street
London N7

Robert Hazell
March 1978

ACKNOWLEDGEMENTS

So many people have helped us in providing information and in reading through different chapters of this book that it is impossible adequately to thank them all. From the organizations which have given us assistance we would like to acknowledge the help of Miss Jean Austin, Sir Roualeyn Cumming-Bruce, Captain J. B. Morison and Sir Eric Sachs of the Middle Temple; Commander Flynn of the Inner Temple; and Philip Beddingham, Mrs Heywood and Mr C. R. G. Hughes of Gray's Inn. At the Bar Council we received assistance from Sir William Boulton and Michael Astbury; at the Council of Legal Education from Mr C. A. Morrison and Mrs Littledale; at the College of Law from Mr I. G. Carvell; and in the Lord Chancellor's Office from Mr Cyril Glasser and Mr D. A. Bleach.

Special thanks are due to Oliver Thorold and Jan Nellen who have written valuable papers on the silk system and on the Bar Council and the Senate, copies of which can be obtained from the Editor.

Among our colleagues at the Bar we are grateful for advice and assistance from John Bradburn (Chancery Bar Association), Michael Burton, Barbara Calvert Q.C., Mary Colton, Edward Cazalet, Richard Harvey, Hubert Monroe Q.C., Gabriel Mosonyi, Patricia Phelan, Bruce Reynolds, Gilbert Rodway (Family Law Bar Association), Audrey Sander and Tim Stevenson. Needless to say none of them should be held responsible for the ideas in this book (and indeed many would disagree with much of what we have said).

Others who have helped us in ways both great and small include Jenny Ashe, Cyril Batchelor of the Barristers' Clerks' Association,

Alan Bean, Marcel Berlins, William Cornish, Julian Disney (Law Reform Commission of New South Wales), Adrian Gale, Giles Gordon, Simon Hillyard (Law Society), Jacqueline Hoogendyk, Christine Jackson, Bo Jones, Pierre Lavirotte, Janet Lewis-Jones, William Miller, David Norgrove, Martin Partington, Peter Reeves, Alison Richards, Tom Sargant, Anne Winyard and Michael Zander. And last but by no means least the Editor would like to pay special tribute to the patience and understanding of his family and friends, who have had to tolerate his preoccupation with this book for the best part of four years.

1 INTRODUCTION TO THE BAR

BARRISTERS AND SOLICITORS: THE DIVIDED PROFESSION

Many members of the public have no very clear idea of what barristers do. They may have a vague idea that they are the figures who appear in wigs and gowns to argue cases in court; but very few know what tasks barristers perform outside the courtroom, or by what process they come to be there. It is the purpose of this chapter to explain the different functions performed by barristers in the legal system, to describe the steps in a barrister's career, and to introduce the reader to the various institutions developed by the Bar to govern its branch of the profession, and to represent the profession to the outside world.

Unlike most countries in the world, and indeed unlike many of the Commonwealth countries which have inherited our legal system, England still has a divided legal profession: a lawyer has to decide whether to practise as a barrister or a solicitor – he cannot do both. In days gone by there were many more divisions, with lawyers called serjeants and scriveners, attorneys and solicitors, pleaders and conveyancers. The only division we are concerned with is that which still exists between those lawyers (in the old days attorneys, now only solicitors) who handle the preparatory work involved in bringing a lawsuit, and counsel (barristers, and formerly serjeants) who argue the case in court. Although performing different functions, both branches of the profession historically have been based on the Inns of Court, and indeed originally both attorneys and barristers could be members of the Inns.

A corporate life was almost from the beginning one of the essential characteristics of the legal profession in England. The

Inns of Court trace their origins back to the fourteenth century. By the middle of the eighteenth century the vast majority of their members were barristers, but a few may still have been solicitors or attorneys until 1794, when an order was finally made excluding the latter from membership.[1] Even after that date many solicitors continued to practise from within the precincts of the Inns of Court; and indeed a few firms of solicitors still have their offices in the Temple, and rather more in Lincoln's Inn and Gray's Inn, to this day.

Although in earlier times it had seemed not improbable that these two branches of the legal profession would ultimately amalgamate,[2] and although spasmodic efforts have been made in the last 100 years to bring about their fusion,[3] the separate preserves of barristers and solicitors are today kept rigidly apart. The division of the legal profession depends basically on two conventions; first, that solicitors do not have a right of audience in the superior courts, and second, that barristers do not have a right of direct access to the lay client. The result is that solicitors are general practitioners to whom the lay client goes in the first instance; barristers are specialists, primarily in advocacy and secondarily often in some particular branch of the law, whose services must be enlisted by solicitors if the matter involves litigation in the superior courts, and whose aid may be enlisted whenever special advice is needed.

This does not mean either that barristers have a monopoly of advocacy or that there is not specialization among solicitors. On the contrary solicitors can and frequently do appear as advocates in the county courts and the magistrates' courts, where the overwhelming bulk of civil and criminal work is undertaken. As for specialization, this is to be found in many of the firms of solicitors which practise in partnership – particularly the larger firms and those in London. Almost all firms of solicitors may be said to specialize in a minimum of two subjects, conveyancing and probate; together these bring in 70% of their total incomes. The Bar has no single source of income which is anything like as lucrative as the solicitors' monopoly of conveyancing, and is a much smaller profession altogether. In 1976 there were approximately 28,000 solicitors in practice, and only 4000 practising barristers.

The barrister is thus a specialist lawyer who has no direct contact with the public; he can only be instructed to act for a client by a solicitor – and even if a client knows of a barrister and wants to employ his services he must approach him through a solicitor. Nor is the solicitor a one-way channel of communication; if the barrister wants further information from the client he cannot contact the client direct, but must address his questions (and receive the answers) through the medium of the solicitor.

It was not always thus. Although by the nineteenth century it had become customary for lay clients not to instruct counsel direct, Lord Brougham (a former Lord Chancellor) was still able to tell the House of Lords in 1852 that 'every barrister had the power of appearing in any court in the Kingdom instructed by a client, without any intervention whatever of an attorney or solicitor'.[4] However in 1888 the Bar Committee (the forerunner of the Bar Council – the barristers' trade union) laid down that at least when a contentious matter was involved a barrister could not see a lay client without the intervention of a solicitor; and in the next 20 years this restriction was extended to cover non-contentious matters as well. Now a barrister is never instructed except through a solicitor[5]; and in 1949 a barrister who appeared in the High Court without instructions from a solicitor was disbarred.[6]

In return for this protection of their interests by the Bar (and for the self-denying ordinance whereby barristers refrain from exercising their statutory right to do conveyancing) the solicitors' branch of the profession has never seriously challenged the Bar's exclusive right of audience in the Crown Court, the High Court, and in the appellate courts above. In these courts if a client wants to be represented he must instruct a barrister (he can of course appear in person – a privilege exercised by relatively few litigants). It was not originally the law of the land that this was so; it was simply the custom of the judges, all of them ex-barristers, that they would hear no one other than practising members of the Bar.

The official rationale of this rule is that the efficiency of court proceedings depends on the employment of trained advocates, and also on the mutual trust between judges and barristers which stems from the fact that they share the same professional training and environment. Barristers in industry, however great their experience at the Bar may have been, are not allowed to appear in court as advocates representing their firms; nor can barristers working for local authorities or government departments. Separate counsel must always be instructed from among the practising Bar.

THE STEPS IN A BARRISTER'S CAREER:

(1) *Admission to an Inn of Court*

Just as barristers have a monopoly of audience in the higher courts, the Inns of Court have from the beginning enjoyed the sole right to admit, train and in general control the professional life of barristers.[7] The constitution of the Inns has been described by Sir Frederick Pollock as 'a survival of medieval republican oligarchy, the purest, I should think, to be found in Europe'.[8] They are governed by the benchers, who are not elected but who themselves appoint their fellows and successors. The benchers can refuse to admit a person as a student[9], or to call a student to the Bar; and they can expel any member and disbar a barrister or suspend him from practice.[10]

The powers of the benchers and the Inns have been preserved undiminished down to this day. No one can become a barrister without first being admitted to one of the four Inns of Court (on payment of an admission fee of £75). He or she must then undergo a course of training designed and supervised by the Council of Legal Education, the Inns of Court law school; and he must sit the Bar Exams which are set and marked by the Council. During this period he must also eat 36 dinners in his Inn, and when he has passed his exams and eaten the requisite number of dinners he will (on payment of a further fee of £75) be called to the Bar in the Hall of his Inn. He is then a qualified barrister, but remains a member of his Inn for life (he need pay no further subscription) and remains subject to the disciplinary powers of the Inn. If a barrister practises in London (as over two-thirds of all those in England do) he will practise from chambers which are located in one of the four Inns[11]; and when he is not doing a case out of London he will probably continue to eat every day in the Hall of his Inn. The Inns thus play an enormously important role, not simply in the professional training of a barrister, but in regulating the whole of his professional life.

(2) *Pupillage and a seat in chambers*

Once called to the Bar, the young barrister is still not fully qualified because he or she must then embark on a 12-month period of pupillage, during which he is attached as an apprentice to a practising barrister. It used to be customary to serve all one's pupillage with one pupilmaster, but nowadays it is more common, in order to gain wider experience, to do six months with one master and then six months with another, possibly in a different set of chambers. The pupil will read all his master's briefs and try his hand at writing opinions or drafting pleadings; he will look up points of law for his master and prepare notes for him to use in court. And when his master goes into court the pupil will go with him, to observe all that goes on and occasionally to assist by taking a note of the evidence.

During the first six months of his pupillage a pupil cannot take any work on his own account; after that he is free to accept briefs from solicitors if any are sent to him or (more usually) to his chambers when no one else is available to do them. In chambers which specialize in crime there is almost always a fair amount of small work in magistrates' courts, and the young barrister will quite quickly start appearing on his own in the second six months of his pupillage; but in specialist sets of chambers or common law sets which do very little crime it is unlikely that he will do any work of his own during the whole of his pupillage – he will simply work for his pupilmaster. This work is unpaid; indeed until recently it was the pupil who had to pay. When we were pupils only five years ago, the pupil had to pay his master a fee of 100 guineas for a year's pupillage, plus 10 guineas for the clerk (the office manager in a set of chambers). Nowadays almost no barristers charge pupillage fees; pupilmasters who still do justify the practice by saying that the training they give is cheap at the price. Those with a civil practice who are lucky enough to have a good pupil probably do very well out of the arrangement – they may use verbatim the pleadings and opinions he has drafted without giving him any of the fees.

After his pupillage is over – in fact if he is wise, long before it has ended – the young barrister will start looking for a tenancy. A tenant is simply someone who has been 'taken on' by a set of chambers, a fully paid-up member who has his name on the door and thus officially becomes one of the barristers practising from those chambers. The Bar's rules do not permit barristers to associate in partnership or any other business arrangement which involves sharing each other's work or sharing the profits, and in theory each barrister practises on his own behalf and for nobody else; he is completely self-employed and success or failure depends solely on his own merits and determination. In reality things are rather different and the choice of one's colleagues at the Bar is vitally important. This is because solicitors tend, particularly with small work, not to brief an individual but to send briefs to a set of chambers which they trust, leaving it to the clerk to the chambers to arrange which of his barristers will in fact receive the brief. Even when briefs are sent to a particular person he or she may have to drop out at the last moment, in which case the clerk will try to persuade the solicitors to transfer the brief to someone else in the same chambers rather than see it 'returned' to some other set. For this reason even a barrister who has established an individual reputation must have colleagues on whom he can rely to step into his shoes when he is not available.

Obtaining a tenancy in a good set of chambers is therefore three-quarters of the battle; but nowadays a young barrister will be extremely lucky to obtain a tenancy at all, because the number of those emerging from pupillage and looking for tenancies outstrips the number of available spaces by a factor of over two to one. This is a recent phenomenon which has only become really acute in the last five years; it is currently the most pressing internal problem facing the Bar, and one it has so far proved quite incapable of solving.

Assume, however, that a young barrister is lucky enough to obtain a tenancy. His professional future will depend to a great extent on the general reputation of his chambers and on the skills and energy of his clerk. He is unknown and it is the task of the clerk to make him known and to build up his practice. Obviously the clerk can only go so far, and ultimately a barrister's success will depend on his own performance, on how he handles those briefs which the clerk sends his way; but it is the clerk who obtains those briefs in the early stages, and a clerk certainly has the power at any stage to make or break a barrister's career. This need not in any way be deliberate: a clerk can drive away business simply by being inefficient.

Another very important factor is chance. The Bar abounds with stories of great men who were on the point of giving up the profession when suddenly a brief came which changed their minds; Lord Atkin was one who almost left the Bar in despair, while Lord Shawcross is said to have earned only a few pounds in his first years. Nowadays of course it is much easier to earn a living in the early years, but the element of chance is still important, and can even extend to a barrister's choice of the branch of the law in which ultimately he or she specializes. Most barristers make no deliberate choice at all (except for the broad distinction between Chancery and the common law), and if they do specialize they tend to choose their field not so much by their aptitude or interest in that field as by the offers of places in chambers as pupils and tenants which happen to be made to them (often through family connections or friends).

Many pupils have no very clear idea of what sort of work their chambers do before they start their pupillage there, and if they are subsequently offered a place in those chambers they will usually accept – it is unlikely that any second offer will be forthcoming. It thus comes about that many specialist barristers drift into their speciality more by chance than by design, but the Bar does not find anything extraordinary about this; it is all part and parcel of the haphazard arrangements for recruitment and training, and also connected with the cab-rank principle, that a barrister must accept any brief that comes his way (provided it is marked with a proper fee). Barristers are peculiarly passive in accepting the work that comes to them without seeking out work which they might find interesting; and indeed within the existing rules it is difficult to do otherwise.

(3) *Silk*

If a barrister is successful, after about 20 years he will consider applying for silk and becoming a Q.C. or Queen's Counsel (also known as a leader or simply a 'silk'). This transition is not automatic; the appointments are made once a year at Easter, and many more barristers apply for silk every year than are granted it. Currently about 30 patents are granted each year, and in 1976 there were 370 practising Q.C.s. No reasons are given for refusal of silk; some barristers may have to wait four or five years before being given silk, others are never given it, or simply give up trying.

All barristers who are not Q.C.s are called juniors (regardless of age); and the majority remain juniors for the whole of their professional careers. This does not necessarily mean they have failed; some earn more – a few much more – than the average Q.C., and many junior barristers become Circuit judges and a few become High Court judges without ever becoming Q.C.s. But on the whole the leaders of the profession are all Q.C.s and almost all High Court judges are appointed from among their ranks. Taking silk is a big step in a barrister's career, because he can no longer do paperwork apart from writing the odd opinion (pleadings and all other legal documents can in general only be drafted by juniors); and overnight he becomes far more expensive – not only will his own fees go up in accordance with his new status, but because of the two-counsel rule any client wanting to hire his services will normally be expected to employ a junior too (although the rule itself has formally been abolished its effects will endure for some time to come). It used to be said that among each batch of silks appointed every year there would be a few for whom the gamble would not pay off, and who would never earn as much as they did as juniors; but thanks to legal aid and the crime wave it is doubtful if this is so today, and there are plenty of salaried appointments awaiting those who wish to leave practice, as Circuit Judges, Queen's Bench Masters or Chancery Registrars, or Chairmen of any one of a large number of different tribunals.

(4) *The Bench*

For those who succeed the pinnacle of a career at the Bar is still regarded as an appointment to the High Court bench, which carries with it not only prestige and a knighthood but a coveted pension as well (barristers themselves, being self-employed and prohibited from practising in partnership, have no pension to look forward to on retirement). There are almost exactly 100 judicial appointments of High Court rank or above – there are 12 Lords of Appeal in the House of Lords, 15 Lords Justices in the Court of Appeal, and below them there are 73 High Court judges. The number of High Court judgeships has doubled in the last 20 years – in 1955 there were only 39. Despite this enormous increase, and growing murmurs from the solicitors' side of the profession that they should at least be eligible for these appointments[12], High Court judgeships remain the exclusive monopoly of the Bar – and of a small part of the Bar at that, since well over half the practising Bar is now of less than 10 years' call. In practice High Court judges are almost never appointed from outside the ranks of practising Q.C.s; although success as an advocate does not guarantee a judicial appointment, it is usually regarded as a necessary condition (and until well into this century political service helped).[13]

Solicitors have succeeded, however, in opening up a small crack in the Bar's monopoly of the next tier of judicial appointments, the Circuit bench. They cannot be appointed direct as Circuit judges, but they are now eligible for appointment after first serving five years as a part-time judge called a Recorder. It was only in 1972 that the office of Recorder was opened to solicitors, so that it was not until 1977 that the first solicitor-Recorders were promoted to the Circuit bench; five solicitors were then appointed, but the remaining 265 Circuit judges then in office had all been chosen from the Bar. The Bar's monopoly of these judicial appointments has not therefore been seriously threatened, and it is fair to say that any barrister of 15 years' call or more, who is reasonably competent and who has not blotted his copybook in other ways, can expect to become a Circuit judge if that is his wish; and the increase in their numbers has been so great that in recent years it has been quite difficult to find suitable candidates for the job.

Judicial appointments are not the only monopoly reserved to the Bar; certain posts in the Government and the Civil Service are also traditionally occupied only by barristers. The Lord Chancellor, the Attorney-General and the misleadingly-named Solicitor-General are always appointed from among the ranks of the Bar; and the majority of lawyers in central government departments are barristers (by contrast the vast majority of lawyers in local government are solicitors). The Legal Advisers Department at the Foreign Office is staffed almost entirely by barristers, as is the Parliamentary Counsel's Office, and all senior posts in the Lord Chancellor's Office. This last is the most important department to be colonized by the Bar, because of its immense powers of patronage.

Although in theory barristers and solicitors compete on equal terms for most judicial appointments, in practice the officials in the Lord Chancellor's Department have tended to favour their brethren at the Bar. Among Masters and Registrars of the Supreme Court the numbers are equal, with 22 barristers and 22 solicitors; but there are 41 barristers sitting as Stipendiary Magistrates, and only nine solicitors; 13 barristers sitting as Judges Advocate General, and no solicitors; 12 barrister-Presidents as full-time members of major tribunals, and three solicitors; and eight barristers who are National Insurance Commissioners (no solicitors). If one adds up the total number of full-time judicial and quasi-judicial appointments which are within the gift of the Lord Chancellor's Department the total number of barristers in post in 1976 was 495, and the number of solicitors 187 (of whom all but 56 were County Court Registrars).[14] The opportunities for a barrister to step into a salaried appointment towards the end of his or her career are therefore unusually high.

THE ORGANIZATION OF A SET OF CHAMBERS

Although barristers are not allowed to associate in partnership they work together in sets of chambers sharing the common services of a clerk or clerks and common secretarial facilities. The average set of chambers in London now contains 14 barristers; in the provinces chambers tend to be smaller and on average contain only 11 barristers. The head of chambers is generally appointed by seniority, but seniority is interpreted in varying ways; it may mean senior by age, by call, by membership of chambers or in silk. The head of chambers is almost always a Q.C.; it is he nominally who employs the clerk, and it is usually he who has the last (and sometimes the only) word in the selection of new members of chambers.

A set of chambers of 14 barristers in London will normally occupy between five and ten rooms, grouped around a staircase in one of the Inns, rather like rooms in Oxford and Cambridge colleges. The Q.C.s will usually have rooms of their own, and in non-criminal sets the top juniors may as well; their criminal colleagues who spend almost the whole of every day in court will generally share, as will almost all junior members of chambers nowadays (15 years ago the average size of a set of chambers in London was only seven, and far more people had rooms of their own).

The hub of every set of chambers is the clerk's room, where the clerk sits like a spider in the centre of his web organizing the lives of his principals. Although in theory the clerk is simply the barrister's agent, in practice it is the clerk who gives the orders and the barrister who obeys, at least where young barristers are concerned. It is the clerk who distributes the briefs among the younger members of chambers, and woe betide any young man or woman who challenges the clerk's authority or loses his confidence; their only responsibility is to do the work the clerk gives them, and gratefully to accept the fees which the clerk has charged.

Fee-negotiation is the other very important aspect of a clerk's job. Not only must a clerk be good at getting the work into chambers; he must know what his principals are worth and how much he can charge for their services without frightening the solicitors away. In order to maximize their fees most chambers pay their clerk on a percentage basis: the more he manages to charge the client the more he himself will earn. Most barristers pay 10% of all their fees to their clerk, so that in the big sets of chambers whose gross receipts now top £250,000 a year the clerk receives very substantial sums indeed. However in some chambers the clerk pays the salaries of the junior clerks out of his own fee. Because of the phenomenal increase in clerks' earnings in recent years more and more chambers are trying to put their clerks on fixed salaries; but the majority are still paid on a percentage basis, and the normal percentage is 10%.

The Common Law Bar and the specialist Bars

Barristers can be broadly divided into generalists and specialists. The generalists all work on the common law side, and will do anything that comes their way; this will normally be a mixture (in varying proportions) of crime, contract cases, personal injury claims (arising out of road and factory accidents), landlord and tenant law, and matrimonial work – divorce and the ancillary problems of finance and custody of the children. Sets of chambers can be found, however, which specialize in each of these common law fields: there is a large number of chambers which do almost nothing but crime, quite a number who specialize in matrimonial work, and rather fewer who depend almost entirely on landlord and tenant or personal injury cases. But apart from crime and divorce it is probably true to say that most barristers practising in the common law fields do not limit themselves to any one of these specialities; and even those who do will occasionally be found straying outside their chosen fields, particularly after taking silk.

Almost all provincial barristers are common lawyers, turning their hand to anything which comes their way; and in London all the common law sets of chambers are to be found concentrated in the Temple. Up in Lincoln's Inn are the Chancery barristers, who specialize in trusts and family settlements, company matters, tax and land law. They tend to do more advisory work, and to make fewer court appearances than the common law barrister; the work involves more purely legal problems and is thought to be better suited to people with an analytical or academic turn of mind. As at the common law bar, there are sets of chambers in Lincoln's

Inn which specialize in just one of the traditional Chancery fields, for example tax; but to confuse matters there are also common law tax chambers. There are six sets of chambers in all at the tax bar. The commercial bar is about the same size, consisting of chambers which specialize in shipping and company law, most of their clients coming from the City and a few from industry; and there are six patent sets, manned mostly by barristers with a scientific training.

Planning is another specialist field which provides employment for half a dozen sets of chambers; and some of them also specialize in doing work for local authorities. The Admiralty bar, concerned with collisions and salvage cargoes, provides work for two sets of chambers (London being the world centre for arbitration over marine disputes); and libel is the speciality of two more. There are many other specialist fields in which barristers practise, but these are probably the most important areas in which the Bar provides established groups of experts. The provision of these experts is the basis of one of the main justifications for the split legal profession in England; the system enables the humblest solicitor to obtain first class advice for his client on the most difficult point of law simply by briefing a barrister who is a specialist in the relevant field.

A CLOISTERED PROFESSION

No description of the Bar would be complete without trying to convey something of the atmosphere in which barristers work. It is a completely cloistered environment, which undoubtedly has its charm: the visitor who steps from the busy hum of Fleet Street into the quiet courtyards and leafy gardens of the Temple often feels he is stepping into another world and another century. But the seclusion goes deeper than that. The Bar's geographical isolation within the Inns is symptomatic of a wider social and professional isolation. A barrister with a flat in the Temple could pass the whole of his professional life without ever leaving the confines of the Inn, except to go to the Law Courts across the road. Few people are lucky enough now to live in the Temple, but many barristers remain there throughout the day and never have lunch outside the Hall of their Inn, where the sole company is that of other barristers.[15] The result is that they have little knowledge of the world outside the Temple, and in particular of how ordinary people think and behave. Only a barrister, for example, could have asked the jury in the Lady Chatterley case whether they would allow their wives or their servants to read the book; and only a judge drawn from the ranks of the Bar would be capable of consoling an injured plaintiff who could no longer do the twist with the remark that she would meet a much nicer class of person if she danced the waltz![16]

Just as the judiciary is dominated by the products of Oxbridge and the public schools[17], so the ranks of the Bar are drawn overwhelmingly from the middle and upper classes. Indeed the Bar itself has retained much of the atmosphere of an old-fashioned public school with its little conventions and its obsession with hierarchy and with dress. Barristers not on christian name terms call each other by their surnames without the prefix 'Mr', and they never shake hands when introduced, because in theory they know each other already.[18] Q.C.s in the High Court not only wear different clothes (a silk gown instead of a stuff one, and an elegant tailcoat), but they sit in a different row, so that everyone else has to move back one row in order to leave the Q.C. in splendid isolation at the front.

A junior being led by a Q.C. who has prepared the case very well may be given his 'colours' by his leader in the form of a red bag to carry his robes in instead of the normal blue one.[19] The little courtesies ('May it please your Lordship', 'I am much obliged' are phrases the neophyte finds himself saying unthinkingly after a couple of months) and the legal pronunciation of Latin (different from that used elsewhere) are the equivalent of a sort of school slang – certainly it is a private language which must be completely mystifying to the litigants themselves. Certain places are also out of bounds – notably those pubs in Fleet Street where barristers' and solicitors' clerks congregate: it is better for the barrister not to see how some of his work is obtained. And the Bar has a clearly identifiable uniform – stiff white collar, sober tie, black coat, black waistcoat (with watch-chain appended) and striped trousers. Many barristers nowadays simply wear a dark suit, but it must still have a waistcoat – indeed the Lord Chief Justice's regulations on dress in court require them.[20]

The Bar is very conscious of these little marks of status which distinguish barristers from ordinary citizens – and from solicitors. It is extraordinary, for example, that the Bar continues to tolerate the rule that a barrister cannot sue for his fees. The reason for the rule is that a barrister's fee is an *honorarium*, a gratuity which he is given by his grateful client but to which he has no right enforceable at law. The fee-bag at the back of a barrister's gown is an archaic relic of this theory. It is there so that the client can slip counsel a gratuity without causing him embarrassment. Although fees are no longer paid in this way, barristers are still considered too superior to discuss such mercenary matters themselves: the whole business of fee negotiation is left entirely to the clerk, and indeed it is against professional etiquette for a barrister to involve himself in discussion with solicitors about his fees.

Officially the Bar is no longer the senior branch of the legal profession, but unofficially there is a widespread feeling that barristers are still the superiors of solicitors, both intellectually and socially. This feeling goes back a long way, to the days when the clerks who eventually evolved into the solicitors' branch of the profession were far more lowly members of society; in 1614 an edict of the Inns described them as 'but ministerial persons of an inferior nature'.[21] Today the Bar continues to maintain its unofficial seniority in a host of different ways. Some have already been mentioned: the monopoly over virtually all judicial appointments, the wearing of wigs, the different rows occupied in court. And in other little ways the status differences are preserved: other counsel are referred to in court as 'my learned friend', solicitors simply as 'my friend'. When a solicitor wants to write a letter to a barrister on a professional matter he cannot do so direct, but has to write to him through his clerk. When barristers were consulted in 1973 over the design of new court buildings, they asked that whenever reasonably possible counsel should not be asked to share a room with solicitors for luncheon.[22] And when a conference is held, however busy the solicitor and however junior the barrister, it is always the solicitor who comes to see the barrister, and never *vice versa*; indeed it is a breach of professional etiquette for counsel (save in the most exceptional circumstances) to go to the solicitor.

There are few barristers nowadays who would defend these differences simply for reasons of snobbery; although a senior barrister (now a Q.C.) once told me that he was opposed to fusion because solicitors were not really gentlemen, and we were. But a large number of barristers simply enjoy being different. It may be asked whether there is any harm in this; the answer I think is provided by Lord Goodman in his comment on the wearing of robes.

Most barristers like the importance conferred on them by their wigs and gowns, and will zealously defend the tradition as lending dignity to court proceedings and authority to counsel. This is Lord Goodman's reaction:

> 'I do feel that it is no longer appropriate, and indeed faintly ridiculous, that grown members of a learned profession should wear period costumes. This is particularly so since they adopt the convention of our undergraduate days, that the honourable nature of a garment is reflected by its age and tatters. But I also believe that there is a more important aspect of the wig and gown than the question of maintaining a tradition or discarding it. I think it reflects an attitude on the part of the people who wear it which is no longer a relevant or contemporary one. It serves to maintain differences and distinctions which I believe should be minimized and not stressed.'[23]

Another consequence of the Bar's isolation is that the Bar is almost incapable of seeing itself as others see it. A rare exception was Sir Morris Finer, who attempted in a broadcast in 1970 to persuade the Bar to be more consumer-oriented. 'Consumer-orientation may be a provocative phrase to use to the profession', he said, '... but we need much more of it. The lawyer's consciousness of his inner rectitude – a phenomenon which afflicts the Bar more peculiarly than it does the solicitor's branch – is no substitute. It is apt, indeed, to communicate itself to the lay public as an aloofness or, worse still, a pomposity, which they find it hard to bear'.[24]

The arrogance and complacency of the Bar do more than simply create a bad impression on its clients. They have an important effect on the whole development of the law. The Bar has consistently opposed all measures of law reform which appear to conflict with its own self-interest[25]; and it has opposed many others simply out of conservatism and a resistance to change. Even simple changes in the technical rules of the law are met with unreasoning hostility. An example is the Civil Evidence Act 1968, whose promoters hoped originally to abolish all rules against hearsay in civil cases; but in the words of its architect, Lord Diplock, 'some so-called safeguards had to be built in simply to overcome the opposition of the practising Bar ... the Bar is terribly conservative in this country'.[26] In fact the Bar has since hailed the experiment as an unqualified success. Many other instances could be given of similar obstruction to measures which after their introduction have been widely welcomed.

There is one other way in which the conventions and traditions of the Bar affect the development of the law and its institutions, and that is by ensuring that barristers who challenge the conventions do not reach positions of importance in which they can influence these matters. Outwardly the Bar has a reputation for tolerance and respect for differing views and eccentricities, but this tolerance only exists within clearly defined limits. Almost any senior barrister will privately give examples of colleagues who were passed over or made to wait for silk or the Bench, simply because they did not conform; and anyone whose non-conformism extends to challenging the practices and traditions of the Bar itself puts his career in serious jeopardy. But of course such cases are extremely rare: most barristers are conformist by training, if not by temperament, and for those few who are not the ceremonies, rules and patterns of behaviour in the Inns soon ensure that they pay proper respect to the ethos and traditions of the Bar which are inculcated into them by their elders.

THE GOVERNMENT OF THE BAR

Until less than a hundred years ago there was no organization which could claim to represent the Bar as a whole. The Inns regulated the profession but they did not represent it to the outside world. That function was assumed by a new body set up in 1883 and called the Bar Committee, soon to become the Bar Council. It was elected by the whole profession and financed by the voluntary contributions of individual barristers. In 1894 an approach was made to the Inns for financial help, and after some hesitation they agreed to give an annual subsidy of £600 provided the Council undertook not to interfere with their traditional property, powers, privileges or jurisdiction.

In its early years the Bar Council was mainly concerned to codify into rules of etiquette the major restrictive practices which had developed in the latter half of the nineteenth century – the rule that a barrister might not be instructed except through a solicitor, the two-counsel rule, the two-thirds rule. In this century it continued to devote much of its energies into elaborating and defending these and other rules of etiquette and in redefining its relationship with the solicitors' branch. Neither this activity nor its various campaigns to increase fees brought it into serious conflict with the Inns, though the potential for conflict always existed if the Bar Council ever took a wider or more positive view of its role and moved into spheres which the Inns traditionally regarded as their own.

In the 1960s this began to happen; but the first move for change was in fact made by the Inns, with the establishment of the Senate in 1966. This was intended to be a single body which could act on behalf of the Inns collectively in matters upon which a common policy was essential. However it merely resulted in a proliferation of committees, duplicating and triplicating each other's work; and the Inns, never noted for their ability to work together in a common cause, proved no better at cooperating with the new body than they had with each other. Properly coordinated plans to accommodate the exploding numbers in the profession became more and more urgent, however, as space in the Temple became tighter and tighter. The Inns held the key: they still retained full control over admissions and call to the Bar and over their own property, in which all the chambers in London were housed. The Bar Council could do nothing: it had no power to provide any extra space, nor to influence the terms on which the Inns let their property, nor to control the numbers entering the profession.

In 1972 a committee under Lord Pearce, which had been appointed to investigate the whole unsatisfactory state of the government and organization of the profession, recommended the incorporation of the Bar Council and Senate into a single body, which would be able to take binding decisions in the name of the profession and the Inns together. Not surprisingly the Inns viewed this proposal with considerable misgivings, but after certain of their amendments to the scheme had been adopted in the Pearce Committee's second report they ultimately gave their cautious consent, expressed in the form of 'Understandings' involving no legal obligation. In July 1974 the new Senate was born, its full title being the Senate of the Inns of Court and the Bar. Despite official protestations to the contrary, its creation has undoubtedly involved (at least in theory) a shift of power away from the individual Inns and their benchers and towards the practising Bar; and its chances of success depend entirely on the extent to which the benchers are prepared to accept this new situation and to put their property and other powers at the disposal of the profession. The initial omens were not hopeful and in its first year of operation some doubted whether the Senate would even survive: it had few executive powers and the Inns continued to block reforms in all the most important spheres. However the establishment of the Royal Commission in 1976 underlined the need for a united policy, and it finally brought home the reality that if the Bar did not set its own house in order the government would be forced to intervene.

For years legislation has been talked of as a distant threat; now it is a real possibility. The Bar is the one profession which is completely uncontrolled by statute; it has been tacitly assumed in the past that the profession can be relied upon to serve the public interest without government interference. This is in marked contrast to solicitors, whose activities have been subject to detailed government regulation for over a century. Successive Solicitors Acts have defined the functions which solicitors alone can perform; they govern admission to the profession, and they even limit the amount which solicitors can charge for a wide range of services. By contrast no statute governs the training, admission, discipline or rights of barristers. The first two matters are controlled by the benchers alone; and the Bar's monopoly of audience before the High Court is conferred not by Parliament (like the solicitors' monopolies) but by the custom of the judges.

In recent years the Bar's capacity to equate its own private interest with the service of the public interest has been called increasingly into question, both within and outside the profession. From outside the profession criticism has been directed at the Bar's restrictive practices and at the high cost of going to law. The Bar has twice been the subject of reference to the Monopolies Commission, first under the general reference to report on restrictive practices in all professions made in 1967, and secondly under the more specific reference in July 1974 to investigate the two-counsel rule and the Bar's restrictions on advertising.

The Bar's restrictive practices have been the subject of adverse comment for years, but only recently has the government itself shown concern, not so much on behalf of private litigants but because of the amount of public money which barristers now receive. It was the revelation of the high fees earned by barristers when doing legally-aided work in the Crown Court which was the immediate cause of the setting-up of the Royal Commission on Legal Services. The Attorney-General had to confess to Parliament that there was no reliable information regarding the earnings received by lawyers out of public funds; and his lame answers to this and to a barrage of other questions led the leader-writers of almost all the national newspapers to support Jack Ashley's campaign for a major investigation into the legal profession. The Royal Commission will almost certainly produce recommendations for a greater degree of public accountability; but whether public control should extend to matters concerning the internal management of the profession is a more difficult question to decide. Here too the private decisions of the profession have a public dimension; and the sort of conflict which arises is well illustrated by the most serious internal problem currently facing the Bar, which is the accommodation crisis in London.

RECRUITMENT AND ACCOMMODATION

In the mid-1960s the Bar Council and the Inns embarked on a major recruiting campaign to boost numbers at the Bar, because there was felt to be such a shortage of barristers that the separate existence of the profession was at risk. That campaign (which was not abandoned until well into the 1970s) was only too successful. The recruits have now arrived in droves but there is no room for them in the overcrowded Inns, and one-half of recent drafts will almost certainly be unable to practise.

In 1960 there were 1919 barristers practising in England and Wales. In 1977 the number in practice passed the 4000 mark – a 100% increase in 15 years. At the same time the Bar has experienced an unprecedented increase in affluence; not only have its numbers doubled, but earnings (expressed in current prices) have increased fivefold over the same period. Whereas in 1960 median earnings at the Bar were about £1600 per annum, in 1976 they were about £7500.[27] Most important among the reasons for this increase is the crime wave, coupled with the almost automatic availability of legal aid in all cases involving trial by jury (tried in the Crown Court, where – with very few exceptions – the Bar has an exclusive right of audience). But litigation on the civil side has also increased, because of the growing complexity of legislation, increased awareness by the public of their legal rights, and the creation of new rights and of new courts to enforce them. Much of this increase in litigation has also been financed by legal aid, which has transformed the state of the Bar in little more than a decade.

These are the main reasons for the phenomenal growth in the number of those coming to the Bar – a growth which appeared to reach its peak in 1975–6, and which may at last be slackening. At the same time the number of sets of chambers has hardly increased at all; most sets have expanded in size, but further expansion is now impossible without the acquisition of further accommodation. As a result large numbers of young barristers have been unable to practise simply for lack of space. It is difficult to be precise, but all the available evidence suggests that about one-half of those who go into pupillage intending to practise fail to establish themselves at the end of it.[28] This is a terrible waste, not only in terms of the human misery caused to those who get so far and fail, but also to the nation in the misallocation of resources which is involved. Pupillage is a vocational training which is generally undertaken only with a view to practise; its value for those who are going to earn their living outside the Bar is low, and to train people for a profession in which they will not be able to practise is to squander a great deal of highly skilled manpower.

The high drop-out rate has another effect which is less obvious but equally important. It has always been the practice to warn aspirant barristers of the considerable financial difficulties they will have to face, not only as students but during pupillage and in the first years of practice. Of late the Bar, for perfectly understandable reasons, has placed even greater emphasis on the risks involved. The net result, confirmed by the evidence of University Appointments Boards, has been to discourage the ablest law students from going to the Bar and to favour those who can bypass some of the hurdles because they have connections or private means. A survey conducted in 1976 revealed that more Bar students still arrange their pupillage through family connections or friends than by any other method; and nearly one-half intended to rely in part on financial support from their families during pupillage.[29] Selection for the Bar has always been based disproportionately on connections and financial resources rather than on merit; the current shortage of space has done nothing to alleviate this bias.

One other aspect of the present situation is not new. Enormous oversubscription has always been the pattern of recruitment to the Bar. The accommodation crisis is a recent phenomenon; the high wastage rate is not. In every year since 1945 the number of young men and women who have sat the exams and paid their admission fees and call fees and have eaten their dinners has far exceeded the number who subsequently started – or could hope to start – in practice. In fact until 1960 the drop-out rate was never less than 50% and in some years as high as 70%. Sir Hartley Shawcross was so indignant at these figures that at the 1957 A.G.M. of the Bar he attacked the Inns' admission policy, and suggested that the benchers 'might be unduly influenced by the income derived by the Inns from students'. While this allegation is impossible to substantiate so long as the Inns refuse to publish their accounts, it is certain that with the peculiar system of paying large fees on entry and nothing thereafter the Inns derive an important part of their revenue from the deposits and admission fees and call fees paid by students.[30]

In the 1950s a fair proportion of those called probably never intended to practise; no one knows how high this proportion was. Nowadays a majority of those called undoubtedly want to practise; but not more than one-half will be able to do so. Despite the intense competition the fortunate few who do win through are not necessarily those best qualified to make good barristers; they continue to be those who know the right people, or who are lucky enough to be in the right place when a vacancy occurs.

2 THE INNS OF COURT

THE IMPORTANCE OF THE INNS

In September 1974 the Senate published a leaflet for young men and women who were considering the Bar as a possible career. This is how it described the Inns:

> 'Every barrister must be a member of one of the four Inns of Court – Lincoln's Inn, Inner Temple, Middle Temple, Gray's Inn. The Inns are essentially medieval guilds of lawyers which, unlike most guilds, continue in full activity at the present day. In about the fourteenth century the Judges granted the Inns the sole right to call men to the Bar, that is, to be entitled to practise in the Royal Courts, and also the right to disbar them in the event of misconduct. The Inns have always been responsible for the education of Bar students. A barrister's Inn is his professional home throughout his career. He can lunch and dine with his fellow members in the Inn hall, use the Inn library, and join in the social life of the Inn. The Inns own extensive buildings which they let in part to barristers as chambers and in part to other tenants, professional, commercial or residential.
>
> 'Each Inn is governed by Masters of the Bench, or "Benchers", consisting of senior members of the Inn – Judges and senior practising or retired barristers. The Bench itself elects members of the Inn to fill vacancies, and a Bencher normally holds office for the rest of his life. The Benchers appoint one of their number to be Treasurer, or head of the Inn, each year.'

This very brief description conveys quite a good indication of the pivotal position of the Inns in the organization of the Bar. No one can become a barrister without joining an Inn; not only are the Inns responsible for the admission of students, and for their Call to the Bar, but they are also responsible for their education and training. Until recently they were responsible for professional discipline as well; and they still have enormous power over the organization of the profession by their ownership of all the property from which barristers practise in London.

Yet in their own internal structure, as the Senate accurately describes, they are essentially medieval guilds, which have survived unchanged down to the present day. This antiquated structure has of late given rise to calls for their reform, as the Inns have become increasingly identified with opposition to any kind of change at the Bar. But so far they have remained remarkably untouched by the murmurs of discontent from the profession; and if a barrister from former times were to return to the Inns today, although he would discover that some of the buildings had changed, as institutions he would find them immediately recognizable. In order to understand the Inns, then, one must first examine something of their history.

THE HISTORY OF THE INNS

The origins of all four of the Inns of Court are obscure. The earliest known records of Lincoln's Inn, the Black Books, date from the early fifteenth century, while those of the Middle Temple and Inner Temple stem from the beginning of the sixteenth century, and of Gray's Inn from the end of that century. But the societies had come into existence long before these dates, being set up by groups of lawyers for their own benefit. Each Inn was a place where the lawyers worked and lived, the Inn providing a chapel, a library and a hall, where the lawyers not only ate and drank, but which was also used for debating and mooting (the holding of mock trials).

In the course of time the Inns became important educational and training institutions. The education in those days was long: before being fully qualified it was necessary for a lawyer to spend eight years before call to the bar of his Inn and five years after call before he was considered fully qualified. The formal teaching provided by the Inn was in the form of practical exercises of various types such as readings, moots and debates. Readings were the most important:

these were extended lectures given by senior practitioners before call to the Bench (the governing body of the Inn). Moots were mock trials in which students took the part of reading pleadings (the formal written statement of each party's case), while the oral argument was conducted by barristers, and judged by the Benchers. It was in connection with the moots that the term 'barrister' originated: the earliest known instance of the use of the word is in the Black Books of Lincoln's Inn in Trinity Term 1455, where 'two of the best barristers' (*duo de optimis barrei*) are mentioned.

It would seem that the administration of the Inns by a governing body of Benchers developed along with the Inns' educational responsibilities: all senior members of the Inn were expected to 'read' and then take their place on the Bench of the Inn. It was probably in the Tudor period that the metamorphosis of the Inns into hierarchical bodies was complete, with the three different ranks of Benchers, barristers and students; and it was then that the Benchers claimed for themselves the wide powers over the Inns' members and property which they hold today.

Tudor England was the heyday of the Inns. Not only were they great educational establishments but they also found themselves at the centre of much of the social, political and cultural life of the period. Shakespeare's first nights were performed in their Halls; the voyages of men like Drake, Frobisher and Hawkins were planned there (the Middle Temple still has a table reputedly made from timbers from the *Golden Hind*); and to their celebrated masques and revels the Queen and her Court were frequent visitors.

During this period the Inns were both professional and educational institutions: professional in the sense that they were living and working communities governed by a body of persons, the Benchers, who were almost exclusively practitioners; educational in the sense that they formed living and working communities for students under the direct supervision of the practitioners with whom they spent their days. In this respect the Inns were much like collegiate universities.

Today, however, the Inns are neither professional nor educational communities in these senses. First, with very few exceptions, barristers no longer live in the Inns; the bulk of the residential accommodation which remains is occupied by senior or retired practitioners and judges. More important, the Inns are now governed by bodies consisting mostly (though not exclusively) of persons who are no longer practitioners but who are either judges or have retired from practice. Second, the Inns themselves are no longer educational establishments: formal law teaching is carried out at the universities, or on behalf of the Inns by the Council of Legal Education. Practical experience is gained in pupillage with a practising barrister, but it is no part of the function of the Inn to provide students with pupillage. Indeed, pupil and master are, as often as not, from different Inns: the nexus between them is professional. In fact, the only activity forming part of the barrister's qualification today to which his own Inn is central, apart from call to the Bar, is the requirement of keeping terms, i.e. of eating dinners (the educational value of which is discussed below). The Benchers themselves no longer play any significant part in the education of students.

From their heyday in the sixteenth and early seventeenth centuries the Inns went into a rapid decline, which was complete by the end of the seventeenth century. Busy practitioners became increasingly reluctant to 'read' to the students, and the tests of competence imposed by the Benchers were reduced to a mere formality. Not until the mid-nineteenth century did the Inns, under the threat of legislation, take steps to ensure once more that those seeking call to the Bar had some educational attainment. In 1846 a Select Committee appointed to examine the state of legal education reported that the Inns provided no education 'worthy of the name'[1], and called on them to 'resume anew the original objects of their institution'.[2] The outcome was the founding of the Council of Legal Education in 1852, but still no educational requirement was made for admission to an Inn; nor were there any examinations. Parliamentary criticism continued: an Irish M.P., J. Napier Q.C., told the House of Commons that the only qualification for call to the Bar was 'that a man should eat and drink and be able to write his name'.[3] In 1855 he secured the appointment of a Commission of Inquiry into the Inns of Court. It recommended an entrance exam, as well as exams before call and pupillage; but the proposals, not being acceptable to all the Inns, were rejected. However the Attorney-General, Sir Richard Bethell, was determined to secure reform; and he threatened that if the Inns continued to oppose the Commission's recommendations, he would regard it as the duty of the Government to introduce legislation.

In the next 20 years a whole succession of Bills was presented to Parliament with the aim of reforming the Inns so as to overcome their opposition to changes in legal education. The first private Bills were introduced in the 1860s, proposing the turning of the Inns into democratic bodies with elected Benchers and uniform disciplinary procedures. In the 1870s the issue was taken up by the Lord Chancellor, Lord Selborne, who drafted a Bill to reform the constitution of the Inns and to compel them to join in the foundation of a General School of Law; in opposition in 1874 and 1875 he raised this proposal again and again, but without success, although his 1875 Bill passed through all its stages in the House of Lords. This was not the end of the campaign, for in 1877 another Lord Chancellor, Lord Cairns, introduced his own Bill to reform the Inns and provide a system of legal education for the Bar. This Bill passed the Lords and reached the Committee stage in the Commons before being abandoned. The following year the Attorney-General re-introduced it, but after obtaining a second reading it was not proceeded with.

That was the last attempt to reform the Inns by legislation. By the skin of their teeth they had staved off the parliamentary challenge, and as a result they have remained uncontrolled by statute down to this day. The very first inquiry, that of the Common Law Commissioners in 1834, had advised that 'the ordinary immunities of a voluntary society ought not to be allowed to any body of persons claiming to be the medium of admission into one of the learned professions. If the Body is to enjoy this privilege, it is no longer a private association, but one in which the public has a deep interest, and the proceedings of which, if not adapted to the purposes of general utility, ought to be made so by the interposition of Law'. [4] That principle did not prevail; and in their admission procedures, call requirements and general responsibility for the standard of entry into the profession the Inns remain very much a law unto themselves.

SERJEANTS' INN

Serjeants were a rank of advocate above the rank of barrister: they are known to have existed since the thirteenth century. Until King's Counsel were first appointed in the early seventeenth century[5], the serjeants were the only senior advocates. They held an important monopoly, the right of audience in the common law courts; and all common law judges were appointed from among their ranks. The end of serjeantry was signified by Parliament in 1846 when their monopoly in the common law courts was removed. Finally the Judicature Act of 1873 ensured that all judges would in future be drawn from the ranks of the Bar; and so it was that the last serjeant was appointed in May 1875. Serjeants' Inn on Chancery Lane was sold by the surviving members in 1877 for £57,000, and the proceeds divided amongst them. Lord Lindley was the last survivor of the English order; but in Ireland the serjeants continued until 1921, and the last surviving serjeant, Serjeant Sullivan, practised at the Bar within living memory and did not die until 1959.[6]

It had been the practice that a serjeant upon appointment ceased to be a member of his old Inn, but just before his departure was made a Bencher *honoris causa* (if not one already). The effect was that none of the judges of the common law courts were Benchers or even members of any of the Inns of Court.[7] But with the sale of Serjeants' Inn, the serjeants were homeless. More important, future judges had nowhere to go and remained members of their Inns. The Inns accordingly took back the serjeants and judges, not only as members, but with the same rank of Bencher that they held upon their appointment.

The decision of the Benchers in 1875 to allow the serjeants to return to their old Inns, and to permit future judges to remain with them, was to have far-reaching consequences which are still very much with us. First, the control of the Inns passed from the practising Bar into the hands of the judges and elderly or retired barristers; since that time, barristers still in practice have formed a minority of the Benchers of any Inn.[8] Control of the Inn thus passed to people who were out of touch with the needs of the practising Bar and who, by the nature of their constitutional position, had a strong interest in avoiding controversy. Second, participation by practising members of the Inns in their government was drastically reduced. Third, criticism of the Benchers became even more muted; a man was reluctant to criticize the Benchers even before the change, for he in his turn wished to be elevated to the Bench of his Inn. How much more difficult was it, then, to criticize a body of men containing judges before whom he appeared regularly, and upon whose good opinion his professional advancement (such as taking silk) would depend. Fourth, there was now no independent tribunal to whom an aggrieved member could appeal. The judges have a Visitorial capacity to the Inns, but now they were on the Benches of those very Inns themselves; and in matters of common interest between the Inns, judges who were Benchers of another Inn were not likely to be the most independent of tribunals.

THE LEGAL RELATIONSHIP BETWEEN THE INNS AND THEIR MEMBERS

The Inns are described as voluntary unincorporated associations; but are they simply clubs, in which case their property and assets could in theory be sold and divided among their members, as happened with Serjeants' Inn – or are they trusts, and if so for what purpose, or purposes?

The 1855 Royal Commission on the Inns of Court Inns delved quite deeply into this question, and it reported that two Inns seemed to have no trust at all. When the Steward of Lincoln's Inn was asked whether he knew of 'any deed under which the property of the Inn is held, declaratory of any trust with reference to the property', he replied 'I am not aware of any'.[9] The Commission concluded that the property 'appears to have been acquired by purchase made by the Members of the Inn, nor is there a trace of its being held upon any Trust'.[10] On this evidence, the Inns would appear to be clubs; but if they were members' clubs, one would expect the members to be entitled to determine how the Inn is run, to elect the governing body of the Inn, and to see full accounts, and minutes of the governing body's meetings.

In fact it is now generally accepted that the Inns are not simply members' clubs; but it is far from clear on what trusts the property of the Inns is held. They do not have statutes, like the colleges of Oxford and Cambridge; Lincoln's Inn, as recorded above, possesses no charter at all. Gray's Inn, in its evidence to the Pearce Committee, stated that, 'The historic functions of the Inn and the primary objects of the trusts on which its property is held are the education and training of students and members of the Bar, the study of law and the maintenance of the professional efficiency and standards of the Bar through the active association of its members within the Inns'.[11] The committee thought that the purposes of the other Inns were similar.

If the Inns are trusts, they can either be charitable trusts, or private trusts for the benefit of their members; or possibly part one and part the other. If they are private trusts, or if part of the

Inns' operations is held not to be charitable, then the Benchers hold all or some notional part of their property on trust for their members. Accordingly every barrister-member is a beneficiary; and it is a well-established principle of trust law that a beneficiary is entitled to ask the trustees for an account. Yet the Inns have never voluntarily published accounts to their members, and until recently it was impossible to see them, even on request; even now it is not easy, and most barristers do not know that they have this right, let alone have the courage to exercise it. For instance the Inner Temple, when holding a meeting to discuss the Inn's financial position, decided arbitrarily to exclude all members of less than five years' call; yet these people were just as full members of the Inn as barristers of 50 years' call. The members themselves have, it is fair to add, shown little desire to involve themselves in the financial affairs of the Inns. In consequence when the Pearce Committee reported that 'the Inns have kindly shown us their accounts for 1970' they were able to add, without a trace of irony, that as a result 'for the first time since the Royal Commission of 1855, it is possible to take an overall view of the financial state of the profession and to see how its resources were being used'.[12] In part the situation in which the Benchers manage the affairs of the Inns without reference to anyone else has been allowed to continue because the members have been content to allow them to do so.

That is not, however, the end of the matter; for recently it has emerged that a major part of the Inns' activities may be charitable. There is support for this view in the grant by Lord Clifford cited in the Clifford's Inn case[13], the charters of the Inner and Middle Temple[14], the trust averred by Gray's Inn in a lawsuit in 1871[15] and the similar trusts declared by that Inn to the Pearce Committee 100 years later. For many years, however, the Inns have steadfastly declined to register with the Charity Commissioners, despite the fact that if they are charities they have a legal obligation to register, and despite the finding by a court in May 1967 that the Inner Temple and Middle Temple hold their property on charitable trusts.[16] This was a case in the Mayor's and City of London Court, in which the Inner Temple claimed it was entitled to terminate the leases of solicitor tenants in order to give them to barristers who, according to the Inn, were the beneficiaries of its trusts.[17] The deputy judge, Stephen Terrell Q.C., held that since the Inn was a charitable trust it could not have private beneficiaries who could benefit from the 1954 Landlord and Tenant Act in this way. Interestingly the Inns did not appeal against this decision, although it had very widesweeping consequences for the management of their property, since it meant that they could not evict their non-barrister tenants in order to create more space for the Bar. It has been suggested that one reason why they failed to appeal is that they were reluctant to risk having the Court of Appeal endorse the view taken by the judge of first instance that they were charities.[18] However four years later the Court of Appeal did comment obliquely on the question, in a case involving the charitable status of the Council of Law Reporting[19]: Lord Justice Sachs (himself an ex-Treasurer of his Inn) referred to the charter of the Inner Temple for evidence that the study of law and the advancement of the administration of justice were charitable purposes – and *a fortiori* it would appear to follow that in his view the Inner Temple was a charity.

Opinion is nevertheless still divided among the Inns as to whether or not some of their purposes are charitable. The Benchers of at least one Inn were of the view as recently as May 1974 that their Inn was not charitable; while in the latest edition of Halsbury's Laws which appeared in 1973, in the section on barristers edited by Roger Parker Q.C., it is stated that 'the property of each Inn . . . is held on a charitable trust for the furtherance of the study and practice of the law'.[20] The matter is one of considerable importance, for charities are wholly exempt from corporation tax and entitled to 50% relief on their rates; in return they are subject to certain obligations, notably to register with the Charity Commissioners and to produce annual accounts. So averse have the Benchers been to any form of outside interference, even from the Charity Commissioners, that until 1974 they preferred the Inns to pay the tax rather than undergo any kind of public scrutiny.

In 1974 however inflation finally forced the Benchers to consider the cost of this independence, and applications were made to the Inland Revenue that the Inns be treated as charities for tax purposes. The Revenue agreed on condition that the Inns applied for registration with the Charity Commissioners; and at the time of writing the Commissioners' ruling on their charitable status is still awaited.

In the interim the Inns have ceased to pay tax; and the benefits have been enormous. In one Inn the level of corporation tax paid fell from £120,000 in 1973 to less than £10,000 in 1974; in another from £64,000 to zero.[21] If (as is expected) the Inns are held to be charitable, and one extrapolates these figures backwards over the years the conclusion emerges that the Inns have paid literally millions of pounds in tax unnecessarily.

Since 1902 and the Clifford's Inn case, charitable status had been at least an arguable possibility; in 1967 a court actually ruled that one of the Inns was a charity, and in 1971 the Court of Appeal referred to this decision without in any way indicating its dissent.[22] The Benchers may well have felt that registration as charities would not be in the best interests of the Inns, because it would restrict their freedom of manoeuvre. But the rights and wrongs of that are beside the point, because it is a well-established principle of law that the trustees *must* apply the property which they hold on trust to the trust purposes – and if there is any doubt about those purposes the trustees should apply to the court for directions. The same principle must apply equally to the trustees of the Inns, however undesirable they may have felt the consequences might be. If there was disagreement about the Inns' charitable status (and it is impossible to believe that the question had not been actively discussed before 1974) then it was the duty of the Benchers to apply to the courts for a ruling on the question. As for those who stood to benefit from the Inns' trusts, the matter of concern to them is not so much the possibility that the Benchers have failed to comply with their legal duties as trustees, but the consequence, which is that in so doing they have lost everyone a great deal of money.

THE INNS AND THEIR STUDENTS

Among the potential recipients of benefit under the Inns' trusts the most important single group are the Inns' students: and the educational part of their trusts is one to which all the Inns rightly attach great significance. Gray's Inn put this function first in its evidence to the Pearce Committee[23], and in James I's charter to the Inner and Middle Temple the educational function is spelt out with true Stuart pride:

> 'Whereas the Inns of the Inner and Middle Temple, London, being two out of those four Colleges the most famous of all Europe . . . have been for a long time dedicated to the use of the Students and Professors [i.e. Practitioners] of the said Laws,

to which as to the best seminaries of learning and education very many young men, eminent for rank of family and their endowments of mind and body, have daily resorted from all parts of this Realm . . . .'[24]

Now as then the Inns alone have power to admit persons as students and to call students to the Bar; the Benchers have the sole responsibility for determining the qualifications for admission, the education provided to the students, and the fees which the students have to pay. This is a heavy responsibility, and one which like everything else the Benchers have chosen to carry alone. So far as admission is concerned, the Inns appear to maintain an open door policy; indeed they have been remarkably undiscriminating in their admissions. Until very recently the educational requirements for entry were minimal, and as a result many students, particularly from overseas, were admitted who had no real hope of passing the exams, let alone being effective barristers. Lord Denning's Committee on Legal Education for Students from Africa made special mention of this:

> 'We have received from the territories many expressions of regret that the Inns of Court so readily dispense with educational qualifications. The Attorney-General of one of the territories speaks of "the well-meaning but in my view misguided practice of relaxing the prescribed standards of general education for admission as a student in favour of overseas applicants". The result is that students are admitted who have not sufficient intelligence or general education to be able to pass the Bar examinations. A considerable proportion fail. This brings disappointment and frustration: to say nothing of the loss of the time and money involved.'[25]

(1) *Admission fees*

The money involved was significant not only to the student who had to pay but to the Inns who received it. Because admission fees and call fees in effect buy a life membership and a barrister once called never has to pay further moneys to his Inn, the students provide an important part of the Inns' income; and in the postwar era just over half of all the students called to the Bar have been from overseas.[26] From the Commonwealth students who were called to the Bar in the 1960s alone the Inns received admission fees of around £350,000 and call fees of £200,000[27]; and given the high failure rate they must have received further admission fees of at least another £350,000 from those who subsequently failed to pass the exams. In addition they received deposits from all the foreign students of £100 each; assuming the same failure rate of 50% this comes to £835,000 loaned to the Inns over the decade. If each student remained three years and the Inns earned 8% on their capital they will have received a further £200,000 in interest on these deposits.[28] Thus in one decade the Inns received over £1 million in admission fees, call fees and interest on deposits from Commonwealth students, who thereby purchased life membership of institutions whose facilities they would never use again, once they had returned to their home countries.

In a book called *In Search of Justice* published in 1968 Professor Brian Abel-Smith and Professor Robert Stevens, examining the position of English and Commonwealth students as a whole, came to the conclusion that 'students appear to pay considerably more to their Inns than either the Inns or the Council [of Legal Education] spend on legal education . . . Assuming the income on the deposits is sufficient to pay the Inns' contributions to the Council's School, an estimated £113,000 per annum received from students of the Inns has still to be accounted for. No doubt some is spent on the libraries, the common room, and other facilities used by students, but the major part presumably goes into the General Fund, with only a small percentage going directly for education – one of the two main purposes for which the Inns were established.'[29] This was a very serious allegation to make, because if it were true the effect would be that the Inns were making a profit out of their students which was used to benefit the practising barristers. It is impossible to investigate the charge because neither the Inns nor the Council of Legal Education publish their accounts, nor did they ever answer to the allegation that was levelled against them. Even today it is difficult to estimate what happens to the money paid by students, but in the two Inns whose accounts have been seen expenditure on students does now appear to exceed the income derived from them. Some of that expenditure is however of questionable value; and the most questionable item is the massive subsidy devoted by each Inn to cover the cost of student dinners.

(2) *Dining*

Of all the qualifications for admission to any profession dining must be the most extraordinary. It owes its origin to the ancient tradition, enshrined in Elizabethan times in Judges' Orders, that before call to the Bar a student not only had to spend seven years 'keeping the case' (i.e. mooting), but also had to be 'usually in commons' in the hall of his Inn during term, so that by constant association with his seniors their experience and knowledge of the law would gradually rub off onto him. The period of seven years was reduced to five in 1762, and in 1835 to three.[30] Since then the requirement has not changed, and a student still has to keep terms for three years, which involves eating 36 dinners (there are four terms in each year, and in order to keep a term a student must dine in Hall three times; until about ten years ago students who were not members of an English university had to eat six dinners a term, or 72 dinners in all).

The tradition is an ancient and honourable one; whether it still fulfils its original purposes will be examined in a moment. Before doing so, however, it is worth mentioning the inconvenience and expense necessitated by dining. The Denning Report in emphasizing the delays it could cause cited two cases, one of a Cambridge graduate in Nigeria who was keeping terms during each of his leaves, and who would have to return to England up to six times after passing his final exam before he could be called to the Bar; and one of a graduate of London University in Kenya who would have to return to England to dine eight times before he could be called.[31] The Report made no comment on the cost involved. Since then the requirement has been considerably modified to make it easier for certain categories of students to eat their dinners in less than three years (so that neither of these cases would recur today); but the cost remains high. Despite very heavy subsidies no Inn can afford to offer dinner for less than £1; and a far more important item now is the cost of travelling to London. An ordinary return from Oxford and Cambridge in 1978 cost £6.15, from Birmingham £12.75 and from Manchester £21.25; and it is not unknown for students to fly in from Scotland and Northern Ireland, who cannot afford the time away from their studies to travel by other means.

In the light of this expense, to say nothing of the disruption to students who come from the universities, one would expect dining to confer considerable benefits on those who attend. But in fact opinions vary greatly on the educational and social value of these dinners. As the Ormrod Report rightly remarked:

'This tradition has received a great deal of satirical attention. Its purpose is to help the student to identify with his Inn before he is called to the Bar, to get to know fellow students and practitioners, and to pick up some of the corporate spirit of the Inns . . . Successive generations of students over a great many years have doubted the value of this tradition, but, as each generation has attained some seniority in the Inn, views have tended to change and the tradition has been kept up.'[32]

The satirical attention is not surprising when one considers the procedure involved in dining. Ten years ago a leaflet used to be issued by the Middle Temple containing detailed instructions on how students were to behave, which included the following:

'Members will sit in Messes of four. The Senior Member (a) of the Barristers by date of Call at this Inn and (b) if no Barrister in the Mess of Students, by date of admission to this Inn, will be Captain of the Mess.

'The Upper Table on each side of the Hall nearest the High Table is set apart for Barristers only, although each Captain may consent to Students joining their Messes if there are vacancies.

'After Grace is said and glasses are filled, each member of the Mess raises his glass in a silent toast bowing in turn to each other member, opposite and diagonally and to the side. No member may drink before the toast.

'During Dinner no member of one Mess may talk to any member of any other Mess, saving and except that the Captain may address any other Captain for necessary purposes such as passing condiments and the snuffbox.'

Happily these rules now appear to be largely ignored.

The Ormrod Committee appeared to disagree about the value of dining and its associated traditions:

'It is difficult to evaluate it reliably. It may play some part in the process of identification and in laying the foundations of that corporate spirit which is a real and important characteristic of the Bar. This object would be fostered if the practice of barristers and students dining at *separate* tables in hall was done away with altogether. On the other hand, the necessity to make frequent journeys to London can be a hardship . . . We do not wish to destroy the positive advantage of this tradition, but we think that it is essential that it should be adapted to present day conditions . . . .'[33]

Sir Robert Megarry, in an otherwise approving account of life at the Bar, also expressed doubts about the value of dining: 'Conversation at the students' table tends towards the personal, the trivial and the political . . . Today it is difficult to find any students who can see any value or utility in the ritual of dining in Hall. The food, it is said, is poor or scanty or both, and the conversation does no more than pass the time, but the Inn requires it, so one must go through the pointless ceremony.'[34]

In response to these criticisms the Inns have in recent years made some effort to improve the value of dinners. Moots are occasionally held, and on one or two evenings a term there may be an after-dinner speaker; but only a small proportion of students ever take part in the moots, and since the after-dinner lectures are optional a number of students leave hall before the lecture begins. It is clear that the original rationale of dining, according to which the students learned from the wisdom and experience of older barristers, can never be recaptured, for the simple reason that on most nights there are few if any practising barristers to be seen; they have all gone home to their wives and families, and apart from a token number of Benchers dining separately at High Table the Hall is almost entirely occupied by students. In these circumstances any attempt to restore to dinners their educational purpose can meet with only very limited success; and if the Inns really wish to pursue in earnest their (eminently laudable) aim of increasing the contact between students and practitioners some other means must be found. There can be little doubt that attendance at a residential course, which included moots, debates, lectures and discussions, in the company of Benchers and barristers would fulfil the aim of the Inns much more effectively than attendance at a series of dinners where, as often as not, the student only meets other students and his sole purpose is to eat dinner and leave as quickly as possible.[35]

THE INNS' FINANCES

The Inns are generally thought by barristers to be fabulously wealthy institutions. In fact they are not; but they have only themselves to blame if false rumours abound, because they are quite unnecessarily secretive about their financial affairs. The only time their accounts have ever been made public was in the Report of the 1855 Royal Commission; they were made available to the Pearce Committee, and they have since been submitted in an annual return to the Senate, but they are not generally available to members of the profession. By contrast the accounts of bodies like the Colleges of Oxford and Cambridge are not only in most cases shown to their students but have for some time been made available in the House of Commons Library.

It is difficult to know what the Inns have to fear, because they are not excessively wealthy. Unlike most ancient foundations they have no estates at all[36], and very little investment income apart from their scholarship funds. Their sole capital assets are in fact the land they stand on, the endowments being all for the provision of scholarships. In the Middle Temple the Harmsworth scholarship fund is worth around £1 million, and Lincoln's Inn and Gray's Inn have similar funds; the Inner Temple is forced to finance many of its scholars from its ordinary rental income.

With this capital position the only source of income for the Inns comes in rent – from barristers' chambers, from commercial tenants (solicitors, architects and accountants), and from those residents fortunate to have a flat in the Inns. The total income from rents varies, depending on the mix of tenancies involved; Gray's Inn, with a majority of commercial tenants, had an annual income from rents in 1975 of over £400,000, while in the Middle Temple gross rental income was £300,000, and in Lincoln's Inn and the Inner Temple it was thought to be between £200,000 and £300,000. Gray's Inn had no barrister tenants until 10 years ago; in 1976 it had about a dozen sets of chambers, but the income from them was still less than 10% of the Inn's total rental income, while commercial tenants provided 87%. In the Middle Temple by contrast barristers' chambers provide 75% of the total income from rents, and commercial tenants only about 10%.

Commercial tenants are charged a 'precinct rent', which is rather less than the level of commercial rents prevailing outside; a discount is offered in order to attract good tenants and to compensate them for the restrictive terms on which the Inns let their property (generally professional use only, with covenants against sub-letting). In Gray's Inn, which has for a long time handled all its letting through estate agents, this discount is 10%; in the Inner

Temple it used to be one-third[37], but in the Middle Temple, which now also uses estate agents, it is 10%.

In the three Inns which handled their own lettings commercial rents used to be extraordinarily low. In 1966 office space was still let to commercial tenants for an average rent of about £1 per square foot. In the Middle Temple rents have since been increased substantially; in 1976 commercial tenants paid £7.80 per square foot for good office space, £5.10 for property rated as medium and £3.20 for that classified as bad. Lincoln's Inn has been less successful, with 1976 rents being £2.16 in old buildings and £4.30 in new property (but this latter figure, unchanged since 1969, was in 1976 under review). In the Inner Temple the rents on bad property had been raised by 1976 to £2.92, and on medium property to £4.69; but on good property the rents of commercial tenants were still stuck at £2.50 (the figure set in 1970). It is difficult to find comparable property outside the Inns with which to compare these figures; but the market rent for Devereux Chambers, acquired by the Middle Temple in 1975, was reckoned by the Inn to be £11 per square foot at that time.

Barristers pay significantly less than commercial tenants for their chambers in the Inns. Overall, barristers pay about two-thirds of the precinct rent, but because rent reviews are not synchronized and because of the uneven effects of the Government's rent freeze the discount at any one time can vary from as much as 50% to as little as nothing. In 1976 chambers in the Middle Temple were paying £1.63, £2.87 or £5.28 per square foot, depending on the quality of the accommodation offered (and virtually no rates, because the Temple is its own local authority). The Inner Temple, caught by the rent freeze, had been charging barristers only 94p to £1.41 from 1971 to 1974, with the result that in 1975 it was forced to raise its rents to the Bar by 175%, to £2.60, £3.03 and £3.89. In Lincoln's Inn in 1976 barrister-tenants were paying £2.17 for old buildings and £2.24 (plus a service charge) for new accommodation.

The tenants of residential flats, who are mostly judges or senior members of the Inn (but not necessarily Benchers) pay substantially less. Residents in the Middle Temple paid 51p, 85p or 93p per square foot in 1976, and provided some 15% of the Inn's rental income. In Lincoln's Inn residents pay £1.08 or £1.86 per square foot; in the Inner Temple figures are not available in this form, but the actual rents paid for residential flats ranged in 1976 from

£269 to £685, and had not changed since 1970. Some indication of the privileged position enjoyed by residential tenants is given by the following: in the Inner Temple residential rents have risen by 68% over the ten years since 1966, while professional rents have gone up by some 550% over the same period. Residential rents may of course be subject to rent control, but not to this extent.

Apart from rents the Inns' only other source of income is their students. In the Middle Temple admission fees and call fees provide about £50,000 per annum, and in Gray's Inn about £40,000. In addition the Inns hold sizeable deposits from students; at any one time each Inn probably has the use of about £100,000 in the form of students' deposits. It is extraordinary that the only members of an Inn who pay fees (apart from the Benchers) are the students who can least afford it, while barristers who use their Inn's facilities extensively pay no annual subscription whatsoever.[38] If barristers did pay a subscription it would furthermore be tax-deductible, as a legitimate business expense; students enjoy no such benefit. For this reason the Pearce Committee proposed in its first Report that 'Lump-sum payments on joining and on call should be phased out and periodical subscriptions substituted ... Membership of an Inn and the use of its facilities should be conditional upon the payment of the appropriate subscription'.[39]

In its Second Report however the Committee recorded that 'Lincoln's Inn and the Inner Temple both give cogent reasons why it is not practicable at the present time to replace lump-sum payments on admission and call by annual subscriptions. It would result in an immediate and substantial loss of income with no guarantee that it would be recouped, because of the difficulty of devising any form of effective sanction to ensure the payment of an annual subscription.'[40] The Pearce Committee had proposed as a sanction that the Inns could provide in their tenancy agreements that the discount from the precinct rent would only be allowed if all the members of chambers had paid their annual subscriptions; but this was widely criticized as 'direct interference with the internal organization of chambers'.[41] The Middle Temple told us that there were also accounting difficulties: the Inn would not be able to foresee what proportion of its students would end up in practice, and what proportion would go abroad. But these are precisely the objections to the present system, under which foreign students and those who leave the Bar heavily subsidize those who remain. The transitional arrangements would of course be difficult, but not insuperable; and once the new system was established each Inn would be provided with a fairly constant level of income if all its members still in practice and all its students paid an annual subscription. It is difficult to make more than a rough estimate, but if each Inn receives between £50,000 and £60,000 per annum in fees and the interest on student deposits, and if this burden were spread evenly between students and barristers, the subscription necessary to produce an equivalent sum would be of the order of £30 per annum. Administratively of course subscriptions would be more expensive to collect; but now that the Bar has agreed that chambers should act as a unit for the purpose of paying their members' subscriptions to the Senate[41a], there seems no reason why they should not act in the same way for the purpose of paying subscriptions to the Inns.

On the expenditure side the biggest item is the cost of the administration; in the Middle Temple this came in 1975 to £150,000. The other items of expenditure are repairs and maintenance of the Inn's property (£65,000); the Inn Library, which costs about £55,000; and the Catering deficit, which in the Middle Temple that year was £35,000 and in Gray's Inn was £60,000. Gray's Inn, with its considerably greater wealth, can afford to spend a bit more on everything; it entertains fairly lavishly, it has a very generous loans scheme under which it lends money to pupils, and overall it claimed to spend £60,000 per annum more on its students than it received from them.

THE INNS AS LANDLORDS

In conclusion, what can be said of the Inns as landlords? One criticism which has been made is that they fail to squeeze the maximum possible rent from their commercial tenants.[42] The figures given above would certainly seem to bear this out; but inflation and complaints from their barrister-tenants have made the Inns much more conscious of the need to maximize their revenue from this source (if barristers knew the low level of rents charged to commercial tenants their complaints would doubtless be much louder). The Senate's rent equalization policy should also serve to make the Inns aware of the higher rents which some of them could charge, and (one would hope) of the level of rents outside; and the practice of certain Inns placing their lettings in the hands of estate agents should ensure that in future they at any rate obtain a fair market rent.

It is much more difficult to judge how the Inns should treat their barrister-tenants and their residents. In *Thomson v The Inner Temple* the judge said that members of the Bar took their tenancies on a normal commercial basis. It is arguable therefore that they should pay the full precinct rent; this would significantly increase the income of the Inns at the expense of the Bar, which in the long run would have to pass the cost on to its clients. At the moment the litigating public certainly enjoys a subsidy from the artificially low overheads of the Bar, and it may be that the Bar should charge a full market price for its services.[43] Raising rents to a commercial level would also ease the accommodation shortage by encouraging those chambers who do not need to be in central London to move out.

The Inns have always accepted that one of their responsibilities is to provide accommodation for the Bar; but in recent years that responsibility has become increasingly difficult to discharge. As a result of the efforts made in the late 1960s to convert accommodation occupied by commercial and residential tenants into barristers' chambers, 63 extra rooms became available for barristers in the Middle Temple and 105 rooms in the Inner Temple between 1964 and 1970.[44] In Lincoln's Inn and Gray's Inn only existing office space could be converted into chambers for the Bar; residential accommodation could not be converted because the Inns were unable to obtain planning permission for the change of use from the London Borough of Camden.

For the Temple the planning authority is the City, which so far has not objected to the change of use, but in 1975 the City Press demanded a policy statement on the future of the Temple as a residential community. That statement has now been issued, and the City has warned that in future it will resist changes of use that involve a loss of residential accommodation. The City Architect has therefore been instructed to make an urgent study of the possibility of accommodating barristers' chambers elsewhere in the City; but until that study is completed the City will not oppose any further applications for converting residential accommodation into barristers' chambers.

The number of residents in the Inns is still substantial. In the Middle Temple they occupy about 40% of the total accommodation available; but a number of these flats are simply pieds-à-terre which remain empty for most of the time, and others are occupied not by the actual tenant but by his children or nominees. It seems indefensible that young barristers should be forced to leave the Bar for lack of space in which to practise while these 'residents' occupy chambers which barristers could use; but the Inns have no legal power to intervene, because the residents can seek the protection of the Rent Acts. Meanwhile the opportunity for converting these chambers slips by, because the City's grace-period cannot be expected to last for ever.

Faced by the grave difficulties in the way of using existing accommodation more intensively, the Inns have tended to look for solutions elsewhere, by providing finance to the provincial Bars to enable them to expand, and by seeking to build new accommodation in London. At one time three of the Inns had planning applications outstanding for permission to erect new buildings; there was no attempt to coordinate these applications, or to place them in the context of the future development of the Bar, and all three applications failed. The Middle Temple's proposal to redevelop Fountain Court and part of Essex Street behind has since succeeded in a modified form.

What has been conspicuous in all these efforts has been what the Pearce Committee identified as the 'inability to achieve an overall long-term plan in which all the Inns and the practising Bar would participate together'.[45] Ultimately this can only be achieved if there is a single planning authority responsible for the future development of the profession. The Accommodation Committee of the old Senate realized this, and recommended the establishment of a central accommodation bureau for the four Inns. It also considered a more radical proposal, 'that control of accommodation in the Inns should be transferred to the Senate, who would be responsible, in close collaboration with the Inns, for obtaining, advertising, and allocating vacant chambers, for keeping a central register of the needs of chambers for space, and for organizing and funding future development within the Inns'.[46] The second proposal must be regarded, for the moment anyway, as a non-starter so far as the Inns are concerned, because it would involve such a major transfer of power; but it is disappointing that the first suggestion has also been ignored. It is conceivable, however, that the coordinating functions of a central accommodation bureau may be performed by the new Senate, which has initiated a rent equalization policy between the four Inns, and in the longer term may prove capable of coordinating future development plans.

DEMOCRACY IN THE INNS

The Benchers hold a position in the Inns which must be almost unique not merely politically but also legally. The latest edition of Halsbury's Laws describes their powers as follows:

> '*Authority of the benchers.* The benchers are the governing body who alone have power to fill vacancies in or to add to their own number, to admit persons as students, to call students to the Bar and to exercise a disciplinary jurisdiction over members of the Inn . . . They can refuse to admit a person as a student, or to call a student to the Bar. They can expel any member, and can disbar a barrister or suspend him from practice for a period, and disbench one of their own number . . . The benchers also decide on the amount of the fees which the members of the Inn have to pay, and on the application of the moneys so raised. In all these matters they are entirely outside the jurisdiction of the ordinary courts, but their decisions are subject to an appeal to the Lord Chancellor and the judges of the High Court of Justice, sitting as a domestic tribunal.
>
> '*Immunity of the benchers.* An action cannot be maintained against the benchers by a student or member of the Inn of Court in respect of any act done by them in their official capacity . . .'[47]

Few governing bodies have such sweeping powers. It is worth noting, however, that the Benchers did not establish their supremacy without occasional struggles on the part of the ordinary members of the Inns. Although, as we have seen, it was during the Tudor period that the Benchers first acquired these powers, Holdsworth records that it was only during the eighteenth century that it was finally settled that the government of the Inns was vested in the Benchers, with the other members having no share.[48] Claims by barristers and students to be entitled to inspect the accounts were made in all the Inns during this period. At Lincoln's Inn in 1688 the accounts were inspected by a committee of barristers and students; and in 1719 the Inner Temple allowed four barristers to do the same. In Gray's Inn the committee of two barristers and two students which inspected the accounts in 1720 made strong criticisms 'owing to the want of better collecting and applying the revenue' – a complaint which might be echoed word for word today.

But it was in the Middle Temple that some of the strongest protests were made, with barristers and students demanding in the early seventeenth century the right to assemble in a parliament in the vacation, and to propose reforms in the government of the Inn. After one such challenge to their authority the Benchers ordered the ringleaders to be fined and put out of commons. A contemporary recorded the barristers' and students' reaction as follows: 'Congregating most of the young gentlemen then in commons, they did come up all together the supper following to the Bench Table, and demanded a present repeal of the said order'. On the refusal of the Benchers to repeal the order, 'they hasted down tumultuously, and calling for pots, they threw them at random towards the Bench Table, and therewith stroke divers Masters of the Bench'.[49]

The Judges – who then of course were independent Visitors, being members of Serjeants' Inn – were called in, and although the Bench wished to expel the rebels the Judges persuaded the Benchers to pardon them on a written apology. But the Bench took the opportunity to emphasize that it would entail 'expulsion *ipso facto* for any man at any time hereafter to take upon him, to exercise, or claim, any power, liberty or authority, to govern within the House, otherwise than as subordinate and subject to the orders, control and government of the Masters of the Bench'.[50]

Even in Victorian times the supremacy of the Benchers did not pass without challenge.[51] This century, however, their position has been accepted without question. It was therefore a rude shock when in 1959 *The Times* described them in an editorial as 'notoriously unprogressive bodies', and suggested that they should be limited to the three rights of the constitutional monarch – 'the right to be consulted, the right to encourage, the right to warn'.[52] The Benchers were not slow to reply. In a letter signed by their four Treasurers they asserted that the Inns 'have for centuries recruited the governing bodies from the practitioners in their Halls, and each Bench is today a cross-cut of the Senior and Junior Bar, including those who have achieved judicial office'. This was followed by a number of justifications of their position, including the bold statement that 'There is no profession to which entry is less expensive and whose repute is higher'; and in conclusion the

Treasurers rejected 'all implications that the Benchers in fact or in intention frown upon reforms'.[53]

Only one of these statements will be followed up here (although a number of them are open to question). This is the assertion that the Benchers form a cross-section of the senior and junior Bar.

The Pearce Committee was nearer the mark when it commented that 'Usually only very senior members of the profession, many of them already Judges when elected, become Benchers and thereafter take part in the government of their Inns.'[54] An analysis of the Benchers listed in the *Law List* reveals that the junior Bar, which forms 90% of all barristers in practice, is represented by less than 5% of the Benchers in the four Inns. Even more serious, practising barristers – Q.C.s and juniors combined – account for less than one-third of the membership of the Inns' Benches. They are heavily outnumbered by the judges, who make up 45% of the Benchers; and the judges and the retired barristers between them account for over 70% of the total. Women are represented by just one Bencher in each Inn, two of them being members of the Royal Family.

In these circumstances it is hardly surprising that the Pearce Committee reported 'a disquieting tendency to think and talk about the Inns and the Bar as if they were in some way opposed to each other'.[55] This is because barristers have no say in the running of the affairs of their Inn, and are left with the impression that everything is carried on behind closed doors by a group of old men who are no longer in touch with the needs of the profession. There is no machinery of consultation, let alone representation, and the channels of information are virtually non-existent. There is not even much social contact with the Benchers within the Inns, because they occupy an entirely separate suite of rooms; lunch, for example, would provide an excellent opportunity for Benchers to meet practising barristers by eating with them in Hall – but they either eat in a separate room, or in those Inns where the Benchers do eat in Hall they sit apart at High Table.

In one or two Inns things are beginning to improve slightly. Lincoln's Inn has nearly 20 different committees, all of which have some representation from members of Hall (members of the Inn who are not on the Bench). The Middle Temple likewise encourages members of the Inn who are also members of a committee of the Senate to attend the corresponding committee of the Inn, even if they are not Benchers. But in general it is still true to say that there is a complete gulf between the government of the Inns, which is entirely in the hands of the Benchers, and the ordinary barristers. The Pearce Committee lamented that 'Inn decisions, which frequently are of great importance, often contain no element from the under-fifties, however talented or gifted, whether silk or junior'[56], and referring again to the 'we/they' attitude which it had found creeping into the relationship between the practising Bar and the Inns, it suggested that 'This unhappy development would, we think, be quickly reversed if members of Hall felt that they were more directly concerned with the management and thus the welfare of their Inns and did so at a somewhat earlier stage in their careers.'[57]

The argument for greater involvement in the government of the Inns would not perhaps be so strong if the Benchers were seen to be competent and imaginative custodians of the Inns' interests and responsibilities. But as other sections in this chapter have shown this is unfortunately very far from being the case. The rents charged to commercial tenants within the Inns have until recently been far too low. The legal education funds entrusted to the Inns' care (together with the Law Society) have dwindled to a fraction of the original sum.[58]

More recently, there has been the failure to carry through the idea of an Inns of Court Property Company which, as one of its progenitors has remarked, would have made the Inns a lot of money while providing the Bar with much-needed extra accommodation. And most worrying of all has been the Benchers' ambivalent attitude towards registering as charities, and their seeming uncertainty over what are the purposes of their own trusts: an uncertainty which calls into question their fitness to continue as trustees.

Quite apart from other factors, such as the age of the incumbents, the structure of the Benches is not conducive to good management. Each Bench is too large and unwieldy to be an efficient executive body, and the Treasurer, who is the chief executive, is appointed from among the Benchers not for his competence but simply by seniority. He holds office for one year only, so that however outstanding he may be, he has to hand over to his successor usually when he is just beginning to make his mark; effective continuity is thus extremely difficult.

Even in non-financial matters, the Benchers have not been noted for their imagination or initiative. The sponsorship schemes for students, in which the Benches now take great pride, were not their idea at all, but were introduced by two ordinary members of the Middle Temple. And in the Inner Temple the Benchers did so little for their overseas students that a Committee of Young Barristers was formed in the early 1960s in an attempt to give them better practical training; the Inn authorities were described in a PEP study as 'largely indifferent' to the experiment.[59]

In matters concerning the government of the Bar the general attitude of the Inns has also been one of cautious conservatism. The Benchers of the Inner Temple and Gray's Inn rejected the proposals contained in the Pearce Committee's First Report without making any attempt to ascertain the views of the members of Hall on what was, by any standard, a vital issue for the future of the Bar. This hostility towards a strong central organization was reflected also in the Inns' attitude towards the old Bar Council. For years they starved it of finance – the Inn contributions of £600 per annum remained unchanged at their 1895 level for over half a century. When *The Times* described this level of support as 'derisory'[60], the Treasurers retorted hotly that the 'subventions in the case of each Inn now very substantially exceed the "derisory sum" which you mistakenly cite'[61]; but rather embarrassingly in a letter printed on the same page Sir Lionel Heald Q.C. revealed that this very substantial increase amounted to no more than a rise from £600 to £900. Even in 1973/4, before the creation of the new Senate, each Inn gave only £1400 to the Bar Council.

There may well have been good explanations for this, as there may have been for the abandonment of the Property Company idea, or for paying tax and foregoing the advantages of being a charity; but if there are they have not been divulged. It is not even known if the Benchers take professional advice over the management of the Inns' assets, let alone what that advice might be; the minutes of their meetings are not seen. The case for greater participation by the members of the Inn is not merely the Pearce Committee's argument that under the present system a great deal of talent and expertise goes to waste; but it is quite simply that the members have a right to participate.

It is not sufficient, for example, for the Benchers of Lincoln's Inn and the Inner Temple to decide, without reference to anyone else, that it is impracticable to do away with admission and call fees[62]; their members might prefer for the future to pay an annual subscription – but they were not consulted. Nor were the members of Gray's Inn and the Inner Temple when their Benchers voted against the Pearce Committee's initial scheme. Nor were any members of the Inns when the Benchers decided to reject a common system of legal education for barristers and solicitors (even though the Bar Council was in favour).[63] Nor, to descend to more mundane matters, have the members of any Inn been told of the size of their catering deficit – let alone given an opportunity to express a view on whether they think this is a good way for the Inn to spend its money.

The Pearce Committee hoped that 'all the Inns will hold annual meetings of all their members, to which meetings the Inn's officers would report'.[64] Not one of the Inns has acted on this suggestion, but even if it were adopted, it would not be enough. What the Inns need are elections to the governing body by the members of the Inn. That is the only way to ensure that the government of the Inns is both representative of the Inns' membership and responsive to the needs of the members.

It is a measure of how far we have actually regressed that to the present generation of barristers democratic elections in the Inns will seem the most extraordinarily revolutionary idea. It did not seem extraordinary 100 years ago. It was proposed in the House of Commons by Sir Roundell Palmer, a former Attorney-General, who after describing the Inns as 'clubs more than public bodies [possessing] no corporate character, no legal organization, no acknowledged public trust or public responsibility' condemned the Benchers with the single question: 'Whom do the Governing Bodies of the Inns of Court really represent? They do not even represent the Bar. They are self-elected'.[65] Today those words ring truer still, because the Benches now are dominated by the judiciary in a way they never were in Palmer's day. Precisely because the judges are now so heavily represented, with practising barristers in a relatively small minority, the Inns' governing bodies are hopelessly unrepresentative of the constituency whose interests they claim to defend. If they were confident that they did adequately represent the views of the Bar they would not be so anxious to conceal from the Bar (and the public) what they do. They are caught in a web of secrecy from which the only escape is the introduction of some element of democracy.

Towards the end of the nineteenth century this realization was shared not merely by lawyer-politicians like Lord Selborne (as Sir Roundell Palmer became) and Lord Cairns, but by junior members of the Bar. Fifteen years after Cairns and Selborne had given up in despair their campaign to democratize the Inns a group of junior members of the Middle Temple took up the cause. They complained that the Benchers gave 'no information respecting the affairs of the property of the society to its members, although the latter are in equity, if not in law, joint owners of the property'[66]; and they argued that all appointments to the Bench of the Inns should be made 'by the votes of the members of the society and that the accounts of the revenues and expenditure of the society shall be duly audited and published'.[67] It is a sad reflection on the amount of change achieved at the Bar in the past hundred years that today those demands seem as far from realization as ever.

THE FUTURE OF THE INNS

Because the four Inns provide essentially identical services it has on occasion been suggested that they should be merged into one. Their libraries, it is argued, are underutilized, and their administrative scale of operations is so small that it must be inefficient. While there may be some truth in the premises of this argument the conclusion by no means follows. It is anyway a foolish argument because the Inns are clearly here to stay, and the most helpful contribution is to suggest ways in which their operations can be improved within the existing institutional framework.

Greater cooperation is clearly essential, and in the last five years significant advances have been made. The libraries are now in communication with each other, and they have agreed each to specialize in certain fields. In their role as landlords, the Inns are moving towards a rent equalization policy, and in time they may be able to establish a common services division to carry out the maintenance of their property. In these efforts the Senate has played and will continue to play a crucial role. It is now the focal point of all attempts to promote greater cooperation between the Inns.

All such attempts inevitably involve a transfer of power from the periphery to the centre. The Inns are at much the same stage of development as the colleges of Oxford and Cambridge 100 years ago; they realize that stronger central machinery is essential for the future development of the Bar, but they are reluctant to relinquish any of their sovereignty in favour of the central authority. Yet imperceptibly this is what has got to happen; and the model of Oxford and Cambridge shows that it can be done – and that in the long run both sides stand to benefit.

Within the Inns themselves one simple change would effect a revolution almost overnight: if one could only turn the clock back a hundred years to the days of Serjeants' Inn, when the judges on appointment automatically left their old Inns, the Inns would be governed by barristers again. It is traditional at the Bar to ignore the difference between barristers and judges, and to say with Sir John Donaldson that 'the reality is that "the profession" consists of "Bench and Bar" and not the Bar alone'.[68] The Pearce Committee certainly went along with this, adding for its part that it did 'not want to lose the benefit of the wisdom and experience of those who have become Judges'.[69]

It is high time that this particular fiction was laid to rest. The profession is the Bar and not the Bench and Bar. A judge is a barrister no longer, but a salaried official of the state; and his interests and concerns are very different from those of a busy self-employed professional man or woman. Certainly judges have wisdom and experience; so do all those in other walks of life who have arrived at the end of their professional careers. But in no other profession is it suggested that the wisdom and experience of retired practitioners entitle them to continue to play an active part in the government of the profession – let alone to dominate it, as the judges do in the Inns. The Bar can benefit from their wisdom and experience without abandoning its right to govern its own institutions. Although Serjeants' Inn can never be revived, it would not be difficult to provide that while judges could remain members of their Inns, and even Benchers, they should do so in a non-executive, purely honorific capacity.

This change coupled with direct election of the executive benchers would serve to end almost all the inefficiencies and absurdities of which barristers at the moment complain. If they were dissatisfied with the management of their Inn the remedy would lie in their own hands. But it would not exempt the Inns from continuing to be the proper objects of public concern. It would be naïve to suppose that the moment the Bar takes over the Inns all the abuses will cease; one cannot ignore the danger that the Inns will be regarded simply as clubs, and that the profession will not take seriously its responsibilities for the education and training of students and the career development of young barristers.

If the Bar continues to show itself unwilling to fulfil these responsibilities one further step will be necessary; and this is that the Inns should be brought under some kind of statutory control. The very suggestion will be anathema to most barristers, but provided they conduct their affairs responsibly and with due regard to the public interest they need have nothing to fear. The universities of Oxford and Cambridge are controlled by Act of Parliament, and periodically their colleges have to submit their statutes to the Privy Council for approval; and the solicitors' side of the legal profession has been closely controlled by Parliament for over two centuries. The Bar is a major profession which remains completely unaccountable to any public authority; yet as the Common Law Commissioners said in 1834, 'the ordinary immunities of a voluntary society ought not to be allowed to any body of persons claiming to be the medium of admission into one of the learned professions. If the Body is to enjoy this privilege, it is no longer a private association, but one in which the public has a deep interest, and the proceedings of which, if not adapted to the purposes of general utility, ought to be made so by the interposition of Law'.[70] The interposition of a regulatory Act of Parliament is one solution, and an inevitable solution unless the Inns themselves produce an alternative acceptable not only to the profession but to the public and Parliament.

3 LEGAL EDUCATION

THE BAR'S ATTITUDE TO LEGAL EDUCATION*

The Bar is not greatly interested in legal education. Long after qualifying exams had been introduced for all the other professions it was possible to be called to the Bar without giving any evidence of learning or even aptitude for the law; and even after exams were introduced (in 1872) they were such a nominal hurdle that up until the 1960s people coming down from university with law degrees used to sit the Bar final after a crash course lasting only three months. A barrister's training did not really begin until his pupillage; it was generally believed that only through pupillage could the professional skills be imparted – and of course in those days when a young barrister would probably not receive briefs for several years, it was possible to take a more leisurely approach to professional training. Now, however, that many beginners are appearing in court on a regular basis in their second six months of pupillage the quality of the training they receive is a matter of considerable public importance; but interest at the Bar in legal education continues to be minimal. One frequently hears the opinion expressed that the Bar exams are a waste of time, but very few barristers can be bothered to consider what changes might be made. Pupillage, despite its brevity, is still regarded as the most important element in a barrister's training.

This lack of interest in professional legal education extends also to the institutions in which the education is given. Historically, the result of this neglect has been that all Bar students who had a

* A fuller version of this chapter can be obtained from the Editor.

choice tended to avoid the Inns of Court School of Law, preferring to go to law tutors or to read privately for the exams. Until the mid-1960s the Council of Legal Education (which supervises the Inns of Court School of Law) was little more than an examining body; it kept almost no contact with the universities, and merely provided lectures for the few students who decided to attend. Indeed the Council would have been greatly embarrassed if more people had enrolled; for its first hundred years it had no premises at all, and in the post-War period its limited facilities have been subject to chronic overcrowding.

After the War the Council of Legal Education (C.L.E.) found itself in increasing difficulties because of the policy of the Inns to admit as students 'all persons of good character and of educational attainments which make it likely that with proper training they can become competent barristers'.[1] This policy amounted in practice to an open door to all those who could pay the fees, and it led to the admission of very large numbers of students from the colonies who had no means of qualifying locally. As the Ormrod Report was later to note, 'From being a quiet backwater catering for those few students who chose to attend its courses, the Council found itself with an intake which reached 1200 a year, and a student body of over 3000.'[2] It thus had far more students than any university law school, and indeed more students overall than some of the new universities; but despite these enormous numbers the Council continued to rely entirely on part-timers for all its teaching until the late 1960s. It was only on the reorganization of the C.L.E. in 1967, following the formation of the Senate of the Four Inns of Court, that a Dean and full-time teaching staff were first engaged.

THE ORMROD REPORT

In the same year the Lord Chancellor set up a Committee under the chairmanship of Sir Roger Ormrod (a former doctor who is now a judge in the Court of Appeal) to examine the whole field of legal education, both in the universities and Colleges of Further Education, and in the professional training schools. The committee reported in 1971. It recommended that legal education should 'be planned in three stages, namely: (i) the academic stage; (ii) the professional stage, comprising both institutional training and in-training; and (iii) continuing education or training'.[3]

The Ormrod Committee envisaged that for most students the academic stage would take the form of a law degree. Degree courses would be designed to give the student a basic knowledge of the law and legal principles; no attempt should be made to cover all the law which a student might require in practice, but the student should study basic subjects in such a way that he would learn how to find out what the law was on any given topic as and when he needed to. The Committee also hoped that law degrees would include some study of the relationship of law to the social and economic environment in which it operated.

The vocational stage, by contrast, would 'be strongly oriented towards practice, and should not primarily be regarded as a means of preparing for qualifying examinations; and conventional lectures in law should be kept to an absolute minimum'.[4] The emphasis would be on practical exercises, certain legal subjects of a practical nature and some non-law subjects such as behavioural science and business finance.

THE BAR EXAMS EXAMINED

Part II (the Bar final) has three compulsory papers, two on the professional techniques of drafting pleadings and writing opinions, and one on criminal and civil procedure and evidence. In addition three further papers must be taken from among a list of nine subjects.

Students who intend to practise in England and Wales are given only a restricted choice; they must take revenue law as one option and keep to practical subjects for their other options – and for them attendance is compulsory. Papers on European Community Law and Labour and Social Security Law were first introduced in 1976, the latter as a result of student pressure.

The Part II course is meant to be closely tied to the needs of professional practice. The examination questions are directed to 'testing the candidate's knowledge of the professional approach to legal problems of the kind which he is likely to encounter in the early years of practice at the English Bar, and his skill in the professional techniques of writing opinions and drafting pleadings and other documents required in civil and criminal litigation'.[5] The course might therefore be thought to resemble the vocational course recommended by the Ormrod Committee, but in the opinion of Professor R. M. Jackson of Cambridge it is 'substantially different and very inferior'.[6]

It is fair to say that the two general papers on writing opinions and drafting pleadings are practically oriented; but the substantive law involved is that of four of the six 'core' subjects already covered in the academic stage. It would be better to test a student's drafting ability either in the papers covering the optional subjects, or by a scheme of continuous assessment. Initially we doubted the wisdom of requiring tuition in any further substantive law subjects for Part II. But on balance we are of the opinion that there is a place in the vocational stage for such practical substantive law subjects as the law of landlord and tenant, family law, social security and labour law and sale of goods and hire purchase. Even more important for practice is instruction in the law and procedure of magistrates' courts (particularly when sitting as a juvenile or domestic court); and also in county court procedure. At the moment there is no provision for the former and scant instruction in the latter. Instead students are required to concentrate almost exclusively on the procedure of the High Court – a court in which it is most unlikely that they will appear in their first years of practice. Almost all young barristers start in the magistrates' court and the county court, and it is for practice before these tribunals that they most require preparation.

The balance still leans too far in favour of learning further substantive law subjects at the expense of practice and procedure. Civil and criminal procedure and evidence, which cover the essential tools of a barrister's trade, are all squeezed into a single paper. It is only fair to add that this anomaly has been recognized by the Dean of the C.L.E. and steps to rectify it and others of the problems outlined above are planned when a new Ormrod-style Part II is introduced in 1978–80.[7]

THE COUNCIL OF LEGAL EDUCATION

The lectures at the C.L.E. are given by established academics from Oxford, Cambridge and London, with barristers and judges lecturing more in the procedure subjects. In addition, in 1976, 16 full-time lecturers and nine part-time tutors were on the staff. This group consists mostly of recently qualified barristers, whose role is to take tutorials and theoretically (though not usually in practice) to help students with any problems arising out of their work.

With more full-time staff and greater experience the standard of teaching has gradually improved, but still falls far short of the claim advanced for it in the C.L.E.'s 1976 Calendar ('Today it can be claimed with some confidence that a scheme of education has evolved which offers as good a training for reading in chambers as is practicable').[8] This is a bold statement for an institution whose facilities are so inadequate that it still has no library, and whose lectures have to be relayed by loudspeakers to overspill classes in other rooms. It is not just the C.L.E. which is to blame but also the Inns for their neglect of the situation; having spawned one of the largest law-teaching establishments in the country, they have never yet willed the means for the school to be properly equipped.

The cramped buildings of the C.L.E. and the large number of students destroy whatever potential there may be for a collegiate atmosphere. Nearly all the replies to questionnaires sent out in the summer of 1976 by the Bar Students Working Party contained spontaneous remarks of dissatisfaction about some aspect of the training provided. The survey's results suggested that the majority of students left embittered and dissatisfied with their course, even if they had passed the exams.

PRACTICAL EXERCISES

Apart from the examined part of the course, a series of practical exercises run by the C.L.E. is compulsory for all students (including those from the College) intending to practise at the Bar in England and Wales. These consist of court attendances, forensic exercises and chambers exercises. The court attendances comprise six visits each of a day to a variety of courts: twice to a county court, once to the Old Bailey and once to another Crown Court, once to a magistrates' court and once to the High Court.

The forensic exercises take the form of demonstrations of various court procedures by judges and counsel to groups of some three hundred students, followed by the students themselves doing the same or similar exercises the following evening in groups of 10, instructed by practising members of the Bar. This procedure is designed to develop the student's capacity to examine and cross-examine, to make applications and pleas in mitigation and generally to familiarize students with court procedures. Yet the fact that each student has only five minutes in which to do the exercise considerably reduces its value. Once again the Dean of the C.L.E. is aware of the limitations of the present programme of forensic exercises and plans that the Ormrod-style Part II should give more opportunities for practical training.

The chambers exercises are also run by practitioners, and students are expected to have done the appropriate drafting before they attend the exercise. The purpose is to familiarize the student with barristers' paperwork. As with the forensic exercises, their value varies enormously depending upon the individual conducting them. Some put a great deal of effort into doing it well, correcting draft pleadings and giving individual attention. Others are much more lackadaisical.

THE SOCIAL AND EDUCATIONAL BACKGROUND OF BAR STUDENTS

In 1976 a Bar Students Working Party was formed to submit evidence to the Royal Commission. They sent questionnaires to all those who sat the summer 1976 Bar exams. With a 36% response their data showed the following:

Table 1: A Profile of Bar students in 1976[9]
Inn: Gray's Inn, 24%; Lincoln's Inn, 20%; Inner Temple, 21%; Middle Temple, 35%
Sex: Men, 79%; Women, 21%
Age: 18–23, 50%; 24–30, 33%; 31+, 17%
Colour: White, 79%; Non-white, 21%
School: Fee-paying, 55%; Other, 45%
Graduates: Oxford and Cambridge, 46%; Other graduates, 21%; Non-graduates, 33%
Family connections with the law: 24%
Intending to practise at the English Bar: 62% – of whom 6·5% were non-white, representing some 20% of all non-white students.
Intending to practise at the Bar elsewhere: 12%
Part II students in receipt of local education authority grant: 69%

Table 2 shows the admission and Call figures for the last 10 years. The figures indicate a rising success rate in qualifying for the Bar. Specific figures are not available, but in the early 1960s only some 40% of all students (British and overseas) appear to have succeeded in qualifying as barristers, compared with approximately 80% of those admitted in the early 1970s.[10] The success rate for overseas students in the 1960s appears to have been about 50%, whereas for the most recent group of overseas students for whom figures are available (those called between 1970 and 1975) this seems to have risen to 60% to 70%.[11]

Table 2: Admission and Call figures for British and overseas students 1966–1975[12]

Year*	Admission to an Inn of Court			Call to the Bar		
	UK	Overseas	Total	UK	Overseas	Total
1966	699	741	1440	236	292	528
1967	931	806	1737	247	312	559
1968	759	642	1401	246	279	525
1969	674	581	1255	370	318	688
1970	537	320	857	471	464	935
1971	659	363	1022	556	423	979
1972	745	388	1133	586	425	1011
1973	838	417	1255	561	352	913
1974	840	482	1322	529	212	741
1975	1023	794	1817	663	239	902

* Admission figures are for the Calendar year; Call figures for the legal year – so that the Call figures for 1966 relate to the year October 1965–June 1966.

OVERSEAS STUDENTS

In 1951 out of the C.L.E.'s intake of 1251 students, 842 came from overseas (438 from Africa). Virtually nothing was done to see that these entrants were capable of the course of study, to look after their welfare, or to see that they received adequate training. The educational requirements for admission to an Inn were minimal, and those students who passed the exams were able to return to their own countries as barristers, apparently fully-fledged, yet without any proper academic education or practical training, or experience of the courts and the administration of justice. Very few chambers were prepared to offer pupillage to such people; the Inns maintained that it was for the local Bar to make requirements for practical training or pupillage, although it was well-known that no such local requirement could be made.[13]

As Table 2 shows, in the last decade the proportion of overseas students has considerably declined. In 1960 about 75% of those called to the Bar were overseas students. By 1970 this figure had been reduced to 50%, and by 1975 the proportion of overseas students being called was down to 25%. The main reason for this decline was simply that the number of British students increased greatly over this period; but there were three other factors. Firstly, as former British dependencies achieved their independence they opened their own law schools.[14] Secondly, since 1964 students have only been allowed to sit the Bar exams four times, which has deterred a number of students (mostly from overseas) who had no real prospect of success. Thirdly, since 1970 there has been a priority system of registration at the C.L.E., with overseas students being accepted only on condition that there are places available for them.[15]

The findings of the Bar Students Working Party make it plain that even those black students who want to practise in England feel that they are not treated equally with their white fellow students. One Bar Finalist in the Inner Temple commented: 'It is bad enough for white students; it is unmentionable for the coloured students ... based on whom you know, and since most coloured students don't know anybody they get nothing [in the way of pupillage] ... one member of the pupillage panel suggested to me to go knocking from chambers to chambers: "That is the way", he said "you get fixed up".' Only 25% of those seeking pupillage had one arranged, while 50% of their white counterparts had arranged pupillage at the time of the survey.

FINANCE

The Bar Students Working Party's findings show, in order of precedence, that family (51%), local education authority grants (43%), savings (26%) and part-time working (26%) form the major sources of support for students.[16] In the current economic climate, the provision of grants is becoming more limited. Awards for study at the C.L.E. are discretionary. The working party found that only one-third of local authorities would be prepared to consider granting awards for Part I to a non-law graduate. Four local authorities have refused finance for Part II, even for law graduates. If with continuing restrictions on local government expenditure others follow their example it will have very serious implications for the socio-economic base of prospective barristers, causing it to become still narrower.

Table 3 shows the minimum reasonable expenses which the Working Party calculated a law graduate going to the C.L.E. for Part II would have to pay, up to and including Call to the Bar:

Table 3: Expenses of a law graduate during the Part II course at the C.L.E.[17]

Joining an Inn	£ 82
Admission fee to C.L.E.	7
Dining fee (8 terms)	24
Tuition fees	395
Exam fees	30
Books	40
Call fee	75
Living in London for 8 months:	
Rent @ £10 per week	340
Food @ £9 per week	306
Travel @ 90p per day	112
TOTAL	£1411

If to the total of £1411 is added a sum for general living expenditure, a student in 1976 had to find about £1650 to £1750 for the eight months of the academic year. In the circumstances it is not surprising that family support was mentioned more frequently than any other single source of finance for the Part II year by the students who responded to the Working Party's questionnaire.

THE ROLE OF THE UNIVERSITIES

The link between the legal profession and the universities in England and Wales is far more tenuous than in other countries. The normal European pattern is for a law degree to be the basic qualification for any practising lawyer. This has never been the case in this country, and one of the main themes underlying the Ormrod Report was that we should move towards establishing an all-graduate profession.

In fact so far as the Bar is concerned this proposal reflects the existing trend. In 1949 only 57% of those called to the Bar in that year had been to university. By 1970, 79% of British students were graduates (about 90% of them law graduates); and the figures for entry into practice show an even higher proportion. The C.L.E. estimated that about 95% of those commencing practice at the Bar were graduates, and about 80% law graduates.[18]

By contrast admissions to the solicitors' side of the profession in the late 1960s showed a much lower percentage that had been to university. About 45% of the intake were university graduates (most of them in law). Thus the Ormrod objective that the profession should eventually become a graduate one is for solicitors more difficult to realize; and in 1976 the Law Society announced that it would continue to admit student-members with A-levels only.

The divide between the legal profession and the universities goes deeper, however, than is reflected by the statement that most of our lawyers do not have law degrees. There is not simply a lack of communication but a degree of mistrust between practising lawyers and academics which is unknown on the Continent or in North America. This was a subsidiary reason why the Ormrod majority recommendation that vocational training should be transferred to the universities was rejected by the Law Society and the Bar (the primary reason concerned difficulties over finance). The professions were not prepared to see control pass into the hands of institutions and teachers whom they felt they did not trust.

England is unique in entrusting responsibility for vocational training solely to the profession. In Europe and in the United States even vocational training is regarded as being primarily the province of the universities. As a result law students receive a broader education than they do here.

One of the distinguishing features of foreign systems is not simply the closer formal links between the profession and the universities, but the frequent interchange of personnel between the two. In the United States it is common for successful practitioners to become university professors, and for law teachers to be appointed to the Bench (from the Supreme Court downwards). The Ormrod Committee was only too sadly aware of the gulf which separates the two camps in this country, and recommended that 'a standing Advisory Committee on Legal Education should be established as soon as possible to act as a link between the universities and colleges and the profession'.[19] A committee was set up under the chairmanship of Lord Cross (the present chairman is Lord Justice Lawton); but the differences of opinion which it spans are such that it has not been notably successful in increasing cooperation either between the universities and the profession or between the two branches of the profession itself.

THE CONTENT OF UNIVERSITY LAW COURSES[20]

Not only do the professions in England control all the teaching for the vocational stage, but they also have considerable influence over what is taught in the academic stage as well. In the United States the American Bar Association approves law schools which conform to its standards, but it does not attempt to prescribe the subjects to be taught. In England the professional bodies are able to influence what is taught, by providing that students will only be exempt from Part I of the professional exams if they have taken certain 'core' subjects as part of their university exams.

The consequence of the system of exemptions is that although only 60% of law graduates subsequently enter the profession, university law courses are geared largely to the student wanting to become a solicitor or barrister.[21] This applies not only to the content of the courses but also to their style. The emphasis is on learning what the law is, without much consideration given to why it is, or to asking what it should be. A common expression among law teachers is that they are concerned to teach their students how to 'think like a lawyer'. Because most law lecturers are themselves the product of university law schools (in particular those of Oxford and Cambridge) they tend to follow the same tradition which they were taught. The emphasis is on the study of the common law and the decisions of the higher courts; little regard is paid to modern legislation or to any of the problems of contemporary society.

In the last 10 years, however, a small but growing number of university and polytechnic law teachers have become dissatisfied with this approach; they are not interested simply in teaching professional skills, and they find the content of traditional law courses too arid and too narrow. In order to bridge the gap between the law in the books and law as it actually functions in society a number of attempts have been made to develop a new approach.

The first coherent departure was made by Warwick University, with its attempt to study 'law in context', i.e. to study law from the perspective of social problems – for example, housing, land use or consumer issues – rather than from the traditional legal concepts of property, planning law and contract.[22] Students are encouraged to look at non-legal material in order to find out how the law works in practice; and the work of administrative tribunals, magistrates' and county courts, which have far greater significance for the mass of the population than the High

Court, is studied much more closely than in traditional courses.

A second development has been in clinical legal education, which aims to involve students in 'real' legal situations by enabling them to advise clients and take cases before tribunals and the lower courts. This technique has been widespread for some years in the United States, but its future in Britain is uncertain. It was pioneered at the University of Kent at Canterbury[23], but their law clinic closed in August 1977, and now only Warwick and Brunel have a small clinical legal education programme.

Thirdly, there has been the development of multi-disciplinary studies. In certain universities students may now read law in combination with other subjects; at Cardiff for example a student may read law and economics, or law and accountancy, law and sociology, law and politics, law and philosophy, etc. Such mixed degrees are however only offered in about a dozen universities; in general, law faculties are wary about establishing closer contact with the social sciences. It is important not to get these new developments out of proportion. Out of the 29 university and 18 polytechnic law schools in England and Wales only about half a dozen institutions are extensively engaged in developing new approaches and methods of law teaching. The vast majority of law students continue to be taught on traditional lines. In Oxford and Cambridge Roman law is still compulsory; and most of the other large law faculties have seen only modest changes in the last decade, with the wider introduction of European Law, Revenue Law and Criminology being the only significant innovations.

CONCLUSIONS

It is important not to exaggerate what can be achieved by changes in legal education. The education which law students receive determines to some extent the sort of lawyers they ultimately become; but the fact that we have a narrow and conservative profession is caused by much more than our traditionalist system of legal education. The universities have no control over the process of self-selection in which it is generally the more conservative-minded students who choose to read law; nor are they responsible for the important socialization process which occurs when a law student enters the profession and quickly learns to adapt to the profession's received opinions.

Nevertheless more university and polytechnic law schools could take action to broaden their students' outlook; and attempts by universities like Warwick to teach the law in its social context do at least expose students to the idea that the law consists of more than a series of abstract rules and precedents. Such an approach need not be confined to the academic stage, but it should be concentrated there; the main purpose of the vocational stage is to impart skills, and it is by its success in achieving this aim that vocational training should be judged.

The Bar's failure to produce adequately trained barristers in the past stems largely from the profession's lack of interest in the subject, and reluctance to devote adequate resources to it; but in part also it stems from an excessively narrow view of what professional skills comprise. We have already made the point that too much time is devoted to mastering further substantive law subjects and not enough to practice and procedure; but there is another aspect which is completely ignored, which is that the law deals with people. Law teaching is based on an assumed set of facts; but in real life the facts have to be ascertained, in most cases from the client and other people. This is not simply the task of the solicitor; the barrister sees his client in conference, and in court will have to examine and cross-examine people from all walks of life, some of them inarticulate and frightened people who need understanding and encouragement before they will tell their story. This is so obvious it should not need saying, were it not for the fact that some barristers show extraordinary insensitivity when handling their clients and other witnesses. In other professions much thought has been given to interviewing techniques; in the legal profession it would be a fruitful subject of study.[24]

We would like to see a common vocational training for barristers and solicitors. It is true that the two branches of the profession have slightly different requirements, but the common ground is much wider than the points of difference, and these can be adequately catered for by a system of options. The Bar is probably not so hostile to the idea as might be supposed; in a survey in 1966 a 'large proportion of barristers' indicated that they favoured common training.[25] The provision of legal services to the public can only suffer if each branch of the profession continues to be ignorant of the workings of the other. A common vocational stage would not lead to the fusion of the two branches of the profession; but it would enable the prospective lawyer to keep his or her options open for a longer period before deciding which branch of the profession to join, and it would ease transfer for a lawyer who subsequently felt he had joined the wrong one. A common vocational stage would also provide a better training for students from overseas who will be practising in a fused profession.[26] But so far as this country is concerned, the main benefit would undoubtedly be to promote much greater mutual respect and understanding between solicitors and barristers.

Finally mention needs to be made of continuing legal education. At the Bar there is no provision for further education after qualification. The system is one of complete *laissez-faire* – if a barrister wants to become an expert in a subject then he teaches himself. This works reasonably well for able barristers, but the more humdrum practitioner could probably benefit from refresher courses or courses in new legislation. Here again the focus should not be too narrow; barristers also need to keep in contact with other professions and disciplines. The Ormrod Committee thought that interdisciplinary courses (bringing barristers together with those working in the social sciences, medicine, economics, business and finance) were just as important as the acquisition of further techniques. In both fields the Council of Legal Education could play a leading role.

4 PUPILLAGE

Pupillage is an apprenticeship during which a young barrister is attached to an experienced practitioner (called his pupilmaster) in order to learn the practical aspects of a barrister's calling – to find his way around the courts, to study advocates in action and to try his hand at some of his master's paperwork. Until 1959 anyone called to the Bar could commence practice without doing pupillage at all. Apprenticeship with a practising barrister was traditional, but it was not obligatory; and in post-War years over a third of those starting to practise at the Bar did so without serving a pupillage.[1] In 1959 the Inns made pupillage compulsory, by amending the Call declaration to include an undertaking not to practise at the English Bar without doing twelve months' pupillage (with a practising barrister of at least five years' standing). However this still did not preclude young barristers from commencing practice while *in statu pupillari*, and a few chambers used to push their pupils in at the deep end by arranging for the occasional brief to be given to a youngster just starting pupillage, in the belief that this would be good for his or her confidence.[2] What it did for the confidence of the client history does not relate; but in 1965 the rules were further amended, so that now no pupil may accept instructions or conduct a case in court during his or her first six months of pupillage.

FINDING PUPILLAGE

Pupillage is thus a mandatory requirement for all those who wish to practise at the English Bar; unless the aspirant barrister can pupillage simply by going round the Temple knocking on doors and asking in the clerks' room. Not surprisingly, he had had no success. 'Many counsel and their clerks consider it bad form for an intending pupil to go around canvassing for openings in clerks' rooms, or to write out of the blue to a head or senior member of chambers. It does not seem to be widely appreciated that an intending pupil may be forced so to act for want of any other way . . .'[7]

Fortunately there are now alternatives for those who have no contacts of their own. In 1972 a special committee was appointed under Sir George Coldstream precisely because of 'a widespread feeling that the present arrangements for assisting pupils to find places leave many individuals unable to complete their education as barristers'.[8] The working party recommended that each Inn should establish a Standing Pupillage Committee, to assist students in deciding what sort of pupillage to look for, and to help them find such a pupillage. These committees are now in operation, and the administrators in the different Inns estimated in 1975 that between one-third and one-half of all students might be using the official schemes. However a study of the problem in 1976 showed that family connections continued to be the single most common method of arranging pupillage, and that introductions through friends and direct application were still more common than use of the Inn Pupillage Committees: of the respondents who had arranged pupillage at the time of the survey only one-fifth had done so through their Inns.[9]

All this is a great advance on the previous system (or rather lack of it), but it is not the comprehensive counselling service recommended by Sir George Coldstream's Committee. It suggested that each Inn should keep not only a register of pupilmasters, but also a register of all students requiring pupillage, and that *every* student should be seen by the Pupillage Committee. Why have the Inns failed to set up a proper scheme along these lines? The main reason is doubtless that it would require a lot of time and expense: more clerical work would be involved in maintaining a double register, and membership of the Pupillage Committee would certainly be a burdensome responsibility for barristers and Benchers if every student had to be interviewed, some of them more than once.

Another reason why the Coldstream recommendations have not been fully implemented is that most people still think that the present system works tolerably well. It must be acknowledged straight away that thanks to the Standing Pupillage Committees no student now should fail to get pupillage simply because he or she does not have the right connections.[10] The main deficiency remaining in the present system is that it continues to depend on the old system of introductions, and there is still virtually no cooperation between the Inns in trying to find a joint solution to what is a common problem (they are almost completely ignorant of the details of each other's schemes). The bodies that presented evidence to the Coldstream Committee were unanimous in recommending a central system of registration, both of would-be pupils and of available pupilmasters. Only in this way can a rational and efficient system be devised for matching up the overall demand for pupillage with its supply.

The Young Barristers' Committee of the Bar Council devised what is the simplest but potentially the most effective scheme. It suggested that the Bar Council should compile an up-to-date register of all barristers willing to take pupils, giving a brief description of the type of work done by each. Each student would then be given a copy of this register and would have to identify the four pupilmasters with whom he would most like to do pupillage, and then return the register to the Bar Council together with four copies of his *curriculum vitae*. The potential pupilmaster would then interview those students who had applied to do pupillage with him, and unsuccessful candidates who had not been accepted by any of four their first choices would be able to reapply for further interviews under a clearing house scheme.

The beauty of this scheme is that there is complete freedom of choice and full information available to both sides, so that it should ensure open competition for the best pupillages; and pupils will (hopefully) be selected according to merit and their prospects of success, rather than their connections with, or introduction to, a particular barrister or set of chambers. Furthermore the scheme is designed to be used by everyone, so that there can be no risk of those using the scheme being labelled as in some way 'second class' pupils. The other great advantage is that the selection is done by pupils and pupilmasters themselves, and not by third parties, whose choice is inevitably limited, and who cannot help but let their own preferences creep into the introductions they arrange.

A centralized scheme of this kind was urged upon the

Coldstream Committee not only by the Young Barristers' Committee (whose report was drafted jointly by a Labour and a Conservative Lawyer), but also in broadly similar terms by the Bar Council and the Under-Treasurers of the four Inns.[11] The reason why their recommendations were not accepted was probably due in part to the uneasy relationship then existing between the Bar Council and the Inns, neither of which thought the other was capable of providing an adequate pupillage service. Now, however, that the Bar Council has disappeared, and the new Senate which has taken its place has been expressly designed to represent not only the Bar but also the Inns, the issue can be looked at afresh. It should be the task of the Senate, on behalf of the Inns, to compile the register of pupilmasters and to act as a clearing house for the pupils' returns; while the Inns would continue, through their Pupillage Committees, to perform their very important function of counselling and giving advice. This would of course involve more work for the Senate, but it would make less work for the Inns, who would no longer be responsible for the compilation of their separate registers. The maintenance of a register is clearly something which can be done more efficiently centrally, and is preeminently the sort of service which the Senate should provide, since its whole *raison d'être* is to promote greater cooperation between the Inns and to avoid unnecessary duplication of effort.

Of course a central scheme of registration will also depend on cooperation from the Bar, which is almost invariably hostile to filling in forms and to centralize coordination of any kind. The Bar has already shown a poor initial response rate to the registers compiled by the Inns, and the sad fact has to be faced that most barristers probably would rather not have pupils. But it has now been fairly widely broadcast that if a barrister does not take pupils he may be prejudicing his chance of judicial or other preferment; and there are elements in the proposed scheme which might make having a pupil a far more attractive proposition. In the first place barristers may have been reluctant to take pupils in the past because they had so little information about a pupil's potential; pupils came into chambers through an introduction from friends or relations rather than on merit. The system of open competition based on interviews and a *curriculum vitae* should do much to remedy this. Secondly, the burden of having a pupil would be considerably reduced if the responsibility for training pupils were shared among the members of chambers as a whole – a proposal which was first made by the Ormrod Committee, and which is considered in the next section.

THE QUALITY OF THE TRAINING

When I first appeared in a magistrates' court to represent a client of my own I had only been in such a court twice before, during 15 months of pupillage. This was because all three of my pupilmasters had practices confined almost exclusively to the High Court. Such an experience is quite common among pupils, and something about which the Ormrod Committee expressed specific concern:

> 'The danger that the pupil will not receive a sufficiently wide experience is a real one. Most pupilmasters are aware of this, and try to ensure that their pupils have the opportunity of spending part of the time with other members of chambers, particularly the younger ones who are doing the sort of work which the pupil will be doing when he has completed his pupillage, for example, in county courts and magistrates' courts.'

The experience of most of those who have contributed to this book is that this latter statement is untrue. The Ormrod Report continued:

> 'We think that this attitude should be encouraged, and that it should be generally accepted . . . that part of the obligation of the master to the pupil is to ensure that he gets as much, and as varied, an experience as the chambers can provide.'[12]

One way in which the committee suggested this might be achieved would be 'by altering the basis of pupillage, so that the pupil becomes a pupil of a set of chambers (rather than of one member), or by the head of chambers assuming responsibility for seeing that the pupils in his chambers get as wide an experience as possible . . . While there are definite advantages in a pupil having a specific master, the emphasis should be upon "reading in chambers" rather than solely with an individual barrister.' In order to prevent an inexperienced young barrister like myself from being let loose on an unsuspecting public this proposal should be incorporated in the code of ethics as a professional obligation. A very firm lead needs to be given from above directing that each head of chambers should either assume responsibility himself for the training received by the pupils in his chambers, or should appoint some other member of chambers to do so.

Some of the better organized sets already delegate responsibility for the interviewing and selection of pupils to one of their number; but the idea that he should also be responsible for their training is a novel one. He might of course still assign pupils to a specific master, but he should also ensure that pupils get moved around; and if pupils feel they are not getting a sufficiently broad training the head of chambers or his delegate would be the person to whom they could go for redress. This was the situation envisaged by the Ormrod Committee, which suggested that 'the informal arrangements which exist in some chambers, under which the head of chambers concerns himself personally with all the pupils in his chambers, became both general and formally recognized. This would provide pupils with a person other than the pupilmaster to consult if, and when, they were in difficulties, and would enable the Inns, or the General Council of the Bar, to exert their influence more directly over pupillage.'[13] As yet neither the Inns nor the Bar Council have accepted responsibility for the quality of the training provided during pupillage, except through rejecting the applications of certain pupilmasters to have pupils. This power was adopted originally to prevent the abuse of 'pupil farms' (when out-of-work barristers took in large numbers of pupils simply to live off their pupillage fees); but it appears now hardly ever to be used.

TRAINING OUTSIDE THE BAR

Not only is the training provided within chambers sometimes excessively narrow, but at the moment training for the Bar is confined exclusively to practical experience acquired within the Bar. No attempt is made to introduce the young barrister to skills or disciplines other than his own, or to give him practical experience of related professions, or indeed of related aspects of the legal system. The most obvious blind spot is in relation to the other branch of the legal profession itself. Barristers will spend the whole of their professional lives advising solicitors, but the vast majority embark on their careers without any practical experience of how a firm of solicitors operates.

In most other jurisdictions where there is a split profession this is not the case. In Australia and South Africa it is standard practice (though not a professional requirement) for would-be barristers to spend a couple of years training first in a solicitor's office; in Scotland an intrant is *required* to spend 21 months with a solicitor before he can start 'devilling' (pupillage) for a practising advocate. The Scottish Faculty of Advocates says that it regards the period in a solicitor's office as 'invaluable'[14], and it is not difficult to see why. Solicitors are the consumers of the Bar's services, and any barrister who has worked in a solicitor's office must have a much clearer idea of what solicitors expect and require of barristers, and will be far better equipped to provide his solicitor-clients with sensible and useful advice.

But the solicitors' branch of the profession is not the only part of our legal system which barristers would do well to familiarize themselves with before retreating to the quieter waters of the Bar. There is also the mainstream of the system, the court structure itself, presided over by judges and magistrates, Masters and Registrars; that part of a barrister's life which is not devoted to advising solicitors is spent in addressing arguments to these people in their respective tribunals. The value of spending some time with such officials to see how they work and to learn how they can most effectively be addressed by counsel is self-evident. It has for a long time been possible to be a Marshal to a High Court judge (by personal invitation), and recently a marshalling scheme has been introduced for county court and Circuit judges: but this should now be extended to cover magistrates, Masters and Registrars as well, and it should be made a compulsory part of the training to spend some time with at least one of these judicial officers.

Clearly this kind of training cannot be provided as part of pupillage. It must be organized in the form of a course. This much has been recognized by the Bar, which since 1970 has laid on compulsory Practical Exercises as a prelude to pupillage; but the training the course provides is derisory. The exercises probably no longer deserve the scathing comment of the Ormrod Committee, that the amount of practical training did not even justify compulsory attendance; but they still fall far short of Ormrod's own proposed vocational course, which was intended to last 40 weeks and to 'contain as much practical work as possible'. The

Ormrod Committee's vocational course was moreover intended to introduce students to other, non-legal fields of knowledge which they would find useful in practice:

> 'Two subjects are obviously important to all lawyers – elementary behavioural science, covering such matters as interviewing techniques, the interaction of lawyer and client on each other, normal psychological development of children and their interaction with their parents, and the basic facts of mental disorder; and business finance, so that the basic principles are understood and balance sheets can be read intelligently.'[15]

The Committee's suggestions fell upon deaf ears. The Bar simply does not recognize that it is uneducated in this respect; but even if there were the will to break this insularity, it would be hard to find the finance.[16] As a short-term alternative some members of the Ormrod Committee suggested that the Bar could do something to secure a 'wider experience by providing short courses during pupillage on various topics of value in the early days of practice'.[17] It would be a poor substitute; but it would at least be a step in the right direction.

THE COST OF BEING A PUPIL

Even in 1913 the Haldane Commission described pupillage as an 'expensive process'[18], and although the fee of 100 guineas has depreciated considerably since then, pupillage can still be an extremely hard struggle for those who do not have private means. Every entrant to the Bar spends a minimum of two years after leaving university when he or she earns no income at all. The law graduate has to spend a year working for Part II of the Bar Exams, for which he may or may not receive a Local Authority grant; and he then has to spend a year as a pupil, when he will have to live entirely by his wits – no grants are given, and for the first six months pupils cannot take briefs of their own. Often they will have to wait much longer than that: I was at the Bar for 16 months before I received my first brief. Only those in criminal chambers can normally expect to get briefs in their second six months: and even they will not be paid until long afterwards – usually not until well into their second year.

At the same time as Bar students and pupils are earning no

income they have to live – and the vast majority have to live in London. The Bar Students Working Party calculated that in 1976 the expenses of being a pupil for a year came to about £2,000.[19] Robes cost £130, and a pupil has to pay his own travel (and sometimes hotel) expenses following his master around the country. He also has to pay further fees to his Inn; on top of the admission fee (£80) there is a call fee of £75, and more dinners to be eaten. These are now relatively small items compared to general living expenses, and it is fair to say that they have not been increased in recent years. In former times they must have formed a considerable barrier to entry; but the Bar has always been remarkably unconcerned about the costs to people who did not have private means. In 1969 the Bar Council told the Monopolies Commission: 'As for the young man from a working class home, if he has "the necessary intellectual and moral qualities" ... there is no reason whatever why he should not be able to overcome these financial hurdles.'[20] The Ormrod Committee was not so sanguine. 'Entrants have to face the problem of financing themselves during the period between leaving the university and beginning to earn their livings at the Bar. Although this period is much shorter for most young barristers than it used to be, it is still a formidable difficulty for many, and a deterrent for others.'[21] And the Young Barristers' Committee of the Bar Council has declared unequivocally that: 'The considerable cost of pupillage is an undoubted deterrent.'[22]

Nevertheless the belief is still widespread that it is a good thing for beginners to have to struggle through pupillage, on the ground that those who have the tenacity to continue despite all the difficulties are more likely to make good barristers. The information collected in 1976 by the Bar Students Working Party should put paid to this particular myth. They found that what in fact happens is that many promising candidates never come to the Bar at all because of the financial obstacles, and that those who do come tend to be those who can afford it. 55% of the Bar students who replied to their questionnaire had been educated at private schools, and thus came from families with means; and when asked how they intended to finance their pupillage, the largest single category (45%) replied that they intended to rely upon family support.[23] The effect on the Bar's intake was illustrated by the evidence from University Careers Officers: Cambridge reported an increasing number of students were deciding not to go to the Bar because they could not finance it, and Hull University said: 'Very many able young law graduates do abandon their plans to qualify as barristers simply because they are unable to face both the financial disadvantages and the uncertainty of a career at the Bar.'[24]

In order to do something to alleviate the cost of pupillage both the Young Barristers' Committee and the Ormrod Report made one proposal for immediate implementation – that the pupillage fee should be abolished. Both these recommendations were ignored by the profession; most barristers remained completely unaware of them, and the Bar Council did nothing to draw them to the Bar's attention. However in 1975 two members of the Young Barristers' Committee moved a resolution at the Bar A.G.M. that pupillage fees should not normally be charged, and this was carried by a substantial majority. A subsequent referendum endorsed this decision (by 826 votes to 334), but supported the *status quo* when it came to enforcement; by 428 votes to 363 the Bar decided that each pupilmaster should be allowed to continue to exercise his discretion in the matter. The Senate therefore has no powers to carry the resolution into effect; but it is probably true to say that the vast majority of pupilmasters no longer charge a fee. However even so long as one pupil earning nothing has to pay £100 to a master earning thousands or tens of thousands (and who passes most of the fee on in tax) the Bar cannot rest content. The taking of a pupillage fee should be made a breach of professional conduct, as it is in Scotland.

But abolition of the fee is not enough; pupils should also be paid. In the solicitors' branch of the profession not only have premiums now disappeared, but articled clerks are paid a wage which in 1976 averaged £2000 *per annum*.[25] Pupils should be paid likewise. It is not sufficient, as the Young Barristers' Committee has proposed, that they should be provided with interest-free loans.[26] Nor is it sufficient to rely upon the scholarships currently available from the Inns, so frequently referred to as if they were freely available to anyone in need, but in practice awarded almost exclusively to Oxbridge graduates, and anyway only worth (on average) about £300 *p.a.* The Ormrod Committee put this source in its proper perspective when it said that, despite some increase in the number of scholarships provided by the Inns, it was making only a small contribution to the solution of the problem.[27]

The real solution is to recognize that pupils do work for their pupilmasters, and to pay them for it. Some pupils earn their masters a lot of money by the help they give them with their paperwork, but it is very rare for them to be paid. There should at the very least be a rule requiring pupilmasters to pay their pupils on a devilling basis for the work they do for them (just as pupils are – or should be – paid when they do some piece of work for another member of chambers).

A better arrangement, however, would be for pupils to be paid by a general levy on all the barristers in chambers. The burden would not be nearly as great as might appear, because the expense would be tax-deductible, and if treated like other chambers expenses a greater share could be borne by those at the top who pay tax at higher rates. In the average set of chambers the net effect of paying three pupils a salary of £2000 *p.a.* would be to reduce the other barristers' annual post-tax earnings by only about £250 each.[28] This solution would also tie in well with the Ormrod Committee's emphasis on pupils 'reading in chambers' rather than being attached to one pupilmaster: if all the members of chambers were responsible for paying pupils collectively they would take a greater collective interest in the pupils' training. They would also be more selective in their offers of pupillage, which would no longer be made simply on an 'old boy' basis, but on merit. As the Bar Council itself has said in another context, 'Many young men are admitted into chambers on an informal recommendation and with little knowledge of their potential ability. If the partnership was to pay the young man a salary, then far greater assurance would be required of his abilities and potentialities.'[29]

There is a further advantage to the pupil of being paid, which is not purely financial. Payment would alter the whole status of a pupil, and his own feeling of his worth. At the moment the master/pupil relationship can be profoundly exploitative: I have known one very busy (and successful) barrister have up to four pupils at a time, and thanks to them he was able to accept far more briefs (and earn far more money) than if he had been working on his own. Paying pupils would not only end this exploitation, but it would also give them a greater sense of responsibility for the work which they do. At the moment pupils can take very little pride in their work because it is seldom used, and when it is adopted it is passed off not as the pupil's but as the master's. If pupils were paid there would be a greater incentive to make good use of them, there would be a recognition that the work pupils do is of value, and the pupils themselves would feel that they belonged to the team instead of being hangers-on. In every other European country, and in the United States, young lawyers are given considerable responsibility as soon as they join a firm, and they are paid accordingly. This applies whether the profession is fused or divided. In France for example the rules of the Bar lay down minimum salaries for apprentice *avocats*: at the Lyon Bar in 1975 a *stagiaire* had to be paid at least £1400 in his first year and at least £2800 in his second – and it is up to his *maître de stage* to see that the firm gets value for its money.

Lack of payment for his work is not the only indignity a pupil has to suffer. In many other little ways he is made to feel unwanted, transient, a second-class citizen. In a number of chambers pupils are not allowed to use the telephone, nor can they be telephoned: the clerks are told (or themselves decide) not to take calls for pupils. In one set of chambers where I was a pupil we were not even allowed to share in the chambers' supply of tea and coffee!

If pupils were paid, their whole status would change and all these little pinpricks should cease. Of course it will be argued that chambers would simply cease to offer pupillage if pupils cost money. But they would have to recruit from somewhere, and I suspect that quite quickly chambers would be competing with each other for the best pupils in the same way that City firms of solicitors compete for articled clerks today.[30] A more substantial objection is the argument that pupillage would be far harder to find, because chambers would be looking for value for their money. However this might not be such a bad thing: the effect would simply be to force out at an earlier stage those who are unlikely to succeed later anyway – and in the long run this must be kinder to them.

It is true that some barristers, for the noblest of reasons, feel very strongly that all students who hope to practise (however forlornly) should have the chance to do pupillage; but the numbers of those currently embarking on pupillage so far exceed the numbers of those who can hope to enter practice that some chambers are already deliberately trying to cut down on the number of pupils they take in. They have no room for them afterwards, and feel that it is dishonest to offer pupillage to people who have no prospect of practising. This policy may appear harsh; but I think myself that it is right. Not only is a great deal of individual misery avoided, but a considerable body of highly skilled people is put to better use: it is pointless wasting the time of pupils (and of their masters) training them for a profession in which they will not be able to remain, However, whether a given individual will be able to find a tenancy depends so much at the moment on his being in the right place at the right time that one can sympathize with those who feel that everyone should at least have the chance to draw a ticket in the lottery.

FINDING A TENANCY

The offer of pupillage imposes no obligation on a set of chambers to make room for the pupil subsequently as a tenant. This was emphasized by the Bar Council in 1972 when it reminded barristers that they 'need not be so inhibited in offering pupillage since no corresponding obligation arises in regard to the provision of tenancies, and indeed the substantial increase in recruitment in recent years has enabled chambers to become more selective in this regard'.[31] Chambers are now in fact so selective that officially virtually none of them have any vacancies whatsoever[32]; but it is said that there is always room somewhere for a really outstanding candidate. Whether he or she finds that room however is very much a hit-and-miss affair; and the last part of this chapter is devoted to examining how this situation might be improved.

One method of resolving the problem is to reverse the presumption that pupillage does not necessarily lead to a tenancy; and in the provinces this has to some extent already been done. In a number of provincial cities chambers do not normally offer someone pupillage unless they intend to take him or her on as a tenant afterwards; selection of pupils is accordingly more rigorous than in London, but once selected the pupil knows that provided his work is satisfactory his future career is assured. Several senior members of the Bar (including an ex-Chairman of the Bar Council) have been heard to suggest that such a system should be introduced nationwide, but this opinion has yet to be voiced in public.

Meanwhile so long as the present situation continues, with only about one pupil in two finding a tenancy, some scheme must be devised to ensure that the few places that are available are given to those best qualified to fill them. At the moment it is quite literally a matter of being in the right place at the right time: when a vacancy does occur (by a barrister retiring, or being appointed to the Bench, or by chambers acquiring more rooms) it is almost invariably filled by one of the pupils then in chambers. There is virtually no interviewing of outside candidates; the best pupil currently in chambers is simply invited to stay on. In a few sets (happily now, I think, the exception rather than the rule) it is not even necessarily the best pupil who gets the tenancy. I know of one set, for example, where the last three tenants taken on have all been the sons of former members of chambers.

No formal machinery can eliminate this kind of nepotism, but it can at least give other pupils the opportunity to press their claim when a vacancy does occur. This would be ensured if vacancies were officially publicized. The Bar Council itself in an unpublished report has proposed such a scheme, involving the registration of tenancy requirements and vacancies[33]; and the Young Barristers' Committee has spelled out in greater detail how this kind of scheme might work:

> 'If a set of chambers wishes to take on a new tenant it should be obliged to give the Bar Council three months' advance notice of that intention. This requirement should apply equally to a set of chambers which wished to take on a former pupil and to a set of chambers seeking to recruit from outside.
>
> The Bar Council should then maintain and publish an up-to-date list of these vacancies. Any pupil seeking a tenancy (whether in his own chambers or elsewhere) would then be free to apply to any set of chambers who had notified a vacancy: the chambers would then be free to decide whether or not to interview him and whether or not to accept him.'[34]

This latter proposal was also contained in an unpublished report, which prompts speculation as to whether the Bar Council lacks the courage of its convictions when it comes to laying its more radical or forward-looking ideas before the profession. This is a pity because unless it does share its ideas with the rest of the Bar, professional thinking on the subject will remain as blinkered as ever (or simply non-existent), and chambers will continue to select tenants by the same secretive methods that they have always used in the past. In some chambers the process is secret even from the pupils themselves, in that they do not know who does the selecting (it may be the Head of Chambers, or a cabal of the senior members, or all the tenants together); nor do they know when the selection takes place. This for the individual pupil is one of the cruellest aspects of the whole system: a pupil who is hoping to be taken on as a tenant is kept in an agony of suspense for periods of up to a year or sometimes even longer, not knowing when his or her fate is to be decided, or even whether it will be decided at all. The subject is generally completely taboo, and thus not a matter which can be raised by the pupil, however anxious; he must wait for his pupilmaster to mention it first. Most pupilmasters are now sufficiently aware of their pupils' concern that they discuss their prospects with them almost as soon as they arrive in chambers, but some still remain silent and leave their pupils in complete ignorance of where they stand. Even when a barrister does discuss the matter with his pupil, however, there is often little he can usefully say, since there is normally no chambers policy on whether or not they will recruit an extra tenant, nor is there a given date by which chambers will decide. The pupil sometimes has to weigh up the risk of hanging on as a 'floater' after his pupillage has finished, in the hope of still being offered a tenancy, or of moving elsewhere, either (if he is lucky) as a tenant, or (more and more commonly) in order to do a third pupillage.

With the acute shortage of accommodation chambers are becoming more ruthless towards floaters, however, and it is increasingly common for pupils to be told if there is no hope for them at the end of their 12 months, rather than being kept in continued suspense. The Young Barristers' Committee has proposed that all pupils who are not taken on should be required to leave chambers within a certain fixed period, which they thought should be three months.[35] This would avoid prolonging the agony for pupils, and would also force chambers to make a decision one way or the other at the end of each person's pupillage; and where a particular pupil could show he had been making every effort to obtain a tenancy elsewhere the period could perhaps be extended by a further three months, where necessary.

The crucial thing which at the moment goes more or less completely unrecognized is the necessity of keeping pupils informed of their progress. Pupils have a right to be told as soon as it is practicable whether or not they can reasonably expect to stay on, so that if the answer is negative they can start making alternative arrangements. So often one meets young barristers who have completed their 12 months of pupillage and are clinging on with no idea whether or not they can remain at the Bar, simply because no one in their chambers can be bothered to make a decision about them.

As with almost everything else at the Bar, some chambers are far more conscientious in this matter than others. The same is true with regard to interviews for tenancies: a few chambers are beginning now to invite outside candidates for interview when they propose to fill a vacancy. But pupils can only learn about the vacancies on the grapevine; and that is no substitute for having a comprehensive system of registration which would advertise the vacancies to everyone who might wish to apply. Similarly it is no answer to the charge that many chambers keep their pupils in complete ignorance of their prospects for the Bar to reply that the good sets always keep their pupils informed. In this as in so much else the Bar Council must give a firm lead, and not merely confine its thoughts to internal memoranda. Until it does have the courage to speak out and if necessary to make regulations on these matters pupils at the Bar are never going to get a fair deal.

5 CLERKS AND FEES

WHAT DO BARRISTERS EARN?

In 1977 the Bar published statistics about barristers' earnings for the first time. Until the Royal Commission started its inquiries the Bar Council itself had no precise idea of what barristers earned; it had never tried to find out, and the only available data were figures thrown up by partial surveys commissioned by outside bodies for other purposes. With the advent of the Royal Commission, however, the Council commissioned a special survey of barristers' incomes, at a cost of some £10,000; and the results were published in March 1977.

Before presenting the information from the Bar Council's survey one earlier set of data is worth mentioning, and these are the Inland Revenue Statistics; although five years out of date, they do give an impression of how the Bar compared with the other main professions at that time.

Table 1: Professional earnings in the years 1971 and 1972[1]

	Average earnings		Number of tax returns	
	1971	1972	1971	1972
Solicitors	£5286	£6582	22,448	23,408
Architects	£2969	£3786	13,646	14,777
Barristers	£3681	£3733	3226	3664
Dentists	£3840	£3616	13,539	15,217
Doctors	£3560	£3440	40,484	44,014
Accountants	£3117	£3323	24,134	25,664
Engineers	£2095	£2326	12,051	12,763

The most striking thing about the figures is how much more solicitors earned than any of the other professions. In 1972 the average income of solicitors before tax was £6582, while the average income of barristers was only £3733.[2] The average at the Bar conceals a wide distribution: because of the large numbers entering practice 30% of all barristers in 1972 earned less than £1000, pulling the median income of barristers down to about £2300 (that is to say, one-half of all barristers in practice earned less than this sum).[3] The total take of the Bar from professional practice was very nearly £20 million in 1972, or £13.7 million net of expenses.

The Bar Council's survey shows that by 1975–6 the total gross take of the Bar had risen to about £40 million, and that some 43% of the Bar's earnings came from public funds (49% for juniors, 24% for Q.C.s).[4] The wide distribution of earnings is still very marked. At the bottom end nearly half the profession was earning less than £5000 before tax in 1974–5; at the top some 5% was earning over £20,000. Although the survey concentrated on the year 1974–5, barristers were asked to give estimates of their earnings for the year then just ended of 1975–6, and because these figures are the most recent they are the ones cited here (all the survey figures are in any event fairly approximate).

In 1975–6 the average net earnings of Q.C.s were estimated to be £21,500 (median £19,400). The earnings of juniors were considerably less, the estimated average for 1975–6 being £7300 (median £6100). There was almost no overlap with the earnings of Q.C.s: the upper decile of juniors earned an estimated £14,000 in 1975–6 (the figure earned by the lower quartile of Q.C.s). All these sums are made after deduction of professional expenses (clerks' fees, rent, chambers overheads, travelling etc.) which amount to about one-quarter of gross fees for Q.C.s and about one-third for juniors (not including pension provision and sickness insurance, which are considered below). Taking juniors and Q.C.s together, the average pre-tax earnings of the Bar in 1975–6 were about £8700. No comparable data are available for other professions from such a recent date, but to provide a standard of comparison it is interesting to note that the Boyle Review Body on Doctors' and Dentists' Remuneration recommended in 1975 that the average annual income of G.P.s, net of expenses, in 1975–6 should be £8485.[5] It would thus appear that the earnings of barristers and of doctors have kept broadly in line with each other in the five years since 1971 (see Table 1).

The Bar Council's survey also provides some interesting information on the earnings of barristers in different kinds of practice. The highest earners are to be found among the Chancery and specialist Q.C.s, who at the very top in 1974–5 were receiving gross fees of £50,000 to £60,000 (almost none of which came from public funds). At the bottom the quickest start is obtained by young barristers on Circuit, who are overtaken by the Chancery and specialist barristers in London after about five years in practice; the lowest earners are the common law practitioners in London, but after 10 years they catch up with the Circuiteers, and after 15 years in practice all juniors tend to settle down to similar earnings regardless of the nature of their practice. This is because the high fliers are creamed off at around this stage to take silk, leaving the more humdrum practitioners in all sections of the junior Bar earning approximately the same (average gross fees of senior juniors in 1974–5 were around £13,000).

The survey is also of interest for the light it sheds on the fees earned by barristers from public funds. Ever since Michael Zander's study of lawyers' fees in the Crown Court this has been the subject of intense speculation; it was the outcry which arose in response to his findings that was one of the immediate causes of the establishment of the Royal Commission. Zander's study showed that combining brief fees and refreshers (the daily fee paid to counsel for each day after the first day of a trial) gave the following gross fees earned from public funds by barristers (prosecution and defence) from work in the Crown Court:

Table 2: *Average fees per day earned by barristers in the Crown Court in 1974*[6]

	Contested cases	Uncontested cases
Q.C.s	£161	£145
Juniors with Q.C.s	£91	£76
Juniors alone	£55	£32

It is extremely difficult to use these average daily fees to calculate average annual earnings, because there are so many variables involved, and Zander wisely refrained from making any such calculation. Had he done so it might have looked something like this:

Table 3: *Hypothetical annual earnings from work in the Crown Court in 1974*

	Gross fees	Net earnings
Q.C.s 150 days @ £155	£23,000	£17,000
Senior juniors 200 days @ £60	£12,000	£8000
Junior juniors 200 days @ £40	£8000	£5500

The hypothetical nature of these figures is emphasized by the Bar Council's survey, which reveals a much wider range of earnings from criminal work (especially at the junior Bar) than Zander's average daily fees disclose. In part this is because of the great variation in the extent to which barristers specialize in crime. In London there is a fairly sizeable criminal Bar, but there are many common law practitioners who also do crime, while in the provinces most circuiteers combine criminal work with a general common law practice.

The Bar Council's survey indicates for the first time the annual earnings of these different kinds of practitioners from publicly-funded criminal work. A few prosecutors in London earn huge sums. Some half-dozen juniors of over 15 years' call earned gross fees of between £25,000 and £35,000 from prosecution work alone in 1974-5; but the vast majority of barristers doing criminal work earn far less than this:

Table 4: Estimated annual gross earnings from public funds for criminal work in 1974-5[7]

	London (criminal Bar)	London (common law)	Provinces
Q.C.s	n.a.	n.a.	£13,000
Juniors (15 years and over)	£15,000 to £20,000	£5000 to £10,000	£6000
Juniors (9-15 years)	£10,000	£6000	£6000
Juniors (4-8 years)	£8000	£4000	£5000
Juniors (3 years and under)	£4000	£2000	£3000

These figures show how difficult it is to determine what level of fees barristers should be paid by the Government for providing representation in the criminal courts. In medicine part-timers are paid an agreed proportion of a full-timer's salary: for consultants combining private practice with practice under the National Health Service the proportion is 9/11ths for $4\frac{1}{2}$ sessions a week. The difficulty at the Bar is that the proportion of time devoted to publicly funded criminal work varies from barrister to barrister; for some it is as high as 100%, for others less than 10%. Yet the Royal Commission will have to propose some basis for calculating legal aid fees which keeps the Bar's earnings roughly in line with comparable professions; and in order to make a comparison it is hard to see how it can avoid some calculation of the annual earnings of a hypothetical full-time criminal practitioner. This is the way in which doctors' and dentists' fees are negotiated, on the basis of a target average annual income, and in order to still public criticism a similar process will have to be introduced for the Bar.

A further complication for the Royal Commission is that before one can start making a direct comparison between barristers' earnings and those of people in employment, allowance has to be made for the fact that barristers have to make their own provision for sickness and retirement. If a barrister falls sick his earning power collapses with him; on retirement he receives no pension, but has to live on the money he has put aside during his working life. A deduction must be made therefore for personal pensions' premium and sickness benefit insurance; in 1975-6 Q.C.s were putting aside an average of £1200 for this purpose, and juniors £300.[8]

The Bar has often rested its case for higher fees on the argument that barristers all have to provide for their retirement, but in fact a substantial proportion of the Bar can expect to receive a state pension at the end of their careers as a result of taking up judicial appointments. A High Court judge receives a non-contributory (and inflation-proofed) pension of the same amount as a Permanent Secretary in the Civil Service, but after only 15 years' service; he also receives a lump sum and there is provision for his dependants. Circuit judges, stipendiary magistrates and chairmen of tribunals are similarly provided for on their retirement with pensions of one-half of their final salaries. Obviously some discount must be made for the fact that barristers who receive judicial pensions will not need to provide for their retirement; and the degree of discount will depend on the proportion of barristers who can expect to receive judicial office.

The Office of Manpower Economics in a rough calculation reckoned that one-fifth of Q.C.s became High Court judges and that nearly 40% of those who were juniors at the age of 50 became Circuit judges.[9] But Q.C.s also become Circuit judges, and the High Court and Circuit bench do not exhaust the range of pensionable posts available to the Bar. In 1976 there were 495 judicial and quasi-judicial posts occupied by barristers[10], all carrying a pension and all of the kind to which a barrister is appointed towards the end of his or her career. Because of the enormous increase in the number of these posts in recent years, while the pool of eligible barristers has remained unchanged, the chances of a senior barrister receiving a judicial or quasi-judicial appointment have increased from about one in three to very nearly two in three. Almost two-thirds of those barristers currently of over 15 years' call can expect to receive a judicial appointment and hence a pension when they retire.[11]

This makes the case for higher fees because of the need to provide for one's retirement seem rather thinner, and could be used by (for example) the Treasury to argue that any notional allowance in barristers' fees for pensions provision should be reduced by two-thirds. The difficulty is that the proportion of barristers who can expect to receive judicial office is not constant. The present situation will last only until about 1985, when the bulge at the bottom of the Bar will have worked its way towards the top and will provide a much larger pool from which to make judicial appointments; the ratio will then sink to one in three again or even less. A more fundamental difficulty is that no individual barrister can count on receiving a judicial appointment and so most will continue to set aside money for their retirement just in case they turn out to be among the unlucky ones.

Nevertheless the present situation cannot be accounted satisfactory. The Bar has pressed that its fees (almost half of which come from the State) should reflect the necessity for barristers to provide for their retirement; yet a majority of those currently at the top of the Bar can expect to receive a pension and so will find their retirement provided for twice over. Only two solutions present themselves which would resolve this inequity. Either the generous pensions received at the moment by the holders of judicial office should be shared out among all retired barristers, and their fees correspondingly reduced to reflect this entitlement; or judicial posts should be made non-pensionable, and all barristers be expected to provide for their own retirement, from their fees or judicial salaries or both. The first solution is unlikely to recommend itself to the Treasury, and the second unlikely to find acceptance at the Bar (and certainly not among the judges); but until one or the other is adopted the Bar's claim for enhanced fees because of pension requirements will continue to be undermined by the fact that so many of its members have no need to provide their own pensions.

THE ROLE OF THE CLERK

A barrister's fees in any given case are a matter for his clerk. Until relatively recently a barrister was not allowed to discuss fees at all with his instructing solicitor. Then in 1951 this rule was relaxed to allow Q.C.s (but not juniors) to discuss fees 'in cases of special difficulty'; and in 1966 the rule was further relaxed to allow juniors to discuss fees as well – but again only in cases of 'special difficulty'. In the vast majority of cases the negotiation and fixing of the fees is left entirely to the barrister's clerk.

The clerk is thus a figure of great importance. Fee-fixing is only one aspect of his job: more important still, he gets in the work. It is the clerk who 'sells' his principals over the telephone to inquiring solicitors, the clerk who decides that Miss X rather than Mr Y will do the possession action in Bow County Court on Monday morning and the clerk who determines how much Miss X will charge. In the classic description by Sir Robert Megarry, the clerk 'is a complicated cross between a theatrical agent, a business manager, an accountant and a trainer . . . A good clerk may be worth a fortune to his principals; a bad clerk may cost thousands, or even spell disaster'.[12] The clerk manages every aspect of a barrister's professional life. He is especially important at the beginning of a barrister's career, when it is unlikely (unless the barrister is well-connected on the other side of the profession) that solicitors will send work to him personally, and most of the briefs he receives are sent to him solely on the recommendation of the clerk. If there are a number of beginners in the same set of chambers, the clerk may see to it that one prospers while another does not; he may believe in launching them all together, or one at a time.

At every stage the clerk is in the saddle and the barrister is the workhorse, doing the work which comes his way. If his services are in demand that will not simply be due to his merits but also to the support of his clerk. The clerk may apply the whip or pull on the rein: he may overload a barrister with work, or he may decide to shield someone from overwork by asking for higher fees or simply by saying that he or she is unavailable; and the barrister may never know what has been done or what work has been turned away in his name. The clerk may also consider a particular barrister to be good at certain kinds of work and not good at others, in which case that barrister will not do much of the others; a good example of typecasting is the commonly-held view that women are good at matrimonial work, but not really fitted for commercial cases. Usually the clerk's opinion will coincide with the barrister's preference, but if it does not, the barrister will have little option but to change chambers if he wants to work more in his chosen field. This power of the clerk to affect the lives of his principals continues throughout their careers, and even a Q.C. was forced recently to move because he fell out of favour with the clerk: in his first year in his new chambers with a new clerk his earnings are said to have more than doubled.

Why do barristers tolerate this situation? In the first place, they are not allowed to practise without a clerk. It is one of the fundamental rules of etiquette that every barrister must practise from chambers with a clerk. Secondly, many barristers like having their lives organized for them. To borrow once again from the account by Sir Robert Megarry (who did not perhaps realize the disturbing implications of the situation he was describing):

> 'All that counsel has to do is to do the work his clerk arranges for him. If Gamma's clerk comes into Gamma's room on a Monday and tells him that he has a twenty-guinea brief in Clerkenwell County Court on Friday next, all Gamma has to do is get up the case in time and fight it. He may never have heard of the case or the client or the solicitor before, and he may never hear of them again. The negotiations over the brief may have been protracted and difficult, or they may have been short and satisfactory; of this Gamma may know nothing. If a case is far out of London, it is Gamma's clerk who will see that a room is booked for him at an hotel and that he catches a suitable train. Gamma has nothing to do except his work; and he is set free of all clerkly worries so that he may do that work well. The barrister's clerk is his shield and his buffer.'[13]

USEFUL FUNCTIONS OF THE CLERK

It is of course true that barristers could not operate without their clerks. The clerk performs many useful functions for which the busy barrister simply does not have time, and which he might not be particularly good at anyway (though I suspect most barristers could be a lot more businesslike than circumstances, and sometimes affectation, permit them to be). The question is whether the clerk could perform the functions of office manager without in effect managing the business as well.

One must consider first what are the 'office manager' functions performed by the clerk. Probably the most time-consuming is the book-keeping work, which in a large set of chambers is done by staff junior to the clerk. When a brief is delivered, the clerk records the fact; and when the work is done, the papers are marked out and the appropriate fee-note is prepared. Periodically thereafter (usually every quarter day) a fee-note will be sent to the solicitors until the fee is paid – sometimes not until several years later. When the cheque eventually comes the clerk either gives it to the barrister concerned, or pays it direct into his bank; often this is the first time that a barrister discovers what he has been paid for a particular piece of work done months or even years before. Some of the procedures and book-keeping routines have not significantly altered for decades and possibly even centuries. With the introduction of V.A.T. the old ledgers have now given way to card-index systems; but most of the other methods used in clerks' rooms appear to have remained virtually untouched by modern techniques of office management.

Secondly, the clerk is a 'fixer', juggling with the court lists to try to ensure that his principals can handle all their cases without being in two places at once. Often clerks achieve the seemingly impossible, but if prudent they err on the side of caution and ensure that counsel with conflicting commitments is 'covered' (i.e. that an alternative barrister is available and reasonably familiar with the facts of the case) just in case the impossible cannot be achieved.

Some clerks take more risks than others; no clerk gives overmuch consideration to the wishes of the client. Of course they will try to ensure that the barrister originally briefed in a case will see that case through, but they will also ensure that the chambers diary is kept as full as possible, and this inevitably gives rise to conflicting commitments. In the event of a conflict the clerk's first thought is what action will give least offence to the solicitors concerned: if this means taking Mr X off a case in order to release him for a more lucrative brief, or to please a firm of solicitors who are regular customers, then this may be done with little thought for the possible effect on the lay client. Mr Y can step into the breach and in this way chambers will get two briefs instead of one. Only firm action by the barrister involved can prevent this sort of thing from happening; but not all barristers have the conscience or the courage to control their clerks in this way.

Juggling with lists and deploying his team of barristers so that the maximum advantage is obtained from each is skilled work and is learnt only by experience; the clerk is helped by his network of contacts, and especially by his friendship with the judges' clerks, most of whom were once barristers' clerks. They will help him arrange for Mr X's case to be 'first on', or alternatively for it to be kept out until he arrives; and to ensure the continued cooperation of all those who can make life easier for him the clerk will distribute gratuities at the end of each term to the key personnel in the Law Courts. The wheels of justice run on a little graft like any other business; but most barristers are blissfully unaware of this, as of so much else that goes on in the clerks' room in their name.

OTHER FUNCTIONS PERFORMED BY THE CLERK

These two functions are the obvious aspects of a clerk's job which barristers could not easily perform for themselves (although even for these functions a clerk is not essential: in some of the other common law countries barristers arrange their own appointments, and keep their own accounts). The more controversial aspects of a clerk's work are his role in fixing fees and in distributing work between different members of chambers. The extent to which the clerk allocates work between his principals (as opposed to briefs being sent specifically to an individual barrister) varies from chambers to chambers. But no one would deny that a fairly considerable proportion of the work is distributed by the clerk in almost every set, particularly among junior members; the more senior members can usually tell how much of their work comes to them personally. The delivery of a brief with a barrister's name typed on it does not necessarily mean that the solicitors asked for that person in the first place, since it is common for solicitors to telephone chambers before delivering a brief in order to find out who is available – and they then type on the brief the name of the barrister selected by them after discussion with the clerk.

It is one thing, however, to face up to the fact that much of our work comes to us *via* the clerk; another (much harder) task altogether to suggest alternative ways in which 'non-specific' work might be allocated among the different members of chambers. Alternatives do exist, however; in Ireland, South Africa and most states in Australia barristers manage without clerks at all. These and other alternatives are discussed at the end of the chapter, in the context of the whole system of chambers organization.

THE DETERMINATION OF FEES

Fees can be discussed as a separate issue. The clerk's right to be the sole negotiator of fees in all ordinary cases is based on a variety of different reasons, the most important of which is simply tradition. 'Fees are clerk's business, and counsel gratefully and trustingly leaves it to him.'[14] Closely allied with this is the feeling that it is distasteful for a professional man to be involved in haggling over his own fees; architects and accountants, doctors and dentists, solicitors and surgeons may negotiate their own fees, but not the Bar. There may also be a measure of self-interest in the arrangement: clerks may have the nerve to demand fees which are higher than many members of the Bar would ask for themselves.[15]

In fact the importance of the clerk as a fee-negotiator has considerably declined in recent years because of the advent of Legal Aid. In legally-aided work no fee is marked on the brief in advance; instead counsel's fees are determined after the event by the appropriate Legal Aid authority. In some cases the clerk may be able to negotiate with the appropriate body but in most cases the fee is simply accepted – until recently without the clerk (or for that matter counsel) being aware of the criteria according to which the fee is computed. However, in 1976 a scheme was introduced in the Crown Courts under which counsel fills in a form after each case to indicate to the taxing authorities the amount of preparation involved, etc., so that barristers doing criminal work are now aware of the considerations which guide their legal aid payments; but in the event of dispute it is still the clerk who argues the case for revision of the fee.

In another large class of cases the fees are more or less stereotyped and leave little room for argument. Thus in all interlocutory (i.e. pre-trial) work in personal injury and divorce cases there are published scales of fees for each item of work which a barrister may be instructed to do. For example in 1975 the standard fee for drafting a statement of claim in a 'running down' (road accident) case was raised to £12, and for writing an opinion to £13.[16]

In fact the fees for almost all paperwork are fairly standard, which is why there is normally no previous agreement as to fees when counsel is asked to advise or to draft a pleading; the clerk sends out a fee-note after the papers have been returned to the solicitor, and provided the fee is reasonably close to the market rate for the work done there is not usually any difficulty.

Brief fees are a different story. These are wide open to negotiation and vary enormously – from £15 (the norm for a small case in the magistrates' court) to £25,000 (the figure paid to a leader in a recent commercial action which involved months of preparation). The brief fee is the fee for preparing the case and for the first five hours of the hearing: if the case lasts for longer than one day the barrister is paid a further fee known as a 'refresher', which may range from £25 to £200 per day. The brief fee must be marked on the brief before counsel goes into court; oddly, the refreshers are often not agreed until after the case is over.

Brief fees give clerks the most scope for negotiation – negotiation in which the barrister can play no direct part, except in cases of 'special difficulty'. The Bar Council's justification for excluding the barrister is that he is not himself competent to judge what is a proper fee: 'The basis of the rule is not that it would be "ungentlemanly" for counsel to deal directly with fees. The basis of the rule is that this is a matter better left to someone able objectively to assess what is a proper fee.'[17] This is an extraordinary argument, since only the barrister who has done or is about to do the work knows how much work was or is involved. This is particularly the case with advisory work. Sometimes the barrister feels the clerk has charged far too little; sometimes that he has charged far too much.[18] The question is, whose opinion is right – the barrister who has done the work, or the clerk who knows what the market will bear? Most barristers would agree that the market rates for various categories of work are quite out of proportion to the skill and effort involved: advisory work, except at the specialist Bars, is on the whole grossly underpaid, while certain classes of court appearance (e.g. Crown Court criminal work) have in the past been over-remunerated.[19] One reason why fees have become such an indefensible lottery is that they are negotiated by clerks who do not themselves do the work.

The disparity between brief fees and fees for advisory and interlocutory work was glaringly revealed in a study in 1975 by Michael Zander, on the costs of personal injury cases in the Queen's Bench Division between 1970 and 1974.[20] Although a strenuous critic of many aspects of the Bar, Zander was forced to admit that barristers are badly underpaid for interlocutory work. Of advisory work he concluded, 'the range of fees for this work shows that it is very inexpensive . . . in 77% of cases fees were not over £10'; and of drafting he reported, 'in only two per cent of cases was any fee over £15. Again, therefore, this class of work per item is remarkably cheap'. Since Zander's study interlocutory work has become even cheaper, as the modest increases permitted in the level of fees have been far outstripped by inflation.[21]

What barristers lose at the interlocutory stages they hope to make up on the brief fee when an action comes to trial. Inevitably because so few actions come to trial (the proportion is only between one and two per cent)[22] brief fees are disproportionately large. I remember a fairly typical junior's brief in a big divorce case in 1974, for example, being marked at £750 (with refreshers, presumably, of £100 or £150 a day). That barrister said not a word during the three-day hearing, his client's case being conducted entirely by the Q.C.; but he justified his fee on the basis that the case had taken three years to come to trial, and during that period he had drafted numerous pleadings and affidavits and attended a number of conferences, for all of which he had been underpaid. This sort of experience is by no means uncommon, and higher brief fees could doubtless be quoted. Their recipients would adopt the same justification: that the brief fee is a reward to counsel to compensate him for selling his services at below their true value in the earlier stages of the action.

Michael Zander's sample of personal injury cases provides evidence of just how great the increase in counsel's earnings is when an action comes to trial. The total fees paid to counsel in those actions that settled prior to any hearing were on the average only £32. By contrast the average fees in contested cases were £284, and in cases that settled at the door of the court £271. Virtually the whole of the difference is accounted for by the brief fee, and refreshers (where appropriate).[23] The average brief fee in Zander's sample for a junior on his own was £80; the average fee when he appeared with a Q.C. was £107. The junior has far less work to do at the trial when being led; the only possible justification for his increased fee is that Q.C.s are briefed only in 'heavy' cases which will have involved more difficult advisory and drafting work, and hence the element of subsidy in the junior's fee has to be greater. The average brief fee for a Q.C. in personal injury work was found to be £193.

This swings-and-roundabouts system of remuneration severely penalizes litigants whose cases come to trial and subsidizes those whose cases are settled beforehand. It also engenders in barristers a cynicism about the whole Alice-in-Wonderland system of fees which leads to passive acquiescence in one of the most anomalous rules of all, which is that once a brief has been delivered the brief fee has to be paid, even if the case subsequently does not go to trial. Although the brief fee is meant to be payment for the preparation of the case and the first five hours of the trial, a barrister is entitled to his full fee even if the case is settled on the day after delivery of his brief and he has not had time to undo the ribbon.

The only justification for this rule is that when a case is settled at the last moment a barrister will not normally find alternative court work for that particular day. But he can get on with his paperwork; in such circumstances a barrister may deserve to be paid for preparing the case for trial, but he certainly does not deserve to be paid for the first five hours of a trial which does not take place. Nor does he deserve to receive any brief fee in those cases which settle well before the last moment and before the barrister has started to prepare the case for trial.

The rule is one reason why briefs tend to be delivered at the very last moment to counsel, leaving them with insufficient time to prepare the case properly. If there is any hope of a settlement the solicitors will hang on to the brief, thus saving their client the expense of paying counsel for a trial which never takes place. The rule of etiquette used to be mandatory that the brief fee might not be remitted or reduced, whether or not the case proceeded to trial. But in 1964 the Law Society protested that 'A fee to counsel should not be payable . . . for work not done or for a service not rendered,'[24] and as a result the rule was relaxed so as to permit counsel to accept no fee or less than the agreed fee if a case is settled after delivery of the brief.[25] There is still no obligation on counsel to do so, and to judge by Michael Zander's study this privilege of waiving one's fees is seldom exercised in personal injury cases. He found that in 46% of the cases in his sample in which a trial brief was delivered to counsel there was subsequently no trial; but the average brief fees demanded by counsel and allowed on taxation in such cases were £190 (a number of such cases involved Q.C.s, and so there were two brief fees).[26]

It is difficult to dissent from Zander's conclusion that these were costs which were wholly or largely thrown away. If only barristers were paid adequately for the work which they do, and there was a rule forbidding them from being paid for work which they do not do, this sort of abuse would not occur. But it is unlikely that barristers will be paid a fair rate for advisory and interlocutory work until they are allowed to negotiate their own fees.

Why should a barrister not negotiate his own fees, if he wants to? At the moment he gets the worst of both worlds: he is in theory responsible for all the fees negotiated on his behalf, but he is not allowed to play any direct part in the negotiations, and often he does not know what his fees are until he actually receives them. It might surprise barristers to learn that they are responsible for the fees charged: in 1963 the Bar Council had to issue a reminder that counsel is always 'responsible for the actions of his clerk', and as part of this responsibility 'he is undoubtedly responsible for the amount and description of fees charged for the work which he has done'.[27] Yet 10 years later, when a pupil wished to spend some time in the clerks' room in his chambers to see how they actually operated, this was considered undesirable and not permitted by the Bar Council.[28] Counsel is responsible for the results of his clerk's activities but he is not allowed to observe the activities themselves.

Solicitors have also expressed their desire to have direct access to counsel to discuss fees, not merely in cases of 'special difficulty', but in all cases if they want to. In an unpublished Memorandum of the Council of the Law Society the Council recommended 'that the Instructing Solicitor should have an unrestricted right to approach direct junior or leading counsel in order to negotiate the amount of the fee ... It is not envisaged that in every case the instructing solicitor would wish to negotiate a fee direct with counsel, but he should be free to do so where the circumstances require it.'[29] Nor in fact is the attitude of the Bar Council as inflexible as its published rulings would suggest: it has arranged in small cases in the Crown Court for barristers who wish prompt payment to lodge their own briefs with the taxing office, and it has devised the 'pink form' scheme for Crown Court work whereby barristers record the time spent in preparing and arguing each case, and also mention any special factors which might entitle them to some extra payment.[30] Yet only 10 years ago the Council was suggesting that a barrister is not competent 'objectively to assess what is a proper fee'.[31]

The rule that barristers should not negotiate their own fees is clearly being eroded and the Bar Council recognizes the fact; but the Council cannot move too far ahead of professional opinion. It is a matter ultimately for the Bar to decide. So long as barristers remain frightened of their clerks and are prepared to leave fee negotiation to them they cannot complain if they feel unfairly rewarded. Only when barristers assume control of their own fees will they be in a position to ensure that their fees reflect fair remuneration for the work they actually do.

CLERK'S FEES

The senior clerk in almost all chambers is paid on a commission basis. Until very recently this commission was charged as a separate item on the client's bill, and varied in amount from $2\frac{1}{2}\%$ on large fees to just over 10% on small fees. Thus for a conference costing the standard fee of two guineas the client in addition had to pay a clerk's fee of five shillings; this separate item originated in the tradition that when a conference was held in chambers on a winter evening it fell to the clerk to provide the candles.

The practice of charging the client a separate fee for the clerk was heavily criticized for many years. The Evershed Committee said in their Final Report that 'the practice of making a separate charge to the client in respect of clerks' fees is now an anachronism and ought to be abolished . . . the time has come when counsel and his clerk must bow to the weight of public opinion'.[32] Typically the Bar showed no sign of doing so. The practice was defended zealously against all comers, and then quite suddenly abolished almost without a murmur. As late as 1968, 15 years after the Evershed Report, the Bar Council dismissed the proposed change contemptuously as being 'attractive to those who prefer tidiness to tradition'[33]; but only three years later the change was implemented as a side-effect of decimalization.

The clerk now receives his commission entirely from the barristers who employ him; and the normal rate of commission is 10% of all their fees, i.e. of their gross earnings, before deduction of expenses. Some chambers pay their clerk a salary, and a few pay only 5%, but the normal rate is 10%. As a result clerks earn an enormous amount of money. Even in those chambers where they are expected to pay the salary of the junior clerk, or to repay or surrender some of their percentage, the take-home pay of barristers' clerks far exceeds what they could hope to earn in any other walk of life; and in many chambers it exceeds the average income of the barristers they work for. In 1960, when the average set of chambers contained seven barristers, a clerk on 10% would earn two-thirds of the average gross earnings of his principals. Now the average size of a set of chambers is 14, and so the clerk on 10% with no deductions earns one and a half times as much as the average member of his chambers; and in the big criminal sets with 20 or 25 members the clerk may earn even more.

Some clerks earn as much as £20,000 or £30,000 a year. It is difficult to confirm the exact range because many barristers do not even know what their own clerk earns. What can be said with certainty is that the earnings of clerks are out of all proportion to their training and qualifications. In an independent study commissioned in 1969 a firm of business consultants was asked to suggest a salary-range for the senior clerk in a set of chambers where four of the clerical staff earned less than £2000 and the fifth earned under £3000. Taking as a guide the level of salaries paid to the other members of the staff and having regard to the expectations in other employment of individuals with a clerk's qualifications, the consultants concluded that the clerk should be receiving a salary of the order of £3000 to £4500. In fact the clerk was earning £14,000 (and that was in 1969).

The Evershed Committee (and others) have criticized the system of paying clerks on a commission basis. '[A] counsel's clerk's remuneration . . . is directly related to the earnings of his principal, so that he has a direct personal interest in the amount of the fees earned by his principal . . . it is obvious that there must be some danger, under such a system, of undue increase in counsel's fees as a result of the energies of over-zealous clerks.'[34]

The percentage system is wrong, not simply for the reasons stated by the Evershed Committee but because the percentage is now much too high, having evolved at a time when the average clerk worked for less than half the present number of principals. As a result some chambers have tried to reduce the clerk's percentage, but they have run into considerable resistance. In 1977 the senior clerk in the chambers of Sir Michael Havers Q.C., the shadow Attorney-General, was dismissed because of his refusal to negotiate a phased reduction of his fee from 10% to 8%: he had been earning £40,000, but paying the two junior clerks £7500 and £3000 out of his fees. His subsequent action for unfair dismissal was followed by the Bar with bated breath, but he lost on a point of law;[36] and it will be interesting to see whether other sets of chambers are now emboldened to follow Sir Michael's example.

The Senate has also been concerned to reduce the inflated earnings of clerks. In 1976 discussions were started with the Barristers' Clerks' Association on the following items: (i) re-negotiation of the minimum fee of 5% agreed to by the Bar when separate clerks' fees were abolished in 1971; (ii) to ensure that in future clerks' fees do not increase in direct ratio to the size of chambers; (iii) to provide that clerks' fees bear a 'reasonable ratio' to barristers' net fees rather than their gross fees as at present. At the time of writing the response of the Barristers' Clerks' Association is not known, but it is unlikely that the Senate will get very far.

It is in any event a misguided initiative, for the only way in which the Bar will rid itself of the present anomalies is by scrapping the percentage system altogether. There is no reason why clerks should not be paid a salary commensurate with their ability and their earning power in related fields. Some clerks are already paid on a salary basis, but most are bitterly opposed to the idea not simply because it will involve a very considerable reduction in their remuneration, but also because of a feeling that being a salaried employee will somehow represent a diminution in their status. Because of the power of the clerk few chambers have yet had the courage to go over to paying their clerk a fixed salary[36]; but in those chambers which have there is no sign that the clerk is any less diligent in maximizing the earnings of his principals, even though he no longer has a direct interest in doing so.

CHAMBERS EFFICIENCY

Most barristers' clerks start working in a set of chambers immediately after leaving school; no educational qualifications are required, and they normally owe their introduction to family or friends. To begin with, junior clerks do no more than carry barristers' books across to the Law Courts, and perform simple clerical tasks like filling in fee-notes, and answering the telephone. Quite quickly they graduate to fixing lists and negotiating the simpler fees, and soon they can perform all the functions of a senior clerk; but they may have to wait a long time before they can step into his shoes, or build up his network of contacts. Until recently clerks had no kind of formal training, but the Barristers' Clerks' Association has now introduced a simple exam for recent entrants. However, the lectures which prepare them for this exam are given by other clerks; at no stage do they undergo any kind of outside training in business methods or even the simplest procedures of accounting.[37] Thus are the techniques handed down, senior clerk to junior clerk, from generation to generation. Small wonder that in 1959 *The Times* felt obliged to comment: 'The office inefficiency of many barristers' chambers is a disgrace to the profession . . . This is because they are run not by barristers but by their clerks, who are wholly untrained in modern business methods.'[38]

Most sets of chambers (which now have an annual average turnover of over £100,000) do not even prepare accounts for audit, let alone make use of any of the other services provided by accountants. There is seldom any analysis of chambers expenditure. In the set of chambers examined by the business consultants referred to above, chambers expenses were not even recorded by double-entry book-keeping. The consultants also remarked on the lack of information about the progress of papers through chambers.

It is difficult to tell to what extent more sophisticated card sorting systems would give the clerks better access to such information, and in general to what extent clerks would be assisted by other modern business techniques and equipment. All one can say for certain is that no one has ever tried to find out. The majority of barristers take little interest in what goes on in the clerks' room and consider it none of their business to do so: indeed they are not allowed to make it their business. In a recent ruling already referred to the Bar Council has said: 'It is not desirable that pupils should spend a period of time in the clerks' room in order to gain experience of its working.'[39]

Of late however there have been signs that attitudes at last are beginning to change. The rapid escalation in barristers' expenses has prompted more barristers to take an interest in the management of their chambers, and the Senate has come to recognize that it too has an interest in promoting higher standards of chambers' organization. In guidelines drafted to assist new sets of chambers the Senate has suggested that large sets should consider the establishment of a chambers management committee, and of an annual audit. As mentioned above, the Senate has also started discussions with the Barristers' Clerks' Association with a view to renegotiating the basis on which the clerk's percentage is calculated.

LATE PAYMENT OF FEES

The Senate has also tried to do something to speed up the payment of barristers' fees. Late payment of fees has been a constant and bitter source of complaint within the profession, and with present rates of inflation the delay in payment of one to two years has caused a severe reduction in the value of fees ultimately received by the Bar. Young barristers are owed thousands of pounds and their seniors tens of thousands.[40] They cannot sue the solicitors for their fees (because they are in the nature of an *honorarium*) and their clerks are either inefficient in collecting the money, or reluctant to put pressure on solicitors, or both. Some barristers believe their clerks sometimes refrain from speedy fee-collection in order to control their own income tax liability.

The solicitors say that clerks do not send out fee-notes speedily enough, and that they fail to pursue them with reminders. In order to ease this problem the Bar Council published a guide in 1974 explaining a new standard procedure to be adopted in collecting fees, and a copy was sent to every clerk and to every practising barrister. But a year later when the Council reported on the new scheme it had to record the bitter truth that few clerks were using the new procedure[41]; they were not prepared to pursue solicitors for fees, for fear of frightening their custom away. Presumably even fewer barristers (if any) had had the courage to tell their clerks to change their ways.

The curious thing about this episode is not that the Bar has killed the Bar Council's scheme stone dead (the Council must be used to that), but that the one effective solution to the problem was never even mentioned. This is that counsel should be able to sue for their fees. If a barrister could issue a writ against either the solicitor or his client the problem of late payment of fees might be solved overnight. But this is considered unthinkable; it would end the special status of a barrister being a person who works only for an *honorarium*; it would involve a change in the law; and, worst of all, the corollary of allowing a barrister to sue for his fees in contract is that he could then be sued for breach of contract.

The Bar is unique among the professions in being immune to actions for breach of contract. It used to be thought that barristers were immune to all lawsuits in relation to their professional work.[42] Now the position is that although a barrister cannot be sued for the negligent conduct of a case in court or for negligent handling of the preparatory work involved in ligitation he can probably be made liable for other negligent advice.[43] But he still cannot be sued for breach of contract; though it is questionable what a barrister would have to fear from such an action.[44] There may be some anxiety lest he lose his independence as an advocate, and that the client might be able to control the conduct of the case; but the surgeon loses none of his clinical independence by virtue of the fact that his patient can sue him for breach of contract. In any event under the present system counsel only acts subject to instructions from his client, and if the client is adamant that counsel should do something which is contrary to his professional conscience, he can (indeed he must) withdraw.

Secondly it may be feared that if counsel were liable in contract a barrister briefed in a case might be sued if he had to drop out at the last moment (as not infrequently happens, because of conflicting commitments). But if it proved necessary there could easily be an implied term in every contract based on the present rule of etiquette that expressly permits a barrister to return a brief: 'Briefs are as a rule delivered and accepted on the understanding that it is possible that a counsel may be prevented from attending the case.'[45] However, for reasons which appear below it is questionable whether it is right to allow a barrister to return a brief unless he has his client's consent to do so.

RETURNS

This is the vexed problem of returns. Because of the distance maintained between counsel and client, and the fact that it is never the barrister who has to explain to the client that he is unavailable (his clerk tells the solicitor, and the solicitor tells the client), barristers simply do not realize how disappointed and worried clients are when their counsel, who has nursed their case from the beginning, for months and often for years, is then unable to present the case in court on the day of trial.[46] For the Bar returns are an everyday occurrence (indeed they are the staple diet of the beginner), and barristers take pride in their ability to step into each other's shoes and to get up any case overnight. It is the solicitor who bears the brunt of the client's anxieties and recriminations; and it is the Law Society which has expressed the greatest concern about this problem.

It is fair to say that the Bar Council has expressed concern also, and has tried to meet the problem by providing in the rules of etiquette that:

'It is a paramount duty of a barrister not to embarrass his client and to allow sufficient time for another counsel to be engaged and to master the brief. A barrister is under a duty to give warning to his instructing solicitor as soon as there is any appreciable danger that he may not be able to attend to a brief and to return the brief if required.'[47]

This rule, however, is more honoured in the breach than in the observance. The clerks overload their principals with engagements in the hope that where two cases conflict one will settle or go short, so that the barrister will still be able to do both cases and collect two fees instead of one. If this hope does not materialize, one brief will have to be returned; and if it is returned at sufficiently short notice the solicitors will probably have to accept someone from the same set of chambers – so that the clerk still earns both fees.

This is how the Law Society described the problem:

'In spite of this rule, it is a common source of complaint that counsel who has accepted a brief does not conduct the case in court and that inadequate notice is given to the solicitor of counsel's inability to appear. It sometimes happens that the notice is so short that the instructing solicitor is obliged to assent to the brief being transferred to another junior in the same chambers who may be of much less standing and experience than counsel to whom the brief was originally delivered, and one whom neither solicitor nor client would have briefed in the ordinary way . . . Where counsel who has been briefed does not attend to conduct the case the situation may well arise that justice is not done. In such cases the client forms a poor view of the Bar and of justice . . . The client should be entitled to the services of counsel who has accepted instructions to conduct his case and it falls short of the ordinary principles of justice if the client has to make do with the next best available . . .

The Council suggest that the problem requires a more realistic attitude by the Bar. Some counsel appear to attach insufficient importance to the responsibility of carrying out their part of the bargain and, in the Council's view, this probably again results from the traditional view that Counsel is not engaged contractually but upon the basis that his services are honorary.'[48]

But the Law Society also shrank from recommending that there should be a contract between counsel and his client. Instead, they suggested that a client whose counsel was not available on the date of the hearing should be entitled to an adjournment. At the moment this is not the case: what is called 'counsel's convenience' is not a valid ground for granting an adjournment. The courts are run largely for the court's convenience, which means that of the judge. There is a hallowed convention in the English legal system that a judge must never be kept waiting. Each day the lists are filled with extra cases just in case the first ones settle or go short; and as a result litigants and their solicitors and counsel are kept hanging around outside courts for hours and sometimes days, waiting to 'come on'.

To be fair to our court administrators, the situation used to be infinitely worse. We do now have an appointments system, of a kind; but excessive obeisance is still paid to the principle that it is better for the parties and their lawyers to wait for hours than for a minute of judicial time to be wasted. As a result a barrister not infrequently has to return a brief which in fact he could have done. This is the reason why clerks take risks and briefs are not returned until the last moment. If only judges could be persuaded that their time is often less valuable than that of the many people who are kept waiting to appear before them, and that an empty afternoon is an unexpected bonus instead of an administrative disaster, some at least of the problems would be solved.

Nevertheless conflicting commitments will still occur, and the Bar also needs to undergo a radical change of attitude. Barristers should recognize that from their clients' point of view they are not interchangeable, and the Bar as a whole needs to press that 'counsel's convenience' should become a valid reason for granting an adjournment, if the client insists. Of course if this rule were adopted there would be greater delays and expense – not only to judges but to the other parties to a case. They would have to be compensated in costs. Some clients might accept substitute counsel because they wanted to avoid this expense, or because they simply wanted to get their case over. But if other members of the litigating public are prepared to pay in order to have counsel of their choice on the day, why should they not be allowed to? In the Law Society's opinion the additional delay and expense 'would be a hazard that the public and the profession would accept in preference to the present unsatisfactory position'.[49]

Interestingly, the Bar Council has also expressed the view that 'the conflict should not normally be resolved against the interests of the lay client'.[50] But it has never taken any public initiative in support of this view. In the 1967 joint report with the Law Society, the Bar Council contented itself with the subordinate role of saying that it would support any representations which the Law Society might make 'to persuade the courts to give greater weight to the desirability of the client being able in a proper case to have the counsel of his choice'.[51] The matter has never been pursued any further, which is not surprising in view of the Bar Council's half-hearted attitude.

If the Bar felt sufficiently strongly about it something could and undoubtedly would be done. But until the Bar begins to regard its clients as people or even simply as consumers whose views should occasionally be respected, the system of returns will continue to make serious inroads into the principle that the Bar provides its clients with a free and unrestricted choice of counsel.

ARE CLERKS NECESSARY?

Clerks are such an entrenched feature of the chambers' organization in this country that it is difficult for most English barristers to imagine how they could possibly operate without them. Indeed they would probably be amazed to learn that in other countries where there is a separate Bar, divided from the solicitors' branch of the profession on exactly the same lines as our own, the barristers manage to get along without clerks at all. In Ireland, for example, barristers arrange their appointments and negotiate their fees directly with solicitors, and no one has suggested that this has corrupted their professional or ethical standards.

South Africa provides an even better comparison, because there the Bar has an identical chambers structure to that in England (in Dublin and Belfast the barristers all practise from a common Library). Their chambers (called 'Groups') are about the same size or slightly larger; they employ the usual telephonists and typists, and there is an office manager called the Group Secretary, who may also do the accounts and send out fee-notes. When a solicitor wishes to brief counsel he talks to the barrister direct – each barrister keeps his own diary, and it is contrary to professional etiquette for him to arrange to be in two different courts on the same day. Fees are a matter of direct negotiation between barrister and solicitor; and to protect young barristers there are scales of minimum fees for most of the standard types of work. Young barristers, in South Africa and in Ireland, receive most of their early work either through contacts (in South Africa almost every barrister works in a solicitor's office before going to the Bar) or on the recommendation of their pupilmasters or other more senior barristers – people who are in a better position to judge the true worth of a beginner than the clerk, who has never seen him in action in court, nor read his work on paper.

The same system operates in Australia (in those states which have a separate Bar). There they do have clerks, but they are simply administrators; the barristers negotiate their own fees and arrange their own timetables. Beginners are passed down returns by their seniors – not necessarily even from the same chambers: with no clerk eager for his percentage there is not the same anxiety to keep a brief in chambers that exists in England. The barrister giving away the brief is merely anxious to find the best possible substitute available, in order not to let down 'his' solicitors. And, as in South Africa, the vast majority of young barristers do not go straight to the Bar but work first for a firm of solicitors for a couple of years, in order to gain practical experience and to ensure a steady supply of work when they do start at the Bar. Again, it has never been suggested that the South African and Australian Bars have any but the highest ethical standards.

In all these countries barristers do the same work as in England and they operate under essentially the same code of conduct. In none of them do they obtain their work or negotiate their fees through the medium of a clerk. The conclusion is inescapable; that in these two crucial respects the English clerk is dispensable. How they acquired their present position of power it is hard to say; but the sooner barristers have the courage to manage their own affairs without being ruled by their clerks the better life will be for themselves, and the better the service will be for their clients.

PARTNERSHIPS

It has sometimes been argued that the formation of partnerships at the Bar is the only way in which the power of the clerks might be curbed. If barristers practised in partnership the clerk would become a salaried employee of the partners, and the partners would decide (subject to the wishes of clients) how to distribute the work among themselves. But as the foregoing description of Bars in other countries shows, it is not necessary to establish a partnership in order to cope with the problem of clerks. Nevertheless partnerships do have other advantages, and no study of chambers' organization would be complete without mentioning them. The brief space allocated to the subject here should not lead the reader to underestimate its importance.[52]

The first thing which is worth remarking is that in many respects chambers are already partnerships in fact, though not in law. The most important respect is that chambers share a common fund of goodwill. If one member of chambers damages this, all will suffer; if one member prospers, the others will benefit also. In matters of organization chambers are also run as partnerships. Most chambers have a collective insurance policy to indemnify their members against liability for negligence; and chambers expenses on rent, secretarial facilities, law reports, postage etc., are apportioned not by keeping individual accounts, but *pro rata*. The only respect in which chambers are not already partnerships is that the rules of etiquette strictly forbid barristers from sharing work or fees as partners.

It might then be asked, what further advantages would accrue from allowing barristers to practise in partnership in this full sense? In the first place, partnership might lead to wider recruitment. Pupils could be paid a salary just as articled clerks are paid by solicitors. The costs of entry to the beginner would be significantly lower; and chambers would take far more care in selecting recruits according to their ability rather than their connections, and also in training their pupils (because most of the pupils would soon themselves be partners).[53]

Secondly, there could be a more even distribution of work between the senior and junior members of chambers. At the moment successful barristers are grossly overworked while their juniors, who may be equally able, are relatively underworked (and consequently underpaid). To fill in time and eke out their income some 'devil' for their seniors, i.e. they do their paperwork for them in return for 50% of the fee. This unofficial delegation of work takes place wholly without the client's or the solicitor's permission, and indeed without their knowledge. The client pays for the opinion of a senior barrister and receives that of a junior one, or even of a pupil. Admittedly the senior barrister signs the opinion and takes full responsibility for it; and most (but not all) check the work of their devils quite carefully. But the fact remains that what the client receives is not what he would have received, had the barrister whom he briefed done all the research and drafted all the documents himself.

If barristers practised in partnership this delegation of work would be expected and permissible. When a client goes to a firm of solicitors he knows that the partner in charge of his case will not write every letter or file every document personally; and the same understanding could exist at the Bar, subject to the proviso that if the client requested the exclusive services of a particular partner he would of course be entitled to them, but at a price.

The third advantage of partnerships is that they can provide pensions for those partners who have retired. Barristers, being self-employed, have to provide for their own retirement. Many, it is true, end their days in judicial or salaried employment, and so receive a pension from the State; but preferment of this kind cannot be guaranteed and some may not even seek it. For those who, for one reason or another, cannot aspire to pensioned appointments the problem of adequate provision for their retirement is a constant worry. Partnerships would help to ease this burden.

Partnerships would also stabilize the earnings of barristers during their working lives. The range of earnings at the Bar is wider than in almost any other profession[54]; this is the case not only between individuals but in the same individual over his lifetime. Whereas a solicitor's earnings start at a reasonable level and steadily increase throughout his life a barrister's income starts at zero (as a pupil) and it tails away again in the last ten to twenty years before retirement.[55] Partnership would produce steadier earnings over a barrister's lifetime, and it would also permit a more even distribution of earnings between the different members of the chambers. This would significantly increase their aggregate post-tax income, by robbing the higher-rate taxpayers to subsidize those who pay less tax (and pupils who pay no tax at all). Over a lifetime a barrister's total take-home income could be increased and the years when he was a net contributor to the partnership would be cancelled out by the years when he was a net beneficiary. Of course there would be all sorts of problems about computing the shares of the different partners; but most of the other professions work in partnerships which manage to resolve these problems, and it is worth the effort because partnership as a form of association between professional people has considerable advantages.

Until recently, however, the advantages were not so prominent at the Bar, because when an individual barrister retired all the fees paid to him after his retirement used to come to him free of tax. A successful barrister who retired after a good year could expect to receive very substantial sums in this way.[56] There was little inducement to contemplate change. This fact permeated all discussion of the partnership issue, until it was resolved by the Finance Act 1968, which abolished the tax concession.

The issue first became a live one in 1959 when the Lord Chief Justice, Lord Parker, expressed himself to be in favour of allowing partnerships.[57] He was in fact merely echoing a suggestion in the Addendum to the Evershed Report[58]; no action was taken on that first occasion, but the opinion of the Lord Chief Justice was not something which the Bar Council could afford to ignore. A committee was accordingly set up under the chairmanship of Geoffrey Lawrence Q.C., then Chairman of the Bar Council, to investigate the matter. The committee was in fact split on the question of principle, as to whether practice in partnership was compatible with the individualist traditions of the Bar; but Sir Geoffrey Howe and Sir Patrick O'Connor felt able to agree with the majority recommendation that partnerships should not then be permitted, because of the tax advantages then existing. They added the rider that if the tax laws were altered in the future the whole matter should be reconsidered. On the matter of principle they declared they 'were not satisfied, however, that practice in partnership was incompatible with the essential virtues of the present system of practice, or would produce any general disadvantage to the profession, or be harmful to the public interest'.[59]

The report of the committee presented to the profession at the Annual Meeting of the Bar in July 1962 made no mention of this dissent. Its full text is as follows:

> '(a) The institution of partnerships at the Bar is wholly incompatible with the traditional conception of members of the Bar as individual practitioners enjoying an independent and individual status.

(b) The institution of partnerships at the Bar could not be effected without working, in the long if not the short run, fundamental changes in this traditional conception.

(c) The present system has been shown by experience to foster the strength and independence of the Bar while affording a satisfactory service to the public.

(d) No case in favour of partnerships has been made out which is sufficient to justify the changes that would be the result of the institution.

(e) There is no real demand for partnerships at the Bar.

(f) Accordingly partnerships at the Bar should not be permitted.'[60]

That remained the Bar Council's policy (if that is not too grand a word for such an inadequate document) until the Finance Act 1968 ended the tax concession. A second committee was then set up to consider the matter afresh; and indeed fresh minds (under the able chairmanship of Sydney Templeman, later the first President of the new Senate) produced a report of a wholly different calibre. The committee heard evidence from other organizations (including the Law Society, the American Bar Association and the B.M.A.); and unlike its predecessor it did accept 'that there were some advantages for the individual barrister in a partnership organization; an income could be guaranteed for a beginner, work could be distributed evenly between partners, and provision could be made for sickness and retirement'.[61]

But the Committee also envisaged there might be disadvantages: that an individual might find it difficult to gain and prove his individual experience and reputation if he started as a salaried employee; and that the high standards which follow from individual responsibility and competition might be eroded. It is doubtful, however, whether these fears would be realized in practice. Most solicitors practise in partnership, but nevertheless manage to gain individual experience and reputation; and of course nobody would be forced to join a partnership – a barrister who wanted to shine quickly on his own could join a set of chambers run on traditional lines. As for standards, these surely will continue to flourish not so much because of individual responsibility, but rather as a result of tradition and training: does a solicitor practising in partnership have lower standards than a solicitor who is in practice on his own? The reverse is probably the case; and at the Bar the spirit and example of other members of chambers are tremendously important. Even under the present system, if a barrister fails to do his best for a client he not only damages his own practice, but he lets down his chambers – and that can be a far more dreadful sanction.

These are minor considerations, however, compared with the committee's main objection to partnership, which really is the only argument of substance (and which was not even mentioned in their predecessors' report). This is the difficulty that members of the same partnership could not be allowed to represent conflicting interests, and similarly a partner could not appear as an advocate before another partner (or pensioned ex-partner) acting in a judicial capacity. In the committee's opinion 'these limitations would inevitably and seriously reduce the number of barristers available to a member of the public in any particular case, especially in the provinces and in specialist fields such as revenue law, admiralty law and company law'.[62] The committee therefore concluded that partnerships at the Bar, although possibly of advantage to barristers, would not be in the interests of the public.

The committee's conclusion stems from a fear that partnerships at the smaller specialist and provincial Bars might create a monopoly situation in which the client's freedom to go to counsel of his choice would be severely circumscribed. The best solution to this problem would be to devise a new form of professional organization which is identical to a traditional partnership except that the partners are not deemed in law to be each other's agents. This would enable barristers although practising in partnership together to continue to accept briefs on opposite sides in the same case (as members of the same set of chambers do now). It should not be beyond the wit of man to devise such a scheme, which would preserve for the client the same freedom of choice that he has now.

But even if such a scheme was not possible, it is doubtful whether monopoly situations would in fact develop at the specialist and provincial Bars: for it is extremely unlikely that chambers in this sort of situation would want to go into partnership – for the simple reason that it would not be in their best interests to do so. It is precisely those chambers which frequently find themselves representing opposing parties which would lose out by becoming a partnership – for they would drive away business by so doing.

Consider the situation in a provincial town which has only one set of chambers. Its members frequently find themselves opposing each other in the local Crown and county courts; some prosecuting, some defending – some for landlords, some for tenants. If they formed a partnership, once a prosecution brief was delivered in a particular case no partner could accept a brief for the defence; once a partner was briefed for a tenant, no colleague of his could appear for the landlord. The work would go elsewhere; and for that reason the chambers would almost certainly decide to retain their present form. Precisely the same would happen in a set of specialist chambers: it is highly unlikely that the number of advocate 'units' available to the public at the smaller specialist Bars would seriously diminish.

But even if this assumption is wrong, and specialist chambers did decide to go into partnership in a way that seriously restricted competition, the Bar Council would not be powerless to act. In the past the Lord Chancellor has intervened to break up a specialist set of chambers that threatened to establish a monopoly (evidence that the authorities already regard chambers – quite rightly – as *de facto* partnerships); and where the Lord Chancellor acted unofficially the Bar Council could act officially, once it is vested with the proper powers. Rules could be adopted regulating the formation of partnerships at those Bars where there is a risk of a monopoly situation developing; while all other sets of chambers should be free to form partnerships or not as they choose.

It may be that few chambers would exercise this right, at least to begin with; but that is no reason for denying them the right altogether. Barristers should have freedom of choice to associate in partnership with their colleagues if they wish; and it is wrong of the majority to prevent them unless they can prove that there will be some clear detriment either to ethical standards, or to the quality of services offered, or to the availability of those services. None of these things has been proved; and indeed foreign experience from the European Bars, and from Canada, provides evidence to the contrary. No barrister would be obliged to join a partnership; but those who personally do not favour the idea should not deny the right to others who deem it to be in their interest.

6 THE CRIMINAL BAR

Most people – even if their sole source is the cinema or television – have some conception of the criminal lawyer. He has long been cast by the fiction writers as having the most glamorous role in the law. Fiercely championing the innocent and skilfully trapping the guilty, the type has commanded universal fascination, from the courageous defence work of Erskine down to the theatrical performances of Marshall Hall. But to others – particularly those within the legal profession itself – the criminal Bar tends to be thought of as being a collection of hack orators, not lawyers, a group of extrovert performers who are intellectually inferior to their civil law colleagues.

Neither view wholly expresses the truth. The criminal Bar is not a profession staffed by those keen to participate in exciting theatre: the legal process has a disappointing knack of being able to strip the fascination from the most heinous or glamorous of crimes, and any espousing of causes is frowned upon as being inconsistent with counsel's duty to be dispassionate. Neither is the work of the criminal Bar necessarily inferior: the qualities required of its practitioners are just as specialized and demanding as those of the civil and Chancery lawyers. It is however probably fair to say that the general standard of advocacy in the Crown Court compares poorly with the standard in even the lower courts of civil jurisdiction.

The crucial difference between civil and criminal work is that every criminal case comes to trial, whereas the vast majority of civil cases are settled without a court hearing, usually because it is reasonably clear which side will win, so that the other side settles on the best terms it can get. A criminal case is never 'settled' in this way – even if a defendant pleads guilty he still has to appear in court to be sentenced, and as a result almost all criminal work at the Bar is court work and advocacy rather than giving written advice or drafting pleadings. Different skills are therefore required; there is less emphasis on the law and more on establishing the facts, and for the criminal barrister a sound understanding of human nature is just as important as his knowledge of such matters as the rules of evidence.

THE COST OF CRIMINAL LEGAL AID

The bill for almost all criminal work is met by the State although an accused is sometimes required to make a contribution to the cost of his defence. The work is well paid, and most barristers with a common law practice are keen to undertake it. Indeed today, with the fall in civil litigation, legally aided criminal work is the bread and butter even for many Q.C.s. In 1971-2 the total cost of legal aid in criminal cases was £9½ million. Over the next four years the number of defendants granted legal aid nearly doubled and the earnings of lawyers more than trebled, reaching £33 million in 1975-6. In that year the Crown Courts dealt with 58,000 men and 5000 women. For their defence the legal aid fund paid out £17½ million to the lawyers involved (both counsel and solicitors); but prosecution lawyers benefited as well, with prosecution costs in the Crown Courts and above totalling £11½ million in 1975-6.[1]

With the rising crime rates it is inevitably the criminal lawyer who profits, and the steady flow of work provides a quick living in the Crown Courts even for young barristers, who ten years ago would not have hoped to appear before a jury in their first years of practice. The Notes of Guidance issued by the Lord Chancellor's Department in 1972 – to assist those responsible for the taxation of costs in the Crown Court – illustrate the scale of fees: a junior barrister could expect in an average case lasting a day anything between £45 and £55, whilst if the matter was only a plea of guilty requiring a speech in mitigation, he could expect £35 to £40. The 1972 scale has, however, never been increased (although in individual cases it is frequently exceeded), and so the earnings of the criminal Bar are unlikely to grow at the same rate as they have in the past decade or so; the boom years are over, and the State has recently shown its determination to reduce the costs of trial by jury by one means or another.

The amount of money spent on criminal legal aid in the magistrates' courts alone now amounts to more than half of the total amount spent on the entire civil scheme. Between 1971–2 and 1975–6 it increased from £3 million to £14 million.[2] In the higher courts the increase in caseload over the last decade has been even greater; while the number of indictable offences coming before magistrates' courts rose by 87% between 1965 and 1975, the number coming before the higher courts increased by 135%. With such an astronomic growth in criminal work, it should be the duty of the Bar to keep the bill as low as possible so far as is consistent with the requirements of justice. In two ways in particular, however, the legal aid fund has been frequently abused at considerable cost by counsel.

The first is as a result of the longstanding and unjustifiable requirement (now formally abolished) that Q.C.s should appear in court only with a junior barrister; almost invariably in criminal cases the junior's presence has been wholly unnecessary. If the Q.C. is doing his job properly, he should read all the papers and prepare the case himself; he should also do nearly all the advocacy in court. That leaves very little else to do, and the junior seldom does any more than take a full note of the evidence given at the trial. When such trials last for several weeks or, as they often do, months, and when a junior is paid in the region of £60 per day for his efforts, it is clear that legal aid has been financing the most expensive note-taking system in the country. Now Q.C.s are permitted to appear on their own, substantial sums may be saved by the taxpayer each year without any diminution in the quality of justice.

The second way in which the legal aid fund is abused is in trials involving more than one defendant. In such cases, each defendant will frequently be represented separately even though there is no conflict of interest between the co-defendants and no real reason justifying separate representation. In February 1976, for example, Judge Clarke Q.C. – at the end of a trial of seven defendants at the Central Criminal Court on charges of causing an affray – called for an inquiry into the reasons as to why it had been necessary for them to be represented by thirteen counsel.[3] Barristers should assume a greater degree of public responsibility in trials involving several accused and inform the court if they believe that separate representation is not justified. The financial temptation not to do so is strong, but it is in the Bar's own interests in the long run to be seen voluntarily to take a sensible attitude.

THE CAB-RANK RULE

In virtually every case in which he is instructed, the criminal barrister will play one of only two roles, to prosecute or to defend. It is a fundamental rule of etiquette that he must accept instructions to appear in any case unless he is already engaged in another matter or is otherwise legitimately unable to do so. It may be that the case offends his politics or his views, but that is not a valid consideration for refusing. Many people cannot understand how any barrister could properly defend, for example, an I.R.A. bomber or child killers such as Ian Brady and Myra Hindley, but the answer is simple: anyone is entitled to a proper defence and it is not the duty of counsel to pre-judge their guilt. The justification by Erskine of his decision to appear on behalf of Tom Paine remains the supreme formulation of this part of the barrister's code of conduct: 'From the moment that any advocate can be permitted to say that he will or will not stand between the Crown and the subject arraigned in the Court where he daily sits to practise, from that moment the liberties of England are at an end.'[4]

Just as barristers are often asked how they can appear for unpopular clients an even more frequent question is how they can defend people whom they know to be guilty. The answer given by the Bar is that there is a vital distinction between believing one's client to be guilty and actually knowing him to be so. So long as the client does not tell his barrister that he is, in fact, guilty, and wishes to deny his guilt to the court, counsel must represent him to the very best of his ability and try to secure his acquittal. Barristers are, of course, only human and may often form a private suspicion about their client's guilt or innocence, but, being trained simply to present a case – any case – as favourably as possible, this really does hardly ever interfere with the efficiency of their performance. The criminal trial is an adversary process fought like a game according to precise rules; playing it soon becomes a matter of routine and rarely gives rise to emotional involvement.

Of course it does happen that barristers may refuse a brief through their clerks on some pretext. Appearing for too many unpopular clients or causes is generally regarded – especially if a barrister is hopeful of judicial preferment – as professionally unwise. The system for appointments to silk and judicial office – namely private consultation between the Lord Chancellor and the judges – is one based on pure patronage; the Lord Chancellor's Office keeps track of the career of every senior barrister, and it does not do to step out of line too often. The result, as one Q.C. pointed out at the 1969 A.G.M. of the Bar, is that there is among most barristers 'a desire to please'.[5]

In 1972, at the time of the Angry Brigade trial, allegations were openly made by the Press that 15 Q.C.s had refused defence briefs. The Bar Council felt obliged to make inquiries through the Barristers' Clerks' Association, and the Chairman wrote to *The Times* that 'The Queen's Counsel had not . . . "refused" the brief because of their dislike of the case, and they would have been in breach of their professional duty if they had done so. It was simply that they were not free to take it on.'[6] The explanation glosses over what is a very real difficulty in I.R.A. and similar trials which involve a number of defendants and frequently last for several months. Any barrister who does not wish to appear in such cases can find conflicting commitments which prevent him from doing so. The result has been that in the Angry Brigade trial and in some of the biggest I.R.A. cases only a minority of the defendants have been represented by Q.C.s, despite the seriousness of the charges against them. (It is only fair to add, however, that in selecting their counsel such defendants sometimes prefer sympathetic personalities to seniority or experience.)

PROSECUTING COUNSEL

On commencing practice, a barrister is normally required to join one of the six circuits into which the country is divided. Prosecuting work may only be done within a particular circuit by a barrister who is a member of it, although now the parallel rule for defence work has been abolished and one may defend anywhere. Until 1964 if counsel was instructed to appear for a defendant in an area where he did not normally practise, he was required to pay a special encroaching fee to the circuit on which the case was to be tried. With prosecution work such trespassing is unlikely to happen; the prosecuting authorities – whether the local police solicitor or, in more serious cases, the D.P.P. – will only nominate counsel to appear on their behalf from lists of experienced practitioners which are compiled on a circuit basis. Appearing for the D.P.P. is by the express invitation of the Attorney-General; frequently, however, such patronage is dispensed by the clerk of the Attorney's chambers who will switch the prosecution brief if the barrister originally instructed is unable to do it. Although in practice this may be a convenient method of re-allocation, it makes the Attorney's clerk a powerful figure in the Temple, and it is undesirable that the Crown's briefs should be peddled in this way.

In civil cases, the roles of counsel for the plaintiff and counsel for the defendant are not really very different. Both are out to win, and will take advantage of what tactical manoeuvres are legitimately open to them. In criminal trials the approach is meant to be different. Prosecuting counsel is not like counsel for the plaintiff and should not be out to win; prosecutors assume responsibility for the case and should 'regard themselves as ministers of justice and not struggle for conviction'.[7]

Prosecuting counsel should prosecute fairly. Fairness is a variable standard depending upon how it is interpreted, but broadly it means not pursuing or constructing a case with insufficient evidence and refraining from taking unfair advantage or making unfair points. Prosecuting is a responsibility that is easily abused; the great trouble of our prosecuting system, and no doubt of any other, is that the way in which that responsibility is discharged depends entirely upon the person who happens to be doing the prosecuting.

One way in which the prosecution can hamper the defence is by not disclosing documents to them. Prosecuting counsel, especially in difficult cases, will always have more background material than the defence and it is up to them whether to release it openly, or on a counsel to counsel basis, or not at all. Such material, which will have been discarded by the prosecution on the ground that it is not relevant to the case against the defendant, may be of great relevance from the defence's point of view, particularly if the defence is alleging that someone else was responsible for the crime. In the Maxwell Confait case, for example, two subnormal teenage boys were convicted of strangling Confait who was a homosexual transvestite; Confait's landlord was a fellow transvestite who had had a jealous relationship with him, and both the landlord and his wife had made lengthy statements to the police which tended to implicate the landlord. These statements were never disclosed to the defence before the trial, and the landlady's was only handed over after she accidentally referred to its existence during her evidence in court; yet the defence's case at the trial was that the landlord may well have been responsible for the killing. Some years later the landlord committed suicide and the boys' convictions were quashed when their case was re-opened by the Home Secretary on other grounds.[8]

This case illustrates a weakness which runs through all our criminal trials: they are not an inquiry into the truth, only an examination of the admissible evidence against a particular accused. The only protection we have against a jury basing its verdict on an incomplete, or even inaccurate, picture of the crime is our reliance on prosecuting counsel to disclose information to the defence, and to present a fair and balanced view to the jury.

THE POLARIZATION OF THE CRIMINAL BAR

The other real danger posed by our present system of selecting prosecuting counsel is that a barrister may become a permanent prosecutor virtually retained by the Crown. At the Old Bailey the D.P.P. has 12 such full-time barristers with a reserve squad of a further 18. They are appointed by the Attorney-General and are called Treasury Counsel. In 1975 the author of Barrister's Diary in the *Law Society's Gazette* described the consequences of this retainer system as follows:

> 'They have the conduct of virtually all the D.P.P.'s work at that court and most of the more important of the cases of the Commissioner of Metropolitan Police. The volume of that work means that they have practically no other clients. They appear day by day before the judges of that court, several of whom sit at no other court. As a result of this state of affairs,

the principal court of criminal jurisdiction in the country has become a cosy little club unlike any other Crown Court in the land. When the same few counsel appear to prosecute, day by day, year by year, before the same judges it is small wonder that they appear to an outside observer to have the ear of the court to a degree not afforded to other counsel.'[9]

Most criminal practitioners would agree that this reflects a certain amount of unhappy truth. To a lesser extent it is also true of counsel on other prosecution lists, such as those held by Scotland Yard and regional police forces, or by the Customs and Excise or the Inland Revenue. The strength of an independent Bar has always been that its members should be available to act for anyone, unallied to any particular side. Now, however, particularly at the Old Bailey, there is a growing tendency for barristers to fall into two camps – prosecutors and defenders. This has meant that occasionally prosecutors put their case with more zeal than the rules allow, while defence counsel cooperate less and less with the prosecution, partly because they do not trust them, and partly because, never having prosecuted, they cannot see the prosecution's point of view.

Division of the Bar into two camps also gives rise to the hazards referred to above of an excessively close relationship developing between a permanent band of prosecutors and a permanent Bench. The only solution to this growing polarization is to abolish the post of Treasury Counsel at the criminal Bar, and to dispense all prosecution work to competent counsel on a rota basis.

One-sidedness is found in the defence camp as well. In the last decade or so more people with less affluent social backgrounds have come to the Bar; the result is that the Bar is beginning to be composed of practitioners with a wider spectrum of political views and beliefs. Now there are counsel, and whole sets of chambers, who – whether by accident, inclination or politics – solely defend. The criminal Bar is attracting an emergent left wing. This should be recognized as an asset if the Bar as a whole is to be seen as providing a true consumer service with the facility for clients to shop around for a barrister in whom they have faith to do justice to their case. Whilst such counsel may not be sufficiently a part of the establishment to receive prosecution work (or even to accept it if offered), they compensate by attracting law centres and solicitors dealing with coloured defendants or cases involving drugs, pornography and political charges.

Just as prosecuting counsel in obscenity trials appear sometimes to be picked for their moral devotion to the cause, so today some defence solicitors brief counsel according to the colour of their views. The idea of a dispassionate Bar, unmoved by belief or prejudice, is finally beginning to be viewed as a myth, and it is in the field of criminal law that the polarization of the Bar into opposing sides is most advanced.

THE CONDUCT OF THE DEFENCE

In a criminal court 'all the powers and resources at the disposal of the State are brought to bear on the individual accused'.[10] It is defence counsel who in theory evens the odds. The American Bar Association has put it even more graphically:

> 'Against a hostile world, the accused, called to the bar of justice by his government, finds in his counsel a single voice on which he must be able to rely with confidence that his interests will be protected to the fullest extent consistent with the rules of procedure and standards of professional conduct.'[11]

The restraint of etiquette is important because counsel is not just the defendant's mouthpiece or *alter ego*. He cannot devise factual defences or put forward explanations which do not accord with his instructions, although there is a tendency within the Metropolitan Police, at least, to suspect left-wing lawyers of manufacturing lines of defence, as Sir Robert Mark has illustrated by expressing his alarm at the sizeable number of acquittals brought about by 'highly paid forensic trickery'.[12]

Most legally aided defendants will not choose the counsel who is to represent them; they will leave that to their solicitor. This division is, for the client, one of the greatest drawbacks of a split legal profession. His solicitor, with whom he has all his pre-trial contact and with whom he builds up a relationship of confidence, is not the person who will represent him at his trial – unless it is a summary trial in the magistrates' court where solicitors have a right of audience. His future, or even his liberty, will depend on someone who will be entirely new to him, about whose abilities he knows nothing, and who all too often will only read the case the night before the trial.

In recent years research has been done for the first time into defendants' attitudes to their legal representation. The most common complaint is that so many defendants saw their barrister only for a few minutes just before the hearing. This complaint comes up again and again:

'He [the barrister] was really young like – only 23 or 24. He came down to the cells just before the case but he wouldn't let me speak. I tried to tell him a few things, but he told me not to speak unless spoken to – he told me off. He was really abrupt like.'

'I never saw the barrister at all.'

'Saw barrister for only five minutes before hearing. Pleaded guilty on his advice – he never mentioned that I was pregnant and about to get married.'

'I never saw my solicitor for the last month of my remand and never saw the barrister at all. Had I been able to speak to him beforehand, I might have got something across. In fact he hardly said anything.'

'I would have liked to have seen my barrister for a longer period. I saw him only for ten minutes before the trial . . .'[13]

The most recent study found a fairly positive overall assessment of lawyers in general, but in the higher criminal courts there were 93% who thought that solicitors had 'helped a great deal' or 'a little' compared with only 70% who thought the same of barristers. The authors concluded: 'The Bar has very satisfied clients, but it has more dissatisfied ones than the junior branch of the profession.'[14] Dissatisfaction sometimes arose from the fact that counsel was not sufficiently aggressive ('I don't think he put up any fight – he wasn't very good – he just wasn't bothered about it'); but here again by far the most common complaint was not seeing the barrister until just before the trial ('He was terrible – he didn't help at all. He only saw me for two minutes and he knew nothing about the case').

The figures produced by this last survey on the frequency of last-minute conferences are the first from any study. Of those committed for trial and pleading guilty, 96% had not seen their barrister until the morning of the hearing. It is not surprising that when asked about the plea of mitigation made on their behalf, defendants often felt that barristers had thrown away valuable points. The authors suggested that at the very least barristers should see their clients after the case to explain why particular evidence was not used.

Even more striking was the finding that for those pleading not guilty the position was hardly any different. 79% of those contesting their case saw their barrister for the first time on the morning of the trial, nine per cent the previous day and another nine per cent the previous week. A number of defendants added that when they did see the barrister there had been insufficient time to discuss the case. In a number of these cases the issues may have been fairly simple, and did not justify the expense of a special pre-trial conference with counsel. In others it may be that the barrister only received the papers a short time before, after the barrister originally instructed was unable at the last moment to do the case. Often this is unavoidable, but equally often it is the fault of barristers' clerks who hang on to a brief even when they know well in advance that the barrister originally instructed will be committed elsewhere. The clerk's aim is to keep the brief within chambers by only informing the solicitor of the difficulty at the eleventh hour, so that he will have no time to try and brief someone else, and will more easily settle for a substitute from the same set of chambers. Often this will be a barrister whom the solicitor does not know, and who is a person of less experience; furthermore because the switch is not made until the last moment the substitute has little time in which to prepare the brief.

When someone's freedom or reputation hangs in the balance, switches of counsel need to be reduced to an absolute minimum; the primary concern should always be the interests of the defendant. Clerks must be persuaded to adopt a less selfish attitude and to return briefs in plenty of time: flagrant breaches of this principle ought to result in financial or disciplinary sanction, not only for the barrister but also for the clerk. An added safeguard would be to impose a rule that barristers of under three years' call should not be permitted to accept a contested brief in the Crown Court.

Last-minute meetings between counsel and client are less likely to happen with more serious offences. The system tends most frequently to lead to injustice in the less important cases (though they are far from unimportant to the defendants concerned). There is no lack of examples; the files of JUSTICE are full of them. Typical was the trial of Luke Dougherty, who at Durham Crown Court in 1973 was convicted of shoplifting and sent to prison, despite the fact that he had been on a coach trip at the time of the offence and could have produced a coachload of alibi witnesses to prove it. He had only met his counsel about an hour before the hearing and the strength of his alibi was never properly communicated within that time.[15]

A similar miscarriage of justice occurred at Lincoln Crown Court in 1973 when two young men were convicted of arson and conspiracy to defraud after having made false confessions under police pressure. One of the men only met his counsel about half an hour before going into court and was strongly advised by him to plead guilty so as to attract a lighter sentence. The young man later told BBC Television:

> 'By the time he had explained all this to me it was getting very close to the time when we had to go into court, and therefore I had very little time to make up my mind as to what I should do. I knew I was not guilty, but after what that barrister said . . . I changed my mind all of a sudden and said I would plead guilty.'[16]

Both men received prison sentences but have since been granted a Royal Pardon.

Cases like these reflect the unhappy fact that criminal defence work, however serious the charge, is generally not nearly as well prepared as even the most minor civil claim in the High Court. There is not a comparable amount of pre-trial effort and preparation, nor is there a comparable number of conferences and meetings. In part this may be because the State and not the defendant is usually the paymaster, so that there is a feeling that the defendant is not in a position to demand, or expect, the same standard of preparatory service as that accorded to a paying civil client.[17]

PLEA BARGAINING

Whilst a defendant should always have complete freedom of choice as to what plea he enters, it is nevertheless his counsel's duty to advise him about that plea even if in strong terms. In the words of the Bar's code of conduct: 'This will include advice that a plea of guilty, showing an element of remorse, is a mitigating factor which may well enable the Court to give a lesser sentence than might otherwise be the case.'[18]

Counsel may also in certain circumstances see the judge so as to gauge the kind of sentence he has in mind and then report back to his client so that the risks and advantages of a plea of guilty or a contested trial can be properly evaluated.[19] Most criminal justice systems could not cope with a high proportion of defendants who insisted on contesting their guilt and, to save the State the trouble and expense of proving it by trial, the offer to trade a more lenient sentence in return for a guilty plea and some expression of remorse is a mutually satisfactory compromise. Defendants should be made aware of this understanding so that, if they are guilty, they can decide whether to take advantage of it, but they should never feel pressured.

Some complain however that they have been pressured, and in such cases the error probably lies with the barrister for failing to communicate with sufficient care and patience, with the result that advice was misinterpreted as arm-twisting.[20] The practice of plea bargaining is a classic example of the importance of the relationship between counsel and client and, above all, of the need for barristers to be able to express themselves comprehensibly and sympathetically so that the client does not feel threatened or confused.

THE ATTITUDE OF DETACHMENT

Defendants frequently complain that their counsel were indifferent or unsympathetic. The Bar's reply is that a barrister's function is not to provide sympathy – only advice and representation. The Bar's rules of etiquette insist on detachment and the unprofessionalism of emotional involvement, resting the need for both on the undoubted importance of counsel being able to exercise unclouded judgment. Breaches of these rules even incur charges of misconduct. Some years ago, for example, it was ruled improper for counsel to stand as surety for his client's bail[21]; in 1971, a barrister was summoned before the Professional Conduct Committee for offering to pay his client's contribution to the legal aid fund[22]; and in 1974, another barrister was reported to the leader of his Circuit for giving his client (who was in custody) a tin of sardines one day during the course of a lengthy trial. To be seen in any way to associate too closely with one's client is not only regarded as unprofessional, but is actively discouraged.

In certain circumstances such association, if taken too far, can clearly become undesirable. A celebrated example is that of Dr Kenealy Q.C., who showed such libellous excess of zeal for his client after the Tichborne trial that in the space of a year he was dispatented, disbenched and disbarred.[23] A more recent example is the Irish barrister who in 1957 was disbarred after the Bar Council had been supplied by the Home Secretary with transcripts of tapped telephone conversations between him and two of his criminal clients showing that he had been providing them with assistance which went far outside their professional relationship.[24]

But by and large the enforced coolness between counsel and client is not always necessary or even desirable and the dangers feared are usually remote. A defendant, like any other consumer, is entitled to service, and service not only means competence in court by lawyers' standards but also satisfying the client so far as possible; inevitably that satisfaction will in part depend on the attitude with which he is treated. It is time that the Bar Council realized that the outlawing of even the smallest acts of humanity by counsel on the grounds of misconduct is as potentially destructive of the image of the Bar as the other extreme, and that more discretion should be allowed to counsel with regard to the distance that they choose to keep.

STANDING UP TO THE JUDGE

Perhaps the most difficult situation any defence counsel may be required to handle is a hostile judge who exhibits impatience, intolerance or even positive hostility towards the defence. Regrettably such instances do occur. The best known recent example of a flare-up between judge and defence counsel was in the 1975 I.R.A. trial arising from the bombs planted at Madame Tussaud's and the Earls Court boat show, which was presided over by Mr Justice Melford Stevenson.[25] The defendants were convicted and appealed, one of their grounds being that the judge's behaviour was prejudicial to them. 'Most of the friction which undoubtedly occurred between Bench and Bar', said Lord Widgery, the Lord Chief Justice, 'arose from the fact that the trial lasted 45 working days. The judge clearly thought that this was excessive and that it was due to unnecessary, inappropriate and too prolonged cross-examination by some defending counsel.' The judge interjected forcefully at several stages, but the passage which particularly offended was as follows:

> 'I am getting deeply concerned about the time that this case is taking. I have listened carefully, and, I hope fairly soundly, to a series of suggestions that fingerprints have been fraudulently planted, including in particular this one; I have listened carefully to the cross-examination to see whether it has revealed any factual basis for any such suggestion. Nothing of the kind has been revealed, and I think a general groping cross-examination directed to every police officer, and indeed behind that police officer to every department of Scotland Yard where documents could be stored, is not a proper exercise of counsel's duty . . .'

At the end of the trial he then ordered that defence counsel's fees, when they were later assessed, be cut for wasting time.

Such remarks, by commenting on the merits of the defence, trespass perilously close to the jury's province of determining the facts, and gave rise to the question as to whether or not the defendants received a fair trial. In this particular case, the Bar Council stood firmly behind the barristers involved although Sir Melford Stevenson found support from such unlikely quarters as Mr Bernard Levin.[26] On appeal, the Court of Appeal found that 'there was no question here of misconduct on the part of counsel', who had only been doing their duty, and that in all the circumstances there probably had been a fair trial. The Court went on to give, for the first time, guidance on counsel's position in such situations. It explained that a judge may not take disciplinary action against a barrister himself but must complain to the Bar Council, although a judge 'can of course commit to prison a barrister who is guilty of contempt of court'. It went on to observe that the Bar Council's rulings on counsel's duty and matters of etiquette 'do not bind the courts', and that 'the judge is the final authority in his own court'; if counsel believes that his duty requires him to follow a certain course which is prohibited by the judge, then counsel must either withdraw, comply with the judge's wishes, or seek redress later in a higher court. The autonomy of the trial judge consequently continues unabated, and in cases of conflict counsel remains in the difficult or near-impossible position of having to convince the Court of Appeal that one of their judicial colleagues has so misconducted himself as to make a conviction unsafe.

MISCARRIAGES OF JUSTICE

Practice at the criminal bar is full of opportunity for memoirs and articles and even richer in inspiration for novels and film scripts, but it is an opportunity which is discouraged. The basic rule is that a barrister may not write or broadcast about any case in which he has been involved unless he can do so without disclosing the part he played in it and without betraying any matters of confidence. But although in theory counsel are free, within limits, to write about their cases, there is a remarkable lack of examples in which it has been done, and there is generally believed to be a very fine line between the ambit of the rule and disciplinary proceedings. Perhaps the answer should depend on the motive; if the aim is gain or personal publicity as a barrister, then the objection is overwhelming.

But what if the aim was a desire to communicate out of genuine concern that a miscarriage of justice had occurred? In 1935 it was ruled that defence counsel in a murder trial ought not to sign a petition, or take part publicly in any way, in the campaign for the reprieve of his client.[27] But mistakes do happen in our criminal justice system: ought they really to be accepted under an imposed duty of professional silence? Counsel – because of their working knowledge of the case and legal experience – are in the best position to comment. Is it a valid objection that their comment is destructive of the authority of the judicial process, or that repeating arguments in the press or on television which have failed in the courts is ungracious? In the United States, criminal lawyers have entered with some success into the public forum to campaign for clients when the circumstances truly warranted it. Fortunately in this country not everyone obeys the letter of the rule: Patrick Meehan, for example, had as his defence counsel an advocate who was also an M.P. and who, after his conviction, took his case up in Parliament with some success. After serving several years of a life sentence, in 1976 Meehan was released and granted a Royal Pardon. Provided counsel exercise care and restraint, there seems to be no valid reason why they should be compelled to wash their hands of the possible mistakes in our courts merely because their professional engagement in a case has come to an end.

CONCLUSIONS

As with most institutions, the future of the Bar lies in its ability to adapt. Today people feel increasingly free to criticize and less willing to tolerate. They see in the Bar a complacency which runs counter to the spirit of reform and the move towards greater social justice. In relation to the criminal bar, there is a widespread desire for its practitioners to assert and promote the freedom and rights of the individual in the courts, and in particular to stand up squarely to a criminal law which is encroaching more and more into private life and pursuits. The response of the Bar, however, has been a curious lack of impetus. Our legal system, unlike that in the United States, for example, has never developed any coherent defence of civil liberties, and its absence cannot be explained by saying simply that the U.S. Supreme Court has been interpreting a Constitution which we do not possess. A large measure of the difference is due to the attitude of English lawyers who have remained firmly unconvinced of the need for such categorical statements of basic rights. A fundamental change of attitude is required; but whether the Bar is capable of it is open to doubt. Very occasionally, the Criminal Bar Association has risen to the challenge: in 1973, for example, it replied hotly to the Criminal Law Revision Committee's Eleventh Report which had reacted to the soar in crime rates by proposing the virtual abolition of the few rights that exist in this country for the protection of suspects under interrogation.[28]

Such intervention is unhappily all too rare. The Criminal Bar Association is generally too passive and needs to take more of the initiative. It is nowhere near as active or influential as its equivalent within the American Bar Association. In England the impetus for criminal law reform lies almost exclusively with the Law Commission, M.P.s and organizations such as JUSTICE, the National Council for Civil Liberties, Release and similar pressure groups concerned with the rights of defendants. Individual barristers have done a lot of good work for JUSTICE, but so far as the Bar itself is concerned, it is not too cynical to say that in general it only enters the political arena when its own financial interests are threatened. The failure of the criminal bar to play its proper part in this sphere is an abrogation of one of its most important responsibilities.

7 WOMEN AT THE BAR

THE STRUGGLE FOR ADMISSION

Just over 100 years ago 92 women signed a petition requesting permission to attend lectures in Lincoln's Inn. The Benchers of the Inn regretted that this was 'not expedient'.[1] It was not until fifty years later in May 1922 that Ivy Williams became the first woman barrister and was called to the Bar by the Inner Temple.

It had been a long struggle punctuated by the unsuccessful applications of many women, including Christabel Pankhurst, and the successful application of Bertha Cave in 1902 – an oversight by Gray's Inn which was rapidly corrected when the Benchers realized what had happened. She appealed to a tribunal of eight judges presided over by the Lord Chancellor himself; they confirmed the Benchers' decision. Their conclusion was based on a fine old principle of English law: there was no precedent for women being called to the English Bar – and the judges were not going to create one.[2] It was not until the passage of the Sex Disqualification (Removal) Act 1919 that the admission of women was forced upon the Inns by Parliament; and since that date the acceptance of women has continued to be slow and grudging.

THE POSITION OF WOMEN AT THE BAR TODAY

The numbers of women at the Bar have increased slightly in recent years, but this has been almost entirely a result of their own efforts and determination; they have received little encouragement or help from the men, who as Table 1 shows still constitute over 90% of the practising Bar.

Table 1: Numbers of Men and Women in practice 1950–1976[3]

Year	Women	Men	Total	Women as percentage of total
1955	64	1944	2008	3·2
1960	84	1835	1919	4·4
1965	99	2065	2164	4·6
1970	147	2437	2584	5·7
1973	239	2898	3137	7·6
1974	252	3116	3368	7·4
1975	258	3388	3646	7·0
1976	313	3568	3881	8·1

When one looks at the number of judicial appointments held by women the pattern of continuing discrimination is even more striking. After half a century of female infiltration there are still no female judges in the House of Lords or the Court of Appeal (25 men); two women High Court judges (70 men); five Circuit judges (out of 270); and only four women who are practising Q.C.s (out of 370). Table 2 below demonstrates clearly the subordinate role to which the Bar assigns its women:

Table 2: Judicial and other appointments held by men and women in 1976[4]

	Men	Women
Law lords and Lords Justices	25	0
High Court judges	70	2
Circuit judges	265	5
Masters and Registrars (excluding solicitors)	21	1
Stipendiary Magistrates	50	2
Recorders	359	7
Practising Q.C.s	366	4
Benchers of the Inns of Court (1975)	377	2

Ten years ago in 1968 there was one token woman on the High Court bench, one woman County Court judge, and one female Q.C. The appointments in Table 2 are therefore comparatively recent. Such recognition is often belated; many senior barristers would agree that for a woman to be appointed she must not simply be as able as her male counterparts but considerably better. This is clearly demonstrated when one considers the proportion of women appointed to judicial posts (the first six items in Table 2).

Even if one allows for the fact that three-quarters of the women in practice were called in the last 15 years, and are therefore effectively ineligible for judicial appointments,[5] the pool of women who could be appointed is far from negligible. In 1976 there were 80 women of over 15 years' call who were eligible for such appointments, and only 17 who had been so appointed – a proportion of 21%. By comparison among the men of over 15 years' call the proportion who held one of the 800 judicial appointments listed in Table 2 was 53%.[6] No one has ever suggested that the senior women practitioners at the Bar are less able than their male colleagues; it is hard to think of any explanation for the disproportionately low numbers of women appointed other than discrimination.

BARRIERS TO ENTRY

Discrimination continues to exist also at the bottom end of the Bar, with the proportion of women who qualify but are unable to practise being greater than the equivalent proportion of men. The statistics needed to calculate exactly the failure rates of women as compared with men are not all available, but sufficient data exist to make an approximate calculation, and these are set out in Table 3.

Table 3 Success rates in obtaining a tenancy: Men and Women 1970–1976[7]

Year	Call figures (British domicile only)		Net increase in number of barristers in practice		Total net gain	Total starting in practice
	Men	Women	Men	Women		
1969–70	380	91	122	14	136	241
1970–71	466 (est)	90 (est)	110	20	130	222
1971–2	499	87	176	29	205	275
1972–3	465	95	175	43	218	321
1973–4	430	99	218	13	231	299
1974–5	—	—	272	6	278	354
1975–6	—	—	180	55	235	382

Allowing for the fact that columns 3 and 4 only show the net increase in the number of men and women who started in practice each year[8], and using a three-year moving average and a time-lag of one or two years between call to the Bar and finding a tenancy, the success rate of men is of the order of 60%–70%, while that for women is only 40%–45%. This difference could be explained if the number of women who qualified but did not intend to practise at the Bar was greater than the number of men, but in fact the reverse is probably the case; a survey of Bar students in 1976 showed that while only 58% of the men replying intended to practise at the English Bar, the equivalent figure for women was 75%.[9]

The stage at which women suffer because of their sex is not in arranging pupillage but in looking for a tenancy. The survey showed that women do not appear to find it more difficult than men to obtain pupillage; and a survey of women barristers in 1972 reported a similar finding – only 15% reported special problems in obtaining pupillage, while 40% said they had special problems in finding a tenancy.[10]

Women also suffer more than men from the expense of starting at the Bar. Banks are frequently less willing to give them the generous overdraft facilities which are essential in one's first two years; and although Inn scholarships are available, some are specifically closed to women. Of the remainder, few are awarded to women and even when they are the amount received is sometimes smaller than that received by men of similar means and ability. The Awards Committee of one Inn told a working-class graduate that she was 'irresponsible' for coming to the Bar with no resources whatsoever. They asked her patiently and sympathetically: 'Wouldn't you be better off considering becoming a solicitor . . . a civil servant . . . a law teacher?' In fact, anything rather than a barrister. She did not receive an award.

However the main stumbling block is simply prejudice, and this reveals itself most strongly at the crucial stage in a woman's career, when she is looking for a tenancy. Many chambers openly admit a 'no woman' policy, and continue to do so despite the Sex Discrimination Act 1975 (which does not apply to the Bar, since sets of chambers are not partnerships and tenants are not employed). One particular set of chambers which has always been known to have a no woman policy (amended to a 'no other woman' policy after the daughter of the Head of Chambers was admitted) has blatantly refused a woman applicant on the grounds of her sex. Others do not have the same confidence that they are beyond the law and hide their discrimination behind all sorts of excuses. Either the woman was not up to the standard of the men who applied or for sound economic reasons she did not suit the vacancy.

One woman who recently left the Bar after squatting for over a year after finishing her pupillage told me that she had applied to a set of chambers of which the Head is a well-known liberal Q.C., and the senior clerk a woman. When she met the clerk she was told 'I will press your application as hard as possible but I'm afraid our Head of Chambers is against women'. He in turn said 'I will press your application as hard as possible but our Clerk is against women'. She does not know who was telling the truth – perhaps both; but she was not taken on.

As recently as 1972 the majority of sets of chambers in London contained no women at all. Furthermore those chambers which do have women appear to operate a quota system, with the maximum number of women being two:

Table 4: London chambers and the number of women in them[11]

Number of women:	None	1	2	3	4	5	Female Clerks	Female Heads of Chambers
1967	115	37	18	4	1	0	4	1
1972	94	54	21	6	4	1	12	4
1975	74	57	25	16	6	3	14	5

As can be seen from the table, the number of sets of chambers with more than two women is very small indeed. The existence of an unofficial quota system has been recognized in an unpublished paper of the Bar Council's Special Committee on Women's Careers (now disbanded), and was commented upon also in an article by a woman barrister published in the *Law Society's Gazette* in 1976:

> 'Miss A . . . was told by her pupillage chambers that she would not be taken on as a tenant because they already had two women in the chambers. Miss A recognized a brick wall when she saw it and so she left the Bar. The Bar lost a most suitable candidate . . .
>
> Miss F had been a squatter in a set of chambers for well over two years and had established a reasonable practice. Why had she not been offered a tenancy? There were already two women in chambers . . .
>
> Miss G, the best pupil in an established set of chambers, had to stand by and watch less capable men taken on as tenants before her because of the views of the Head of Chambers about women.'[12]

In the 1960s the expansion of legal aid increased the work and expectations of the practising Bar far beyond its capacity, and the Bar Council undertook a recruiting drive to encourage young men of ambition to come to the Bar. Quite a few women came too, together with a few intrepid black students and an increasing proportion of both sexes without recognizable old school ties. The flood of crime and divorce work forced open gates that had remained impervious to purely moral persuasion. Now with the accommodation crisis in the Temple there is suddenly no space for the influx of able people of both sexes, and because of the economic depression there is beginning to be a shortage of work. The successful jealously guard their right to remain overworked, and junior tenants who have only just got onto the bottom rung of the ladder are frequently the least sympathetic to the plight of those still waiting below.

Today the competition for each tenancy is even fiercer than before and the woman applicant stands very little chance alongside her male rivals. She is once again a luxury the profession cannot afford. At a meeting of Heads of Chambers in 1975, attended by about 80 men and two women, one of the elder statesmen said: 'Our prime concern must be for those young men in our chambers with wives and mortgages.' Few will ever accept that a woman is not merely working to pass the time until she has children, or else to provide a second salary in a male-provider's household.[13]

After all, we are frequently told, women form a higher proportion at the Bar than they do in any other profession. This is not in fact true. The proportion of female dentists and doctors (14% and 18% respectively in 1972) is far in excess of the proportion of women at the Bar; although it is fair to say that the Bar scores a lot better than many other professions, including the Law Society (only 3·2% of all solicitors were women in 1972).

This record is merely a poor excuse and certainly not a justification. However, many men at the Bar seem to see it as a total answer not only to the present but to the future aspirations of women barristers.

THE KIND OF WORK WOMEN DO

It is also frequently pointed out that at the Bar women receive equal pay with men for equal work, and always have done. The problem is that women frequently fail to get equal work.

There are still great difficulties facing a woman who wishes to practise outside the traditional fields of crime and divorce. At the Chancery Bar there are only seven or eight women barristers in active practice, while virtually none break into the specialized fields of tax or commercial law, patents or planning. These are the more lucrative areas of practice, as well as being intellectually more demanding; but it has never been suggested that academically women lack the ability to succeed in these fields – if only given the chance.

In the 1972 survey women described the nature of their practices as crime (54%), civil (53%), matrimonial (49%) and Chancery (5%).[14] Not one appeared to practise in one of the specialist fields (unless these were lumped together under 'civil'). It is interesting that the proportion doing matrimonial work is not higher; the general impression at the Bar is that just as women in medicine are eased into gynaecology so women lawyers all too often find themselves in the field of divorce. Most barristers if asked to name the main speciality of women at the Bar would certainly say divorce; if this is untrue then the position is encouraging. One thing the survey did not bring out is that women are often also used to do unpleasant placatory work such as apologizing to judges for the non-attendance or mistakes of senior counsel; anything which involves a human touch is thought to be women's work.

Even at the common law Bar where all the women are concentrated they tend to remain clustered on the lower rungs of the ladder without the encouragement and variety of work given to their male contemporaries. To find the reasons for this it is necessary to look at the three people who decide which barrister is the right one for the job: in ascending order of importance these are the client, the solicitor and the clerk.

The Bar Council does not recognize that prejudice might come from the clerk, but lays the blame squarely with the client:

> 'The prejudice against women emanates from the lay client who wishes to have a male barrister to conduct his case. The same prejudice exists between the patient and the surgeon, hence, no doubt, the small number of women surgeons. Accordingly a solicitor is as a general rule reluctant to recommend women barristers.'[15]

It is true that some clients are prejudiced against women barristers, and may be prompted to complain, especially where a last-minute change of counsel leaves them being represented by a woman where previously their barrister was a man. However it is relatively rare that a client actually declines the services of a woman barrister.

More frequently, as the Bar Council says, solicitors will screen the pool of barristers available for the case, and if they feel the client might be a little awkward they will play safe and brief a man. Sexism can however operate from a different angle, with solicitors taking a fancy to a pretty woman and briefing her in preference and to the envy of her male colleagues. One such squatter was told that her chambers had decided not to give her a tenancy because she had been getting 'too friendly with solicitors'.

An interesting finding in the 1972 survey was that as many women barristers thought they were treated differently by solicitors because of their sex as reported being treated the same (44% and 40%). It is a pity that they were not asked in what ways they were treated differently from men. It is interesting, too, that the number who thought they were treated differently by their clerks was considerably less (25%). It is nevertheless a significant proportion: solicitors do find that they have difficulty in sending women heavier work because clerks try to channel the better cases to men. Clerks generally regard their 10% as better invested in a man than in a woman in the long term. The clerk will be reluctant to help a woman build up her practice when any day she may marry, produce children and leave a gap in chambers. 'It's like backing horses, women often fall at the first fence', was how one of them put it. Childbearing hampers every woman's struggle for equality and the break in her working life which this involves tells against her even in a profession where she is self-employed and the profits are her profits. The power of the clerk in the system is immense and few Heads of Chambers would have the courage to demand the entry of women where a clerk was against it. Even fewer Heads of Chambers will insist that a woman gets her share of the interesting work and is not left simply to pick up the crumbs.

And that is how most of the male bar would have us leave it, with the blame resting principally on the villainous clerks. Yet most of them at heart agree with the clerks' attitudes. As one Head of Chambers put it: 'It's nice to have a pretty face around; the trouble is some young chap is bound to notice her charms and then what will chambers do?' Another Q.C., the Head of a large set, denied any taint of prejudice: 'I've got two women in my chambers, one older and past marrying, the other younger but so plain that the chance is remote' – words spoken in jest, perhaps, but with a grain of truth behind them. Younger men can also be found who protest that it is their clerks alone who quash any attempt to introduce women; but their inaction speaks louder than their words.

We have seen in chapter 5 how barristers like to be covered by suitable alternatives within their own set of chambers; neither they nor their clerks are happy about solicitors taking a brief to another set whom they might suddenly start to prefer. Uncertainties must be reduced to a minimum by keeping the chambers team intact, and women are thought to create uncertainty. The fear that the solicitor or client might not want a woman, or that she might drop out to get married or have children is felt most forcibly by younger men at the Bar. The older, established and successful man is naturally more secure, but his innate prejudice is played on successfully by the younger members of his chambers.

THE EFFECT OF PREJUDICE ON THE MORALE OF WOMEN BARRISTERS

Until 1964 women barristers in the provinces were still excluded from certain activities of their local Bars. On the Northern Circuit they were allowed only to attend meetings and some dinners, and the Midland Circuit admitted women neither to meetings nor to the Circuit mess. Those who opposed the admission of women did so because they would 'inhibit the atmosphere' and 'completely alter the character and nature' of the mess. Moreover it was feared that some women might attend dinner because they felt 'that in so doing they are in some way advancing their professional chances'.[16]

Gray's Inn still holds an annual smokers' concert for men only at which vulgar jokes and songs combine with large quantities of drink to give them the illusion of being some sort of latterday Hell Fire club. A number of years ago a young woman, moved by curiosity, hid in the Hall until the proceedings were well under way and then disclosed her presence. One of our most eminent judges gave vent to his fury and ordered her out of the Hall, amidst the cheering approval of the gathering.

This kind of episode typifies the traditional flavour of the Bar which, with few exceptions, is an echo of the public school, the military mess and the gentlemen's club. Women are just not 'chaps'; and the men are certainly not prepared to make any concessions to make women feel more welcome.

THE EFFECT OF PREJUDICE ON THE LAW

One County Court judge in Berkshire who had a notorious reputation as a misogynist used to refer to women barristers in open court as 'chorus girls' and 'silly girls'. During a road accident case, where the woman driver was represented by a woman barrister, the judge gratuitously gave the court the benefit of his jaundiced view of women drivers. The male counsel for the plaintiff obsequiously inquired if the judge held the same views of women barristers. This sort of male togetherness is frequently used in a competitive way to undermine the professional confidence of women practitioners.

This kind of incident makes one wonder whether a woman driver could ever hope for justice in front of that particular judge. But prejudice can influence the outcome not only of individual cases but also the general development of the law. In a professional negligence case reported in *The Times* in November 1975 Mr Justice Caulfield said: 'Even in present times, when there was a movement by women for equality with men, a sensible wife, certainly in a united family, did not generally make the major decisions. Most wives sensibly left such decisions to their husbands. A solicitor should not take instructions from a wife when a husband was also available.'[17] The judge made it clear that the negligence of the solicitors did not lie in consulting one of two clients, but in consulting the wife rather than the husband. This kind of ruling refuses to recognize women either as equal partners in marriage or even as responsible citizens. Seldom are a judge's feelings on the subject articulated so openly, but similar attitudes are to be found in hundreds of courts and tribunals sitting in judgment every day on cases in which the rights of women are involved.

The popular prejudice is that women are silly creatures, easily swayed by emotion and not open to reason; it was only half in jest that A. P. Herbert pointed out that the law, so fond of consulting the reasonable man, has never yet made reference to the reasonable woman. At the Bar the belief is widespread that women barristers tend to be over-emotional, and that in order to succeed they must suppress the feminine aspects of their nature. 'The fact has to be faced', the Bar Council told the Monopolies Commission, 'that the profession of barrister requires the masculine approach (however fallacious it may be) to reasoning and argument, and women only succeed in such activities if they have a masculine disposition.'[18]

This really is an extraordinary statement. Quite apart from its defects of logic (if the masculine approach is 'fallacious', why does the profession of barrister 'require' it?), its sheer arrogance is something to wonder at. It completely overlooks the possibility that women might have a contribution of their own to make, to the profession and to the development of the law. If there is one thing in which this writer does believe strongly, it is that women barristers can make a separate contribution, and that the Bar will be the loser if women are forced to behave just like the men. The 'masculine approach' of the Bar is characterized all too often by a combination of arrogance and insensitivity; and the sort of qualities which women can bring to their work (and which need not exclude the power to reason) are a greater awareness of people's feelings, a sense of humility and a genuine desire to help their clients rather than to impress them.[19] They might in the process persuade the men to be a little less conscious of their own importance and a little more responsive to the needs of the people they claim to serve.

THE BAR COUNCIL'S SPECIAL COMMITTEE

Few of these ideas will receive much assent from senior women barristers, who were taught to believe that women's acceptance at the Bar is conditional on their conforming to the predominant male ethos. Still less will they be acceptable to the Bar Council, which has never gone on record to say that it welcomes the presence of women at the Bar, and on the whole seems to regard them merely as a cause of embarrassment. Despite acknowledging in 1969 that 'it is no doubt still more difficult for a woman than for a man to find a seat in chambers'[20], the Bar Council made no effort to rectify this state of affairs until continued protests from female students and pupils forced it to set up a committee to investigate their complaints in 1971.

The committee sent out a questionnaire to all the women then in practice. The response was quite good, although some of the results were inconclusive (most of the significant findings are referred to elsewhere in this chapter).

It could have formed the basis for further research, or even (dare one say it?) for action. Instead the survey findings were never reported to the profession, and although the committee continued to appear for several years among the special committees listed in the Annual Statement of the Bar Council, it had in fact died a natural death some time before the Senate finally dissolved it in 1975.[21] The older women members were never happy about having a separate committee to inquire into the problems of women, believing that the Bar is a single profession and that women do not have any special problems which are not shared by men; or if they do, that they only do themselves harm by drawing attention to them. In the circumstances it is not surprising that the verdict of one of the younger members was that in her opinion the committee was simply a front to make the Bar Council look more responsive than it really was.

DRESS

One item which the Bar Council referred to the Special Committee was the question of dress, a topic which takes up much energy in the Ladies' robing room. Meticulous rules are imposed and their strict interpretation endlessly discussed. To be the very model of a perfect lady barrister means looking as indistinguishable as possible from one's male colleagues. Warnings are given at an early stage in one's career to remove dress rings and nail polish when appearing before a certain lady judge. 'Dresses or blouses should be long-sleeved and high to the neck . . . Wigs should, as far as possible, cover the hair, which should be drawn back from the face and forehead, and if long enough should be put up.'[22]

These rules are sacred to the heart of the older woman practitioner, going back to the days when admission to a man's world was such a privilege that women conformed even in their mode of dress. To its credit the Special Committee refused to act as a watchdog of skirt lengths and referred the question of dress straight back to the Bar Council. It is extraordinary how much time is wasted on trivia of this kind while the real problems continue to be ignored.

CONCLUSIONS

Examining the problems of prejudice facing women at the Bar has inevitably involved some repetition of the general problems mentioned in other chapters which face a large number of people coming to the profession. Some of our problems are special but many cannot be isolated from the problems of discrimination which operate just as forcibly against black or Asian lawyers and other minority groups. In the world outside the Temple demands are being made for equality; there is a heightened awareness of women's issues and the struggle for women's rights. Yet the Bar has remained impervious to external change. It is this failure to respond to public need that highlights its insularity and ineffectiveness as an institution. Nothing of any significance has been done to counter discrimination against women, and as a result women are playing little or no part in the creation and interpretation of laws which affect women just as much as they affect men. This has now reached the point where legislation specifically designed to protect women's rights will be interpreted almost exclusively by men.

The Bar Council says that 'If there is still a prejudice against women, it is rapidly disappearing. There are today more women joining the Inns of Court, and more women in practice at the Bar than ever before.'[23] It is true that the number of women in practice has increased considerably in recent years; it is also true that as their numbers grow the prejudice against them is slowly diminishing. Nevertheless the present position offers no grounds for complacency. At the top women are still being passed over for judicial appointments which they deserve; at the bottom they still find it harder to obtain tenancies than men, and are used as part of a lump labour force to service the excess work of chambers without being offered any professional security in return.

Central to the whole problem of discrimination is the issue of childbearing. So long as women are considered liable to drop out of practice in order to have children the prejudice against them will continue to find a rationalization. This was how Diana Cheeld described the problem in her article in the *Law Society's Gazette:*

> 'The Bar, with exceptions, does not take women practitioners seriously. It is assumed that no woman is capable of giving the long commitment necessary for a career at the Bar, because all women have babies. This is unfair to the many women who never marry or have children; it is unfair to married women who decide against a family and it is unfair to married women who decide to combine a career and a family, making their own domestic arrangements accordingly.'[24]

Interestingly out of the respondents to the Bar Council's 1972 survey of women barristers one-half were not married. Of those who were married two-thirds had children, but one-third had not come to the Bar until after raising their families. Of course one does not know how many of the unmarried women subsequently married and left the Bar, or how many of the childless married women went on to have children; but this sort of thing can be found out. The Senate publishes annual statistics of the number of barristers who ceased practice in the previous year; at the moment these are divided simply into two categories, those over and those under ten years' call, but it would not be difficult to provide a breakdown also by sex. We would then know how many women do leave the Bar, as compared with men, and at what stage in their careers; and we would at last have evidence against which to test the hypothesis that women are a bad risk for chambers looking for a tenant. We would then be able to judge the extent to which chambers are justified in discriminating against women and the extent to which they are motivated simply by prejudice.

This is pre-eminently the sort of investigation which the Bar Council's Special Committee should be carrying out, if it were still in existence. The present state of ignorance only serves to play into the hands of those who would perpetuate the *status quo*. Discrimination flourishes but goes unchecked. It is little exaggeration to say that at the moment a woman can succeed in making a career at the Bar only if she makes a deliberate decision not to have a family, *and* if she can persuade clerks and Heads of Chambers to believe her decision.

In a state of greater knowledge about women's careers unjustified discrimination could be penalized with disciplinary sanctions by the Senate. Greater awareness of women's problems, rather than a brave pretence that they do not exist, might in the long run help also to engender greater sympathy for their position. It is absurd that most male barristers have the benefit of both a career and a family, and yet force their female colleagues to choose either one or the other. Women also have the right to both a career and a family, and the Bar cannot claim to treat women fairly until it offers them an equal opportunity with men to do both these things.

8 INDEPENDENCE AND FUSION

THE BAR'S GROWING DEPENDENCE ON PUBLIC FUNDS

In 1975–6 over 3000 barristers received fees from the civil legal aid fund for work in the High Court and County Court, and if one includes work in the magistrates' courts (but still excluding the Crown Court) the total number of barristers receiving legal aid moneys that year was 3816.[1] Almost every barrister in practice thus depends in some measure on public funds; but the degree of dependence where civil work is concerned is very small. Total payments made to counsel for civil work amounted in 1975–6 to only £2½ million or about six per cent of the Bar's total income.[2] Even among those specializing in the work, very few barristers received substantial sums: only 100 counsel earned over £4000 from civil legal aid in that year.[3]

This low degree of dependence on civil legal aid is surprising, because for some time it has been generally supposed that over half the Bar's total earnings come from the Government. Sir Peter Rawlinson told the Bar A.G.M. in 1971 that 'most of its income was now derived from public funds'[4], but in fact the proportion appears to be slightly less than half – the Bar Council's 1976 survey showed that in 1974–5 some 43% of the Bar's total revenue came from government sources.[5] What boosts the proportion to this level is the earnings of the criminal Bar, from prosecution work and from criminal legal aid. Because almost all criminal work is paid for out of public funds the criminal Bar is particularly vulnerable to changes in Government policy; but civil practitioners are not entirely immune, as was shown by the withdrawal of legal aid from certain classes of divorce proceedings which took effect in 1977.

Case-study (1): Legal Aid for undefended divorces

As a result of the Divorce Reform Act 1969 (which abolished the concept of a guilty party) divorce became considerably easier. The number of petitions filed rose from 54,000 in 1968 to 110,000 in 1971. The increase was not solely due to the change in the law, however, for divorce is a social phenomenon which like the crime wave has increased inexorably in recent years. Over the last decade the number of petitions has trebled, reaching 140,000 in 1975[6]; and the amount of business this brought to lawyers is evidenced by the fact that in 1975–6 113,000 legal aid certificates were issued for matrimonial proceedings, with a value of about £20 million.[7]

In June 1976 however the Lord Chancellor announced that part of the golden tide was to be cut off; legal aid was to be withdrawn from undefended divorces, although it would continue to be available for disputes over maintenance or the custody of children. In making this decision the Lord Chancellor was merely recognizing the fact that divorce proceedings nowadays are usually a formality, albeit a lucrative one for lawyers; not only has legal assistance now been deemed unnecessary, but in future not even the petitioner will need to be present for the granting of an undefended divorce.

At first sight it was thought that the withdrawal of legal aid from undefended divorce would deal a body blow to divorce practitioners. In a bitter speech in the House of Lords Lord Wigoder Q.C. said that the Lord Chancellor's announcement would be:

> 'received with gloom at the Bar as being yet another of the many blows which the profession has sustained in recent years ... The fact is that the current scales for both criminal and civil legal aid were fixed in January 1972. Since that date, the average earnings of the rest of the community have risen by 104%. Since that date, the retail price index has gone up by 85%. Since that date, the expenses of the profession have soared immeasurably; and yet the income of the profession has gone up by precisely nought per cent. ... Those of my friends who have had the misfortune to practise in matrimonial work in the county courts, and who are the ones who will suffer if the proposals put forward today are carried into effect, have received perhaps even more of a raw deal. Their fees, the fees they at present receive, were fixed in 1967 ...'[8]

In fact because of the Bar's very limited dependence on civil legal aid the withdrawal of legal aid from undefended divorce is unlikely to be such a drastic blow as was at first supposed. A few individual divorce practitioners may be hard hit, but the work is quite widely spread: in 1975–6, 2864 barristers received payment from the legal aid fund for matrimonial work in the county court (and 1903 in the High Court).[9] The Lord Chancellor estimated that the total saving might be about £6 million, but much of this goes to solicitors for their preparatory work, and many solicitors themselves represent their clients at the actual hearing – a study of undefended divorces in 1973 (based on one urban and two rural county courts) found that 54% of the petitioners in the sample were represented in court by a solicitor and 45% by a barrister (less than one per cent being unrepresented).[10] If this picture is repeated nationally and if barristers draft the petition in about half the cases in which they appear then the Bar stands to lose only £$\frac{1}{2}$ to £$\frac{3}{4}$ million from the withdrawal of legal aid in undefended divorce cases.[11]

Case-study (2): Crown Court fees

Crown Court fees are a different story. We have already seen that some 85% of the public funds received by the Bar come from criminal work, and the lion's share of criminal work for the Bar comes from the Crown Court. While total payments to counsel from the civil legal aid fund came in 1975–6 to £2$\frac{1}{2}$ million, the Bar's earnings from publicly funded work in the Crown Court alone amounted to some £15 million.[12] Over 95% of those tried in the Crown Courts are represented on legal aid[13], so that in this sphere the Bar relies entirely on the continued generosity of Governments; and in recent years the Government has shown that there are limits even to the capacity of the public purse. The level of fees is controlled by Regulations promulgated in 1968[14], but these are interpreted according to guidelines issued by the Lord Chancellor's Department in 1972 which allow fees substantially higher than those specified in the 1968 Regulations.[15] Since then there has been no increase; and fees which were exceedingly generous in the early 1970s (see chapter 5, Table 2) are now regarded by the Bar as being generally inadequate. Between May 1971 and September 1976 the retail price index rose by 100% and wage rates by 150% while the Crown Court scales remained the same. The Government simply sat back and allowed them to be eroded by inflation. In 1974 at the request of the Lord Chancellor the Chief Taxing Master reviewed the 1972 guidelines, but the Lord Chancellor subsequently stated that he was not prepared to implement the recommendations of the review; and in July 1976 the Home Secretary proposed an increase in the upper limit for brief fees (unchanged since 1960 at £64.50) of 10%. Not surprisingly this offer was rejected by the Bar; but the outcome of these negotiations demonstrated how powerless it is to act in the face of determined inaction on the part of its public paymaster.

In practice the reduction in real earnings has not been as stark as the foregoing figures suggest. The 1968 Regulations do not restrict the fees of Q.C.s and of juniors instructed with them; and they contain an escape clause which allows higher fees where the taxing officer certifies that owing to 'exceptional circumstances' the sums payable under the Regulations would not provide fair remuneration. In 1974 the brief fees in contested cases in the first- and second-tier Crown Courts already exceeded the maximum more often than not[16]; and the proportion of 'exceptional' cases has probably increased considerably since then. However in 1976 this device was challenged by the Home Office on the ground that inflation does not constitute an 'exceptional circumstance' and in February 1977 a specimen taxation was taken before the courts.[17] If the Senate and the Law Society lose this appeal a confrontation seems inevitable, and the Bar may have to threaten to withdraw its services from the Crown Court (something which will cause much soul-searching if it means individual practitioners breaking the cab-rank rule). One reason why things have come to this pass is the Bar's insistence on being paid on a piecework basis, so that neither the taxing authorities nor the Lord Chancellor's Department nor the Bar know when negotiating the level of Crown Court fees what the average annual earnings of barristers from Crown Court work are. Negotiations over doctors' and dentists' remuneration, by contrast, are based on a target figure for average annual income; that figure is regularly reviewed, and if in 1977 it had been the same as in 1971 doctors and dentists would not merely have had good reason to complain but they would also have attracted considerable public sympathy for their cause. Barristers command no such sympathy; fees earned from Crown Court work still seem enormous in public eyes (witness the universally hostile reaction of the press when the average daily fees were published by Michael Zander in January 1976), and any public campaign by the Bar would elicit little support.

If criminal barristers who are paid almost exclusively by the State wish to protect their earnings from inflation then the most sensible thing might be for them to negotiate some kind of salary structure for themselves; the authorities would save the administrative costs of taxing counsel's fees in each individual case, and the criminal Bar would have the security of a steady income, and of a pension on retirement. To individual practitioners who are sick and tired of the lottery of payment on a case-by-case basis such a scheme would not be as unwelcome as one might expect (and certainly not as unwelcome as it would have been five years ago); but to the leaders of the Bar it is unthinkable, since in their view it would seriously undermine the independence of the profession.

THE INDEPENDENCE OF THE BAR[18]

Professional independence is a slogan which is wheeled out in almost any discussion on reform of the legal profession, often with little thought as to what it means. If independence means not being reliant on government money then the criminal Bar ceased to be independent some time ago; but barristers would rightly deny that receipt of public funds has compromised their professional independence. Salaries, it is argued, are rather different; they would give the Government direct control over barristers' earnings, and the next step might be a National Legal Service. However, the judges work for salaries payable out of public funds (and have suffered just as much from pay restraint as other recipients of top salaries); and in recent years the Bar Council has given its blessing to barristers working on salaries in law centres, while retaining their right to appear as advocates in the lower courts.[19]

The real fear is not that barristers' professional independence will be compromised by state funding, but that they will no longer be able to earn unlimited incomes. However as we have seen in the preceding section this ability is already circumscribed when it is the State that pays; under the present legal aid system not only can the earnings of practitioners in a particular field be severely restricted (as in Crown Court work) but they can also be cut off altogether (as with undefended divorce). The right of the

Government to adjust the flow of legal aid in this way in order to improve its cost-effectiveness cannot seriously be challenged; nor can anyone question the necessity for some control over the fees paid to practitioners from public funds. The criminal Bar at the moment has the worst of both worlds; its earnings are controlled by its public paymasters, but it has little effective say in the negotiations over the level of earnings because it does not itself know (or will not admit) what its annual earnings are.

Another objection which could be made to paying criminal barristers an annual salary is that there will no longer be any reward for ability or effort, nor any incentive to work hard for one's clients. If true this latter argument does not say much for the present ethos of the criminal Bar; but in any event a salary structure can incorporate a great deal of flexibility. It is not even essential to pay fixed salaries; what is required is a system for assessing fees paid out of public funds by reference to some estimate of what practitioners 'ought' to earn on an annual basis. The Boyle Review Body's calculations of the various items in a G.P.'s income do not result in all doctors, regardless of experience, skill or type of practice, earning exactly the same; but they are based on the objective that the average annual income of doctors in a given year should be £x. There is no reason why barristers' fees should not be assessed on the same basis.

This should not pose any threat to the Bar's independence. When we speak about professional independence the only meaning that matters is freedom from the possibility that the Government may intrude in the relationship between the lawyer and his client, or prevent or inhibit the lawyer from doing his professional duty. One of the most important rules in the Bar's code of conduct is that 'a barrister should, whilst acting with all due courtesy to the tribunal before which he is appearing, fearlessly uphold the interests of his client without regard to any unpleasant consequences either to himself or to any other person'.[20] Equally sacrosanct is the cab-rank rule, that a barrister is bound to accept any brief in the courts in which he professes to practise (provided it is marked with a proper fee). No organizational structure can guarantee the observance of these rules; a lawyer paid only private fees may still sacrifice the interests of his client to his hopes of preferment, or simply through subservience.

It would be idle to pretend that there are no dangers in the State becoming a direct paymaster; what is important to realize is that the method of payment guarantees nothing. Independence is more a matter of values held by lawyers than of organization; its preservation at the Bar depends not on methods of payment but on the individual consciences of practising barristers, and on their collective code of professional conduct. It is the spirit that counts, not the organizational structure; the independence of the Bar will last just as long as its capacity to withstand improper pressures, from whatever source.

It should not be thought that all pressures from government are improper or a threat to the Bar's independence. The proposition that lawyers should be free from government interference is sometimes extended to the affairs of the profession generally; but here the Government does have a legitimate claim to intervene. The legal profession enjoys important monopolies conferred by statute or long-standing custom, and the Government is perfectly entitled to see that these monopolies are regulated in the public interest. The inquiries into restrictive practices by the Monopolies Commission and the more general investigation by the Royal Commission are examples of this. The Bar's long history of self-government fosters the belief that it enjoys some kind of immunity from such accountability; but in truth it is as much open to governmental scrutiny and intervention as any other institution in the public domain – perhaps rather more so because it serves so vital an aspect of public life as the administration of justice.

The Government must be allowed to govern even in relation to the legal profession; and the fact that lawyers receive so much of their incomes from public funds gives it added responsibilities in this sphere. The Bar is of course entitled to defend itself as best it can when the financial interests of its members are threatened, but it does not help its case by always crying wolf about the threat to its professional independence. The only kind of professional independence that matters is the lawyer's freedom fearlessly to fight for the interests of his client; yet all too often what the Bar means by threats to its independence are in fact merely threats to its self-interest. Clear thinking and honest argument are essential if the fundamental aspects of professional independence are to be preserved.

THE SPECTRE OF FUSION

A good example of the sort of muddled thinking which occurs

is the argument which conflates professional independence with independence from the solicitors' branch of the profession. An instance is provided by Sir Peter Rawlinson's address to the Bar A.G.M. in 1976, when he said: 'Fortunately, in the United Kingdom the independence of the advocate and of the adviser who instructs him is much advanced by the separate role allotted to each. It is on the continued existence of such private practitioners that much of the liberty of the subject depends.'[21] This kind of special pleading merely confuses the issues rather than clarifying them. It is not presumably part of Sir Peter Rawlinson's case that countries with unified professions such as Canada, New Zealand and the United States are less free than our own, yet he appears to suggest that the liberty of the subject in England is somehow dependent on the maintenance of the divided profession.

Unification of the two branches of the legal profession is a subject which invariably arouses intense passions at the Bar. It is a debate which has gone on for well over a hundred years, but in which the real issues remain as shrouded in myth and prejudice as when they were first discussed in the middle of the nineteenth century. The debate continued vigorously until the turn of the century, while the division of function between the Bar and the newly-emerged solicitors' branch remained uncertain and negotiable[22]; but once the lines of demarcation were firmly established interest in the issue subsided. Since then fusion has remained a slumbering volcano, overshadowing all debate about the future of the legal profession, but erupting only intermittently; in the post-War period the sparks have flown in the correspondence columns of *The Times* in 1953, and again in 1966; the matter has been debated by the Law Society, with Lord Goodman (pro) set against Sir David Napley (anti) at their annual conference in 1974; and now of course fusion is an important item on the agenda of the Royal Commission.

The Bar has always seen fusion as a death-warrant. 'If fusion took place barristers would disappear', Patrick Neill Q.C. proclaimed when Chairman of the Senate in 1974[23]; while Andrew Leggatt Q.C. maintained it would involve 'the elimination of the specialist corps of advocates which barristers at present comprise'.[24] Both these statements are wildly exaggerated, bearing little relation either to what has taken place in those common law jurisdictions which have adopted fusion, or to any scenario which is likely to unfold here. They are good examples of the Bar's scaremongering response, which serves to divert attention from the real issues. For in truth fusion is really only a heading for discussion of the various demarcation agreements which separate the two branches of the profession; each of these agreements is a separate issue and each is negotiable without bringing about the collapse of the whole.

FUSION DISSECTED

The divided profession could be retained while relaxing some or all of the following restrictions:
(i) Solicitors could be granted audience rights in the higher courts.
(ii) Barristers could be permitted to take instructions from the lay client direct (or from certain categories of professional client, such as accountants).
(iii) Barristers could be permitted to form partnerships with solicitors, so that some firms of solicitors had barrister-partners.
(iv) There could be a common system of education and training, with lawyers only becoming barristers after (say) five years' practice as a solicitor.

Only the third and fourth of these alternatives deserve the title fusion, since they involve an institutional link-up between the two branches of the profession; but even then fusion would be a misnomer, since it implies a complete abolition of all the distinctions between barristers and solicitors. In fact all the above changes could be introduced without coming anywhere near 'eliminating' (Leggatt) or 'abolishing' (Neill) the specialist services provided by a separate Bar. Each aspect of the present demarcation needs to be discussed as a separate issue; if the advantages of a restriction outweigh its disadvantages, it should be retained; if not, it should be modified or abandoned, without fear that abolition of one restriction will bring down the rest like a house of cards. The Bar is more durable than that.

(1) *Audience rights*

Solicitors have rights of audience in the County Courts and in magistrates' courts, but not in the High Court, Court of Appeal or House of Lords, nor in the Crown Court save when appearing for the defence on committal for sentence or appeal from the magistrates' court. The present very limited right to appear in the Crown Court is the result of horsetrading between the Bar Council and Law Society during the passage of the Courts Act 1971[25]; it is based on political compromise rather than principle. If defence solicitors can handle committals for sentence and appeals from magistrates then presumably prosecution solicitors could do so equally well. An obvious further relaxation would be to allow solicitors to represent defendants who are pleading guilty in the Crown Court (as 60% of all defendants do).

The Crown Court will be the main battleground. The Bar's monopoly of audience rights in the High Court is not nearly so valuable; most of the work is advisory or interlocutory, and few solicitors would want to appear as advocates in the rare cases that come to trial. In the Crown Court on the other hand they might well find it worthwhile to do more advocacy if they were able to take cases on a regular basis.

The Bar will argue that solicitors lack the knowledge and experience to conduct such proceedings. But just as barristers learn the ropes in the lower courts and then gradually expand their skills to the higher courts, solicitors who wanted to appear as advocates would presumably do the same. The Bar's defence is further undermined by the appointment of the first solicitors as Circuit judges in January 1977; for solicitors can now preside full-time over courts in which they do not have the right to appear. This situation is unlikely to pass without comment from the Royal Commission; at the very least some relaxation of the restriction will probably be recommended, if not a grant of full rights of audience.

The Bar's only remaining defence is that this competition would deprive young barristers of work on which to cut their eye-teeth. This argument has been advanced in the past in relation to every extension of the jurisdiction of the County Court[26], and usually been rejected; and the Bar has always survived. If barristers are indeed the specialist advocates which they claim to be they will continue to survive, for they will be well able to meet the competition from solicitors; if not, most of the argument for a monopoly of audience rights collapses.

(2) *Direct briefing*

Like most other restrictive practices the rule that a barrister cannot be instructed without the intervention of a solicitor dates from the last quarter of the nineteenth century, when the new Bar Council was busy codifying custom and practice (not always universally observed) into an enforceable set of rules.[27] It is a self-denying ordinance which redounds primarily to the benefit of solicitors, and which the Bar has since had occasion to regret, and has even threatened to repeal. When the Law Society launched its attack on the Bar's restrictive practices in the 1960s, invoking the principle that 'the interest of the lay public should form the paramount consideration', the Bar Council retorted that it shared this concern to the full and considered 'that joint scrutiny could with advantage be directed to certain matters arising from . . . the solicitors' branch of the profession. In this connection, the rule of the Bar which prevents members of other professions and other persons legally qualified from having direct access to counsel without instructing a solicitor, calls for examination.'[28]

No such examination in fact took place; the threat to re-examine the rule was simply used as a bargaining counter in the subsequent negotiations with the Law Society in order to obtain a better overall settlement for the Bar.[29] As a result barristers still cannot accept instructions except through a solicitor from anyone except a patent agent or parliamentary agent.[30] Tax experts, accountants, architects, banks, insurance companies and the like cannot approach counsel direct; they must always go through a solicitor, who may act as no more than a post box but who will always charge for the privilege. The Bar gains nothing from this restriction and should press for some relaxation at least where professional clients are concerned.

(3) *Partnership between barristers and solicitors*

To permit barristers to enter into some kind of formal association with a firm of solicitors goes considerably further than either of the changes considered above. But a number of barristers do almost all the advisory work for certain firms of solicitors (particularly in the specialist fields) and are in effect consultants to those firms; and it has been argued that barristers in such a position should be allowed to enter into a consultancy agreement with their solicitor-clients, or even to become litigation partners in the firm. Such an arrangement would of course involve complex questions of professional accountability and discipline, but the overseas practice rules of the Bar permit partnership with a foreign lawyer; and the rules governing barristers in law centres permit them to work alongside solicitors as part of the same professional team.

The overseas practice rules are interesting because they overturn almost every canon of conduct at the Bar. Subject to certain conditions, a barrister may accept instructions from the lay client or a foreign lawyer direct, without the intervention of a solicitor; he may negotiate a fee directly with the lay client or a foreign lawyer; he may take an annual retainer or a fixed fee, or even a contingent fee; he may practise without a clerk; and as we have seen, he may enter into partnership with foreign lawyers.[31] The purpose of these rules was to permit barristers to compete on equal terms with solicitors for work in the E.E.C.; but they were not adopted without considerable misgivings by the Bar. It was urged that barristers ought not to become solicitors, doing solicitors' work; and that if the lines of demarcation were blurred abroad, it might not be long before they were regarded as unnecessary at home. Against this it was argued that the Bar's restrictive practices could not be exported to Europe, because European countries would not understand or accept them, and the Bar should not be hamstrung by its own rules when overseas; and these arguments won the day.[32] The Royal Commission may wonder whether English clients would understand or accept many of the Bar's rules and practices if they could look at them afresh with European eyes.

(4) *General practitioners and specialists*

Much of the argument about fusion revolves around the continued provision of specialists. Under the present system solicitors are said to be the general practitioners, and the Bar to provide specialists available for consultation and the conduct of cases where particular experience and skill is needed. In the words of Patrick Neill Q.C., 'If fusion took place barristers would disappear. There would then cease to exist a body of trusted and respected lawyers, who provide specialist services in advocacy and advisory work (the closest analogy being to the services provided by consultants in the medical profession).'[33] The difficulty with this argument is that a large proportion of the Bar has no great experience or skill, certainly not enough to merit the title of specialist. Young barristers start taking briefs after six months' pupillage, aged only 23 or 24; their success in passing the Bar exams is no guarantee of expertise. Over half the Bar is now of less than ten years' call. It is absurd to pretend that all barristers are specialists when a great many are less experienced and less competent than the solicitor who briefs them. In other professions (including medicine) specialists are people who acquired general practitioner qualifications and *then* specialized, often after taking further exams.

For barristers to have a credible standing as specialists the legal profession needs to be restructured, to provide a body of general practitioners and specialists drawn from those practitioners. This would mean that all lawyers would start with a joint education and training as solicitors, and then those who wished could after, say, five years, decide to practise only on instructions from other lawyers and become barristers. A system of this kind would be compatible with the Bar being a separate body, with the same organization and professional rules as at present; and it would provide a stronger justification for some kinds of legal work and some appointments being reserved for barristers (though one would hope that if barristers were truly specialists in this sense they would be more confident about surviving on their merits and might not feel the need for the restrictions and monopolies which exist at present).

In South Africa and in Australia it is normal practice for barristers to spend a couple of years with a firm of solicitors before going on to the Bar. In Scotland it is a professional requirement. Not only does this arrangement help to provide them with clients in their early years, but it gives them a much sounder knowledge throughout their working life of how solicitors operate and how the Bar can best advise and help them. Interestingly one of the advocates of introducing such a system in this country is Sir David Napley, who in 1976 became President of the Law Society. Although opposed to fusion, he has declared himself 'in favour of a system under which all lawyers would undergo common training, but that after a specified number of years in practice as "lawyers" they would be entitled to apply to be classed as experts, and would then have to satisfy an independent authority that they had the necessary competence and expertise'.[34]

FUSION DEFUSED

Fusion is generally viewed by lawyers as a shotgun marriage

between a reluctant Law Society and an even more hostile Bar which would destroy the separate identities of both. The word itself is unfortunate, implying some kind of forced union, when all that is usually envisaged is a dismantling of some or all of the rules which at present keep the two sides of the profession apart. It by no means follows that they will rush together the moment the barriers are down; and in fact all experience both here and abroad argues to the contrary. It is extraordinarily unlikely that the Bar will disappear overnight; for even in fused systems a separate Bar can exist and indeed flourish.

The best testing ground for observing the effects of fusion is Australia, which provides a rich variety of different systems among its different States. Victoria is the system most commonly examined, but the other States are no less instructive. In Victoria the profession was fused by the Amalgamation Act 1891. Since then all lawyers have qualified and been entitled to practise as barristers or solicitors or both; the interesting thing is that those who wished to specialize as advocates continued to practise as 'barristers', and to refuse instructions except through a 'solicitor', and so it has remained ever since. The divided profession has continued but it is a *de facto* rather than a *de jure* division; those who choose to practise as solicitors have exactly the same rights of audience in all courts as barristers, and those solicitors who regularly appear in the courts are in effect practising as both (and are known as 'amalgams'). These amalgams nevertheless brief members of the Bar in cases where they think this is desirable.[35]

It is often argued that because the profession has remained divided fusion in Victoria has been a failure. But on the contrary, what it has achieved is to sweep away the whole mesh of monopolies and restrictive practices and to allow the Bar to survive and be seen to survive on its own merits. In our system a client involved in proceedings in the higher courts is forced to take in and pay for a barrister whether one is needed or not. In Victoria when a specialist advocate is needed and the client can afford one he is briefed; in other cases the solicitor will argue the case himself.

Specialists exist in every legal system, whether fused or divided. It is because of the need for specialist advocates (and subject-specialists) that a separate Bar has continued in Victoria; and there is no reason to suppose that exactly the same would not happen in this country. The Bar can also take courage from the experience of other States in Australia. In New South Wales there is a *de jure* division of the profession but the Bar has no monopoly of rights of audience; it continues to survive. In South Australia and West Australia the profession is unified, but in the 1960s a separate Bar on the same lines as in Victoria has emerged and exists side by side with what is in substance the North American system. Individual partners in firms of 'amalgams' still do most of the court work (briefed by one of their partners, or by another firm)[36], but some practitioners have decided to practise as barristers taking instructions only from 'solicitors'. In both States the Bar is still very small; but it has come into existence to meet a need, and as in Victoria it survives on its merits – there is never any obligation to brief counsel. The client instructs a second lawyer because he thinks his advice or advocacy is worthwhile.

The evidence from Australia and from the fused systems in the United States and Canada should allay the fears of those who believe that fusion would bring to an end the possibility of seeking expert help, whether with advocacy or a legal problem. Even if the English profession were fully fused the Bar would continue to exist. It is inconceivable that lawyers would be forbidden to take instructions from other lawyers, and many (perhaps most) barristers would decide to remain in practice at the Bar, and to take instructions only from solicitors. Solicitors themselves being creatures of habit would continue to instruct counsel much as before for at least a generation. After that firms who needed specialist help in tax or planning or libel – or advocacy – would continue to go to the Bar; and the Bar would continue to flourish in those areas in which it provided services of value. Where its services were not of value, barristers would go to the wall – or become solicitors. But since solicitors would have full audience rights in all courts that would not be such a terrible sacrifice.

Interestingly, younger barristers may have greater confidence than their seniors that the Bar is capable of facing the winds of competition. In a survey conducted just after the announcement of the Royal Commission among barristers called since 1970, one-third of the respondents pronounced themselves to be in principle in favour of fusion.[37] The result is surprising, for one of the depressing things about the Bar is that on most matters affecting the organization of the profession young barristers hold opinions which are no different from those of their more senior colleagues.

The most probable explanation is that those who bothered to

reply to the survey were untypical representatives of their generation; but it is conceivable that the Bar as a whole is more open-minded over the question of fusion than has generally been supposed. If only barristers had a keener sense of legal history more of them might find it easier to retain an open mind on the subject. Until the mid-nineteenth century the Bar was hemmed in by no restrictive practices save for its monopoly of audience rights; yet it lasted perfectly well. The present division and demarcation are almost entirely the product of trade union activity in the last 100 to 150 years. The Bar should have the confidence to compete once again on its merits.

9 A LOOK INTO THE FUTURE

The preceding chapters in this book have been devoted largely to an examination of the internal organization of the Bar. In this chapter the intention is to step back and take a broader look at the future role of the Bar within the English legal system. Little has been said of the wider changes which are taking place within that system, but their effect on the future of the Bar is likely to be just as great as any amount of internal change. R.H.

Too much of the debate about the future of the Bar is rooted in the assumption that however much reform there may be the traditional structure of the Bar ought to and moreover will remain essentially unaltered. One of the purposes of this chapter is to challenge that assumption. The comfortable notion that the Bar will – or even can – preserve its existing role and structure unchanged is without foundation. If one examines those factors likely to affect the profession's future the most important are all found to be outside the Bar's control.

THE EFFECT OF LAW REFORM

Much of the reform which most vitally affects the Bar is not directed to that end at all. Indeed all law reform, whatever its primary purpose, ultimately has an impact on the professional organization of the Bar. Paradoxically that impact is often greatest where reform of the Bar is not the principal end in view. One example may suffice to make the point. Any serious reform of the law relating to personal injuries claims would almost certainly have a far more dramatic impact on the silk system than reform of that system along the lines recommended by the Monopolies Commission. Accordingly, in considering factors relevant to the future of the Bar it is necessary to cast the net fairly wide. Firstly we will examine recent or impending changes in the substantive law.

Family law

Reform over the last decade has been comprehensive. In 1967 jurisdiction in divorce cases was transferred from the High Court (in which barristers have a monopoly of audience rights) to the County Courts, where solicitors may also appear. This move was strongly opposed by the Bar. More widely welcomed was the Divorce Reform Act 1969, which abolished the concept of a guilty party in matrimonial proceedings and directed the courts merely to satisfy themselves that the marriage had irretrievably broken down. As a result divorce became much easier. The increase in the divorce rate and what this meant in terms of increased business for lawyers are described in the previous chapter, as is the loss caused by the withdrawal of legal aid from undefended divorce in 1977.

Since the 1969 reforms the emphasis has shifted from the divorce as such to the resolution of disputes involving children and matrimonial property. There is not much difficulty in the law concerning children, because the courts have a wide discretion in each individual case to do what is best for the child; but the division of property has become extremely complicated, not only in cases involving family businesses or trusts, but at the other end of the scale with problems of income maintenance and social security benefits. Many divorce practitioners flounder in the complexity of modern property and tax and social security law, and one wonders how much longer the division of function and practice in this sphere between the Divorce and Chancery Bars can be tolerated. Recent appointments to the Family Division of the High Court have included judges whose practice was in the commercial and tax fields, and if the divorce Bar is to give an efficient service in property disputes changes of this sort must in future be reflected among its practitioners as well.

Landlord and tenant

The effect on the Bar of the Rent Act 1974 was immediate and obvious. The extension of Rent Act protection to furnished as well as unfurnished tenancies resulted (at least in the London area) in a considerable reduction in the number of possession actions brought in County Courts. Since a large proportion of possession actions were argued by young barristers the effect has been to deprive one section of the Bar of a valuable segment of its work.

Tax

Abolition of Estate Duty and the introduction of Capital Transfer Tax illustrate some rather different effects that changes in the substantive law can have on the Bar. The change in policy represented by the new tax structure has profoundly affected the strategy of tax-planning; in general its scope is much reduced. This must have long-term repercussions on the development of the tax Bar.

Personal injuries

Far more serious than all these in its implications for the Bar as a whole is the possibility of a fundamental reform of the law of personal injuries, following the report of the Royal Commission under Lord Pearson.[1] A very substantial proportion of the 'heavy' work of the common law Bar concerns personal injuries cases; of the total number of actions set down for trial in the Queen's Bench Division some 75% come into this category. Under the present law an injured person can recover damages only if he can prove that his injuries were caused by the negligence of some other person (in industrial accidents his employer, in road accidents another driver). This system has been condemned by the Commission on the grounds that the entitlement to compensation depends too much on chance; that too few victims are compensated (only $6\frac{1}{2}$% of all those suffering industrial injuries, for example); that the system is unduly slow; and that it is expensive to administer.[2] In its place the Commission has proposed that we should follow the example of New Zealand and introduce a system of no-fault liability, under which an accident victim can recover compensation without having to prove that any particular defendant has been at fault.

For road accidents the no-fault scheme would be comprehensive, and financed by an increase of 1p a gallon in the price of petrol. For industrial accidents the Commission proposed less sweeping changes, but relied upon improvements in the existing State industrial injuries scheme, with extensions in its scope and substantially higher benefits. Compensation based on negligence would be retained for work injuries, as a means of supplementing the no-fault scheme; but the Commission envisaged that increasingly less reliance would be placed upon it.

Whether the industrial part of the Commission's recommendations will be implemented is uncertain; employers will be opposed because the improvements in compensation are to be financed by an increase in their national insurance contributions, and trade union leaders have mixed feelings, because assistance with litigation under the present system is an important attraction of union membership which could disappear under the new scheme. But even if only that part of the Pearson recommendations which applies to road accidents becomes law the Bar will lose a substantial amount of work; and if the Pearson proposals for industrial injuries are accepted the loss will be heavier still.

Procedural changes

Changes with regard to the procedure in divorce cases have been discussed above; the transfer of matrimonial work to the County Court and the withdrawal of legal aid from undefended divorces are both of great significance for the Bar. A number of other changes have been introduced in recent years with the same purpose of reducing the costs of ligitation. In May 1977 the jurisdiction of the County Courts was raised from £1000 to £2000, thus increasing the number of civil cases in which solicitors may appear and reducing the scales of costs; and the new restrictive rules as to costs in small cases are designed to discourage legal representation altogether. In the Chancery Motions Court a recent change permits certain categories of case to be adjourned without the need for attendance or legal representation. In the Companies Court it has been suggested that unopposed or straightforward winding-up petitions should no longer be heard by the judge in court but should be dealt with by the Registrar in chambers; were this proposal to be implemented the Bar would lose its monopoly in winding-up work, because solicitors may appear before the Registrar.

Most important of all recent proposals because of what it portends for the future was the recommendation of the James Committee that certain kinds of offence which hitherto have attracted the right of trial by jury should in future be triable only in the magistrates' court.[3] Although the Government announced at the beginning of 1977 that this part of the Criminal Law Bill would be abandoned, it cannot for ever remain indifferent to the soaring increase in the expense of Crown Court trials: in 1975–6 criminal legal aid in the Crown Court and higher courts came to £17½ million, and prosecution costs added a further £11½ million to the public bill.[4] At some time in the future the Government is likely either to make a further attempt to transfer work from the Crown Court to the magistrates' courts, or in some way to reduce the cost of Crown Court trials. The Bar is bound to suffer from any such move; it enjoys a monopoly of audience rights before the Crown Court, and the fees earned there are more than twice those received for similar work before the magistrates' courts.

CHANGES IN THE LEGAL SYSTEM

Equally significant in their effect on the Bar are changes in the legal system. Far and away the most important change in recent years was the reorganization of the provincial courts effected by the Courts Act 1971, following the report of the Royal Commission on Assizes and Quarter Sessions chaired by Lord Beeching. Although this was primarily concerned with the structure of the criminal courts, it also had – and continues to have – indirect effects on the civil courts. Nor should it be imagined that there will be no further reform of the latter. For instance, rationalization of the present chaotic system of matrimonial and family jurisdiction spread between the magistrates' courts, County Court and High Court (Family and Chancery divisions) must eventually be resolved by the creation of a Family Court on the lines of the Crown Court; but in such a court it is most unlikely that the Bar would enjoy any privileges with regard to rights of audience.

Second in importance, and related to the reorganization of the courts system, is the massive increase in the last decade or so in the numbers of the judiciary. In 1976 there were 370 High Court and Circuit judges and a pool of only 370 practising Q.C.s and 750 juniors of over 15 years' call from which to replace them (and to provide 365 Recorders). Lord Hailsham's comments on the difficulty of finding suitable candidates and the tone of much conversation at the Bar suggest that this huge increase has inevitably resulted in a dilution of quality; but it has also had a corresponding effect on the Bar, which in its senior ranks has been seriously depleted by the efforts of successive Lord Chancellors to recruit the Bench exclusively from the Bar. The other effect of the growth in the Circuit Bench is decentralization; the long-established system of centralized justice with a judiciary based on London is being gradually eroded as more and more judges are locally based and preside over increasingly powerful provincial courts.

Third but by no means least in importance is the growing dependence of the Bar on civil and criminal legal aid. This has been analysed in detail in the previous chapter, and it is sufficient to remind the reader that almost half the Bar's total income now comes from public funds; that the bulk of this public money (80%–90%) is earned from criminal work; and that as crime provides a bigger and bigger proportion of the Bar's total employment this dependence on public finance can only grow, not diminish.

THE EFFECT OF THE ECONOMY

The work of lawyers (both in litigation and in advising) is affected not only by changes in the law and the legal system but also by wider changes in the social and economic forces at play in society. The volume of legal work will tend to reflect the overall level of economic activity – periods of slump or boom are felt as much at the Bar as anywhere else. When money is short potential customers will be forced to cut their spending on relative luxuries such as legal services. Cutbacks are a characteristic not only of the private client but also of the Legal Aid fund – witness the cut in legal aid for undefended divorce.

However, over and above these general economic factors certain specific trends can be shown to affect the Bar. For instance, the very considerable rise in land values over the past decade has led to a vast increase in property litigation as more and more people have come to own houses of a value sufficient to make even expensive litigation profitable. Within this general upward trend in property values there has also been a trend to rapidly fluctuating values. To the lawyer it does not matter whether the fluctuation is up or down; so long as values stay generally high the difference in value implied in price fluctuation is a sure cause of increased litigation. This is shown most clearly in the increase in vendor and purchaser litigation. First vendors (as prices rose) and then purchasers (as prices fell) frantically resorted to law in an effort to escape their now onerous obligations.

A further area which has shown dramatic increases in the volume of work is that of insolvency – bankruptcy proceedings in 1975 were 20% up on 1974, and company windings-up 40% higher; the 1976 figures were higher still. For those sections of the Bar specializing in property or commercial work an unsettled economy and unstable prices are therefore birds of good omen; they increase the initial demand for legal services, and since those services are usually paid for out of some 'fund' (i.e. the property in dispute or the bankrupt's estate) and not from either private or legal aid sources, that initial demand is unlikely to be reduced by the need to cut spending on legal services. On the other hand, the remainder of the Bar is disadvantaged by such economic trends; the initial demand for legal services is reduced (fewer men in work means less personal injuries work for lawyers) and this reduction is aggravated by the reluctance of both private and public sources to spend money on legal services of only marginal necessity.

THE SHIFT FROM CIVIL TO CRIMINAL WORK

The common law Bar has however been compensated for the loss or diminution of civil work by the inexorable increase in criminal work. The shift is difficult to measure exactly but some idea of the new order of priorities can be gained from the fact that in 1975 of the total days sat by all judges (High Court judges, Circuit judges and Recorders) 63% was spent in the Crown Court, while High Court civil work accounted for only 9%, and county court work (including undefended divorce) for 23%.[5] The same pattern is discernible at the Bar: more and more barristers are spending more and more of their time dealing with criminal work, and this trend appears likely to continue indefinitely.

The crime wave more than anything else is responsible for the changes which have taken place at the Bar in the last ten years.

To it very largely can be attributed the unprecedented growth in the size of the profession, which increased by almost 75% between 1966 and 1976; the consequent acute shortage of accommodation, particularly in London; the declining standards of advocacy which have been noticed among younger barristers; and the enormous increase in numbers and similar decline in quality of recent appointments to the Bench.

Few professions have had to cope with such an extraordinary explosion in the demand for their services, and the Bar is not wholly to be blamed for having been caught so unawares. Some increase was foreseen, which is why the Bar Council embarked on a recruiting campaign in the mid-1960s; but the Bar was not alone in failing to predict the magnitude of the increase. The Government was equally unprepared, and the whole system of Assizes and Quarter Sessions was swept away by the tide; the prisons were filled to bursting, and many of the other services connected with criminal justice hopelessly overstretched. In the circumstances it is not surprising that the Bar too has had its problems, and it is worth considering what the reaction of the public would have been if the Bar had refused to let its numbers rise so rapidly on the ground that it wished to maintain its standards.

It is inevitable that standards have suffered. The demand for barristers is so great that the second six months of pupillage in criminal chambers has become to all intents and purposes the first six months of practice, and young barristers are appearing before juries at the stage when in the old days they would have been making their first tentative steps before the magistrates. *The Times* was led to comment: 'Few observers of the courts over the past years can doubt that the general standard of advocacy has declined significantly, especially among younger counsel.' The leader-writer went on to complain of 'the growing incidence of barristers appearing in court clearly unprepared and often having received their brief only the night before'[6], but this too is largely a consequence of the crime wave; there are so many more briefs flowing into chambers that clerks can only cover the field by making many more last-minute returns. Of course the system is also abused, and barristers and their clerks forget (or have never learned) how much a last-minute switch of counsel can upset the client. Of course too, returns have always been a feature of the system – but they have now become so entrenched a feature that they are generally accepted as a fact of life.

Looked at a decade hence the accommodation crisis may well be regarded as a temporary, once-and-for-all phenomenon. There is little or no room for any further increase in the size of chambers, at least in the Temple, but the supply of barristers has now caught up with the demand. If civil work continues to disappear at an accelerating rate, because of the various factors outlined in earlier sections of this chapter, a surplus of barristers may even develop. The profession will then be back in the situation which faced it in the 1950s, when the number of barristers in practice steadily declined from year to year. However, criminal business is expected to grow at 9% per annum until the end of the decade[7], and if crime now provides almost half the Bar's total supply of work it will require an extra 150 barristers a year simply to keep pace with the steady increase in criminal demand. Rather than the Bar declining in size, therefore, it is more likely that its numbers will at least remain stable, and may even continue to rise. The reason for this will not, however, be any growth in demand for the Bar's services from the public at large, but rather from that section of the public which finds itself before the criminal courts and from the Government which pays for their prosecution and for their defence.

THE DECENTRALIZATION OF THE ENGLISH LEGAL SYSTEM

As a result of the reorganization of the provincial courts following the Beeching Report the long-established system of centralized justice which for centuries has characterized the English legal system is gradually being dismantled. The Bar's ignorance of its own history is the only explanation for the remarkable complacency with which it has viewed this process. The traditional system whereby the Bench and the Bar were located in close physical, professional and social proximity to each other in London has already passed almost unnoticed into history. The Bar is still predominantly based in London, but the Bench less and less so. The establishment under the Courts Act for the first time ever of a rationally organized Bench of provincial judges with both civil and criminal functions (the Circuit judges) and the increasing preponderance of that Circuit Bench within the judicial system as a whole have altered the entire balance of the legal system.

The recent increase in the jurisdiction of the County Courts to claims of £2000 has shifted the balance further towards the provinces. This tendency will be carried further still by the growing preponderance of criminal work, which is (and always has been) tried locally. By the 1980s it will probably be true to say that the English courts structure is a system of decentralized, provincial justice, central control being exercised only through the appellate courts in London.

The implications of this shift of balance are profound. Three are worth mentioning, none of which has received much recognition (partly perhaps because they are so unpalatable to the Bar). The first is that a centralized Bar, 70% of whose members still practise from London, is manifestly unable to provide an adequate service either to solicitors or to the public in a decentralized system of justice. The dangers to the Bar are accentuated by the fact that the shift in litigation is more and more in the direction of courts in which solicitors have rights of audience. In the long run the Bar is bound to lose a great deal of this work unless it can adjust to meet the situation; but it is unlikely that the Bar will be able – or even willing – to provide sufficient manpower to serve this new structure of local courts. The manpower requirements will be too great, and many barristers will not want to leave London.

Secondly, as solicitors assume a greater burden of local work, the pressure to open the Crown Court and Circuit bench effectively to them will become overwhelming. As Recorders, solicitors have been presiding over sittings of the Crown Court since 1972; yet it is a court in which they have no general right of audience. Now that the first solicitors have been appointed Circuit Judges the situation is even more anomalous, and the right of solicitors to appear in a much wider range of cases in the Crown Court cannot much longer be denied.

The third effect of decentralization is the inevitable destruction of the traditional relationship of mutual friendship and trust between Bench and Bar. That this is already noticeable is openly admitted by the more perceptive and honest members of both the Bar and the Bench, who recognize that much of the Bench is totally unknown to and equally unknowing of the majority of barristers who appear before it. In the specialist fields and at the appellate level the old traditions still prevail. Elsewhere the truth is that they do so with daily diminishing force.

THE SHAPE OF THINGS TO COME

The time has come to try to summarize the effect of all the different factors which will determine the future shape of the Bar. The shift from civil work to crime will continue. In civil law only the specialist Bars have an assured future; the family and non-commercial common law Bars are going to suffer a severe diminution in their traditional work (but the increase in crime will more than compensate the average common law practitioner). However the shift from civil work to crime means increasing reliance on the Government as a source of finance, and also growing decentralization of barristers' work.

Solicitors, emboldened by the diversion of work to courts and tribunals where they have rights of audience, the inability of the Bar to provide an adequate service in local courts, and the gradual breakdown of the traditional relationship between Bench and Bar, may be prompted to mount a bolder attack on the organization and privileges of the Bar at a time when the onslaught of public opinion and the ending of the traditional centralized system have weakened its defences. At the same time the Government, exasperated by the inability of the Bar to provide an adequate service in local courts and to man the judicial Bench, and strengthened by the increasing dependence of the Bar on state finance, will intervene to demand or, indeed, impose fundamental reform and future regulation on a Bar unwilling to reform itself.

Whatever the Royal Commission recommends, changes in the present division of function and practice between barristers and solicitors are inevitable. Given the shift in the fundamental balance of the system of justice, a corresponding shift in the traditional division of work within the legal profession must follow. This will not involve fusion – at least not of the compulsory variety usually contemplated – but a re-allocation of work and function along the lines of the 'permissive' fusion described in the previous chapter.

Any such reappraisal will probably sound the death-knell of the common law and circuiteering Bars. Within the new system of localized justice organized regionally or provincially, the true functions of the Bar will be seen to be threefold:

(i) the maintenance of specialist Bars based in London and providing (as at present) a specialist advisory service for the whole country;

(ii) the provision of a *small* corps of specialized advocates providing their services in cases where 'heavy' advocacy is really required;

(iii) the provision of a small London-based corps of advocates undertaking the bulk of appellate work in London.

All other work – whether or not it involves advocacy – will be undertaken by the locally based 'lawyer' whose main function will be to provide a comprehensive legal service in all cases other than those which require one of the three specialized Bar services described above.

Within a system of permissive fusion, one would expect to find a combination of the existing specialist Bars, some of the existing heavy advocates, and some of the larger or more specialist firms of solicitors emerging to provide the three specialist services of the new Bar. Other barristers and solicitors would similarly combine to provide the new local legal service. Even without permissive fusion the same pattern will emerge in the long run: it will come about gradually through a change in patterns of recruitment to the two professions and a gradual alteration in their respective functions. The machinery of change is not so important as the need to recognize the direction in which that change is going to occur.

The final result will be seen in the composition of the Bench; this will have to reflect the pattern of representation in the various courts. The local court system will be staffed by judges recruited from the local lawyers; conversely, the specialist (London) and appellate courts will be staffed by members of the new Bar. The system will not be inflexible; but that will be the general tendency. Unless the local Bench is thrown open to all members of the legal profession, it will never be possible to man it with a sufficient number of suitably qualified judges.

These then are the trends which the Bar faces in the last quarter of the twentieth century. Most barristers are unaware of their existence, or hope that if they are ignored they will somehow go away. The establishment of the Royal Commission has at least ensured that these developments can no longer be ignored; but it has also given rise to the forlorn hope that they might still be opposed. The Bar is never happier than when playing King Canute, and it seems unable to comprehend the possibility that one day it might be swept away.

At the moment the Bar is strong and prosperous; but only by

adapting can it maintain anything like its present strength and size. If the Bar is prepared to adapt it can also have an influence – an enormous influence – over the legal services provided in the twenty-first century. But if it is not prepared to adapt it will have no influence, and it will slowly die.

NOTES

1: Introduction to the Bar
1. See Bellot in (1910) 26 L.Q.R. 137.
2. Holdsworth: *A History of English Law* vol. VI p. 624.
3. The latest campaign is being organized by a new pressure group set up in 1976 specifically for this purpose, and called the United Lawyers' Association. Lord Goodman is the best-known advocate of fusion on the solicitors' side: for a report of the debate on the subject at the Law Society's Annual Conference in 1974, see the *Guardian*, 21 October 1974.
4. *Hansard* 3rd series (H.L.) vol. CXIX col. 643 (17 February 1852). For a detailed history of relations between barristers and solicitors in the nineteenth century see Forbes: 'Division of the Profession: Ancient or Scientific?' in (1977) *Law Society's Gazette* p. 67.
5. For the few exceptions to this general rule see Boulton: *Conduct and Etiquette at the Bar* (6th Edn) pp. 8–14.
6. Bar Council *Annual Statement* (1949) p. 18.
7. The right to call men to the Bar and to disbar them was vested originally in the judges. It was entrusted to the Inns by the judges in about the fourteenth century.
8. *Essays in the Law* (1922) p. 134.
9. Since 1837 the judges, by consent of the Inn, hear appeals against a refusal to admit.
10. This power since 1966 has been effectively delegated to the Disciplinary Tribunals of the Senate.
11. Despite the general belief to the contrary there has never been a rule requiring London barristers to have chambers in one of the Inns; and indeed there used to be chambers in New Court in Carey Street, just outside Lincoln's Inn. Lord Gifford's set of chambers started in Lambeth in 1974 was a new departure, because it represented the first attempt to establish a local set of chambers designed to serve its own immediate community; but in 1976 these chambers moved back much closer to the legal

heartland, in Covent Garden. In 1965 a barrister was reportedly disbarred for practising outside the Inns of Court: *Daily Telegraph*, 26 January 1965, but it is more likely that the reason for his disbarment was practising without a clerk.

12. E.g. Lord Goodman *Not for the Record* (Deutsch, 1972) p. 84; Lord Chorley *Hansard* 5th series (HL) vol. CCXXXV, col. 964; Chapman *British Government Observed* (1963) p. 63.

13. The main study of political bias in judicial appointments is by Laski in *Studies in Law and Politics*. Henry Cecil describes in detail four of Lord Halsbury's worst appointments in *Tipping the Scales* (Hutchinson, 1964) at ch. 6. A study by the *Economist* in 1956 (15 December) found the political tradition still alive: one-quarter of High Court judges at that time had been either M.P.s or parliamentary candidates.

14. *Hansard* HC deb. 20 May 1976 col. 658. The 'major Tribunals' are the Immigration Appeal Tribunal, the Lands Tribunal, Pensions Appeal Tribunal, Transport Tribunal, V.A.T. Tribunals, and the Foreign Compensation Commission. It is difficult to correlate this list with the total number of public appointments within the Lord Chancellor's patronage, published in *Hansard* HC deb. 1 April 1976 at col. 524.

15. Megarry in *Lawyer and Litigant in England* (Stevens, 1962) estimated that 70% to 80% of the London Bar lunch together in the Halls of their Inns or in the Crypt of the Law Courts.

16. Abel-Smith & Stevens: *In Search of Justice* (Allen Lane, 1968) p. 183.

17. Three-quarters of the present High Court bench were sent to public schools, and a slightly higher proportion were at Oxford or Cambridge: *Sunday Times* 5 October 1975. The proportion coming from the ranks of the working class has always been minimal – in the nineteenth century the number of High Court judges with working-class backgrounds was 3%, and this century it has fallen to 1%: JUSTICE Report on the Judiciary (Stevens, 1972) Appendix II.

18. Megarry *op cit* attaches great weight to these little conventions: see pp. 70–71.

19. The ritual which accompanies this gift is itself illuminating: 'The giving of a red bag is attended with a certain amount of ceremony. The K.C. hands it to his senior clerk and asks him kindly to convey it to Mr So-and-so with his compliments. The senior clerk then hands it to the junior clerk who takes it round to the junior counsel's chambers and makes a formal presentation of the bag to him on the K.C.'s behalf. It is the custom for the junior counsel then to hand a guinea to the junior clerk, who takes it back to the senior clerk and the latter pockets the sovereign and gives the shilling to the junior clerk for his work in the transaction.' (Sir Harold Morris K.C.: *The Barrister* 1930). Nowadays the tip is two guineas, and it is all kept by the junior clerk.

20. Published in full in the Bar Council Bulletin, No. 41 (January 1974): '1. The dress of barristers appearing in Court should be unobtrusive and compatible with the wearing of robes. 2. Suits and dresses should be of a dark colour. Dresses or blouses should be long-sleeved and high to the neck. Men should wear waistcoats. Shirts and blouses should be predominantly white or of other unemphatic appearance. Collars should be white and shoes black. 3. Wigs should, as far as possible, cover the hair, which should be drawn back from the face and forehead, and if long enough should be put up. 4. No conspicuous jewellery or ornaments should be worn.' The wearing of waistcoats was discussed at the Bar A.G.M. in 1974, where an informal vote revealed equal numbers for and against continuance of the requirement: Senate *Annual Statement* 1974–5 p. 25.
21. M. Birks: *Gentlemen of the Law* (1960) p. 106. See also Holdsworth: *History of English Law* vol. xii.
22. Bar Council *Annual Statement* 1973–4 p. 41.
23. *Not for the Record* (Deutsch, 1972) p. 78.
24. In *What's Wrong with the Law?* (B.B.C., 1970) p. 48.
25. E.g. its consistent opposition to proposals to extend the jurisdiction of the county court (where solicitors share audience rights with barristers): see Abel-Smith and Stevens, *Lawyers and the Courts* (Heinemann, 1967) pp. 56–7, 233–5. Some sections of the Bar are still opposed to the county courts having any jurisdiction in divorce matters.
26. Speech to the American Bar Association at the Guildhall, London; 2 May 1975.
27. Royal Commission on Doctors' and Dentists' Remuneration, Cmnd 939 (1960); Inbucon Survey of Income at the Bar (March 1977) Tables 7 and 8.
28. The figures are discussed in detail in chapter 2 of our evidence submitted to the Royal Commission in August 1977 (at pp. 29–30). These should be updated by reference to two further surveys carried out by the Senate, published in its *Annual Statement* 1976–7 p. 18.
29. Senate submission no. 5 to the Royal Commission (December 1976) on behalf of the Bar Students Working Party, Appendix I. The findings are discussed more fully in chapter 3.
30. See Pearce Second Report, para. 44: 'Lincoln's Inn and the Inner Temple both give cogent reasons why it is not practicable at the present time to replace lump-sum payments on admission and call by annual subscriptions. It would result in an immediate and substantial loss of income.'

2: The Inns of Court
1. *Report from the Select Committee on Legal Education* 25 August 1846 HC 686 p. lvi.

2. *Ibid* p. lix.
3. *Hansard* 3rd series (HC) vol. CXXXI 1 March 1854 col. 157.
4. *Sixth Report of the Common Law Commissioners* p. 8.
5. The first appointments were made by James I, and Bacon was the first K.C. appointed.
6. For a delightful memoir of Serjeant Sullivan see C. P. Harvey: *The Advocate's Devil* (Stevens, 1959) pp. 44–5.
7. The Chancery Judges had never been Serjeants and remained Benchers of Lincoln's Inn; but they were so few in number that they were never in a position to dominate the affairs of the Inn.
8. For details of just how small this minority is, see *infra* p. 61.
9. Question 76, Minutes of Evidence, *Report of Royal Commission on the Inns of Court:* XVIII Parlty Papers (1854–6) p. 43.
10. *Ibid* p. 3.
11. Pearce Committee: *First Report* para. 40.
12. *Ibid* para. 19.
13. [1902] 1 Ch. 744.
14. Relevant extracts from which are quoted by Sachs LJ in *Council of Law Reporting v Attorney-General* [1971] 3 WLR 853 at 870–2.
15. Roffey *v* Wigg and others 1871, Public Record Office Ref. C16/747/R106.
16. *Thomson v. Inner Temple* 177 NLJ 647 (15 June 1967).
17. See Landlord and Tenant Act 1954 s. 30(1)(g) and s.41.
18. Michael Zander: *Lawyers and the Public Interest* (1968) p. 68.
19. *Incorporated Council of Law Reporting v. Attorney-General* [1971] 3 WLR 853 at 869–72.
20. 3 Halsbury's Laws (4th Edn) p. 590. His authority for this proposition was *Thomson v. Inner Temple* n. 16 *supra*; but in referring to the case he does not cast any doubt on the correctness of the decision.
21. It is impossible to work out the aggregate saving because two of the Inns declined to discuss their financial affairs with us; but at 1973–4 tax and income levels it must be of the order of £250,000 per annum for the four Inns together.
22. See n. 19 *supra*.
23. Pearce Committee: *First Report* para. 40.
24. See n. 19 *supra*.
25. *Report of the Committee on Legal Education for Students from Africa* (January 1961) Cmnd 1255 para. 17.
26. In the period 1946/7 to 1973/4 out of a total of 18,283 barristers called to the Bar in England 9301 were of overseas domicile.
27. These figures are inevitably approximate because we did not have the time to do meticulously accurate research. 4175 students of overseas domicile were called to the Bar between 1960/61 and 1969/70; and we have multiplied this number by the admission fees (£85) and call fee (£50) prevailing in the Middle Temple in 1966. The level of fees varies slightly from Inn, to Inn and must have

varied over the decade; but the figures given in the text should be accurate to the nearest £50,000.
28. It has been suggested that the Inns may not be within their legal rights in withholding the interest from the students, because of the fiduciary relationship which they have with the students. A solicitor cannot take interest earned on his client's money without the client's authority, express or implied, because of the fiduciary relationship that exists there: *Brown v. I.R.C.* [1964] 3 WLR 511. See also Zander: *Lawyers and the Public Interest* p. 42.
29. Abel-Smith and Stevens: *In Search of Justice* (Allen Lane, 1968) p. 100.
30. 3 Halsbury's Laws (3rd Edn) p. 3.
31. *Report of the Committee on Legal Education for Students from Africa* (Jan. 1961) Cmnd 1255 para. 25.
32. Ormrod Report para. 166.
33. *Ibid.*
34. Megarry: *Lawyer and Litigant in England* (1962) p. 114.
35. For a more detailed account of the possible advantages of such a course see Zander: *The Eating of Dinners* in 8 *The Lawyer* (1965) 21 at p. 23.
36. This is a matter of some curiosity. Most learned institutions that are over five centuries old acquire fairly substantial endowments over the years. Are barristers less generous to their institutions than members of the other professions? Or did the Inns squander the wealth that was left to them?
37. Oral evidence given in *Thomson v. Inner Temple* 117 NLJ 647, reported by Zander in *Lawyers and the Public Interest* at p. 51.
38. Benchers on appointment pay a term fee of about £300.
39. Pearce Committee: *First Report* para. 58.
40. *Second Report:* para. 44.
41. *Ibid.* para. 45.
41a. Senate *Annual Statement* 1975–76 p. 25.
42. See e.g. Zander: *Lawyers and the Public Interest* p. 50. n. 45.
43. This possibility was considered, and rejected, by the Pearce Committee: *First Report* paras 21, 22.
44. Senate of the four Inns: *Annual Statement* 1970–71 p. 8.
45. *First Report* para. 27.
46. Senate: *Annual Statement* 1970–71 p. 9.
47. 3 Halsbury's Laws (4th Edn) paras. 1106–7.
48. Holdsworth: *History of English Law* (Methuen, 1938) vol. XII pp. 15–19.
49. Ingpen: *Master Worsley's Book* p. 124.
50. *Ibid.* For a fascinating account of the government of the Inns during this period see W. R. Prest: *The Inns of Court 1590–1640* (Longman, 1972) chs 4 and 5.
51. See p. 41 *supra* and p. 64 *infra*.
52. *The Times* 10 December 1959.
53. *Ibid.* 14 December 1959.

54. Pearce Committee: *First Report* para. 42.
55. Pearce Committee: *First Report* para. 40.
56. *Ibid* para. 25.
57. *Ibid* para. 64.
58. A question by Sir Geoffrey Howe Q.C. in the House of Commons in March 1966 revealed that the value of the funds had declined from £134,517 in 1905 to £56,250 in 1966.
59. PEP: *New Commonwealth Students in Britain* (1965) p. 191.
60. *The Times* 10 December 1959.
61. *Ibid*. 14 December 1959.
62. Pearce Committee: *Second Report* para. 44.
63. M. Zander: *Lawyers and the Public Interest* (1968) pp. 59–60.
64. *First Report* para. 67.
65. *Hansard* 3rd series (HC) vol. CCVII 11 July 1871 cols 1496–7.
66. *Law Journal* vol. 20 1 August 1885 p. 465.
67. *Ibid*. p. 457.
68. Pearce Committee: *First Report* para. 39.
69. *Ibid*. para. 38.
70. *Sixth Report of the Common Law Commissioners* p. 8.

3: Legal Education
1. *Memorandum of Evidence by the Senate of the Four Inns of Court* to the Ormrod Committee (October 1968), para. 12. The memorandum is reproduced in the Ormrod Report as Appendix F.
2. *Report of the Committee on Legal Education* (March 1971), Cmnd. 4595, para. 41.
3. *Ibid*. para. 185(4).
4. *Ibid*. para. 185(18).
5. Quoted in R. M. Jackson: *The Machinery of Justice in England* (Cambridge, 1972) p. 344.
6. *Ibid*. p. 347.
7. Senate: *Annual Statement* 1975–6, p. 29.
8. *Calendar of the Council of Legal Education*, 1976–7, p. 2.
9. Senate submission No. 5 to the Royal Commission, Appendix I.
10. The figures are inevitably very approximate, being derived from a crude comparison of the Call figures and admission figures over a five-year period. Total Inn admission figures for 1961 to 1965 were 1566, 1782, 1513, 1626, 1703. If one compares these figures with the Call figures for 1963 to 1967 (i.e. assuming a $1\frac{1}{2}$–2 year time-lag between the time a student joins an Inn and the time he is called to the Bar) then the success rate was 41%. If one assumes a $2\frac{1}{2}$–3 year time-lag (i.e. comparing 1961–5 admission figures with the Call figures for 1964–8) the success rate was 37%. For the five-year cohort admitted between 1969 and 1973 the success rate was 82% on a $1\frac{1}{2}$–2 year time-lag, and 80% on a time-lag of $2\frac{1}{2}$–3 years.
11. Rates for overseas students were calculated by the method ex-

plained in note 10, save that a longer time-lag was assumed between admission and Call. Of those called between 1970 and 1975 (the latest five-year cohort for whom figures are available) the success rate was 72% if they were admitted 2½–3 years earlier, and 60% if the time-lag was 3½–4 years.

12. Sources: Inn admission figures derived from evidence submitted by the C.L.E. to the Royal Commission; Call figures from the Senate's *Annual Statement* 1975–6, p. 45.
13. Jackson: *op. cit.*, p. 349, n. 1.
14. A problem is still presented by the expense of some local law schools. The C.L.E. has found that it was cheaper in 1976 for a Malaysian student to fly to England, take his Bar courses and exams here and then return to Malaya, than it was to attend the equivalent institution at home.
15. Senate of the Four Inns of Court: *Annual Statement*, 1969–70, p. 7.
16. Senate submission No. 5 to the Royal Commission, Appendix I.
17. *Ibid.* Appendix III, Table II.
18. Ormrod Report, Appendix B. pp. 112, 115.
19. *Ibid.* para. 185(9).
20. This section draws heavily on an article by Martin Partington, 'Putting the Law into Perspective' in *The Times Higher Education Supplement*, 25 February 1977.
21. This is as much a reflection of student demand as teacher desire. Even where 'core' subjects are optional, nearly all students opt for them: J. F. Wilson and S. B. Marsh, 'A Second Survey of Legal Education in the U.K.', 1975 J.S.P.T.L. 241 at p. 281.
22. See W. L. Twining, (1974) *British Journal of Law and Society*, p.149; and the evidence submitted by Warwick University to the Royal Commission.
23. See W. M. Rees, (1975) *Law Teacher*, p. 125.
24. Interviewing techniques are studied at Warwick as part of their (optional) course on Legal Practice.
25. J. F. Wilson, 'Survey of Legal Education' (1966) J.S.P.T.L. (NS) vol. IX, No. 1 at p. 174.
26. The C.L.E. plans to halt its Post-Final Practical Training Course (designed in part to overcome this difficulty) in the near future.

4: Pupillage

1. The statistics for 1949–54 are in the Bar Council's *Annual Statement* for 1957, p. 36.
2. I can remember when I started pupillage being told by one of the Q.C.s in chambers that on his first day as a pupil he had been left to make an application in the Court of Appeal while his pupilmaster and his leader went off to have a cup of tea!
3. *Report of the Senate Working Party on a Scheme for Co-ordinating the Activities of the four Inns in Assisting Pupils to Find Places*,

hereafter referred to as the Coldstream Report (April 1973), para. 11. No evidence is cited in support of the figure quoted, but it seems unlikely that a committee with such a distinguished membership would have over-estimated that number.
4. Bar Council: *Annual Statement* (1972), p. 60.
5. *Report of the Committee on Legal Education* (March, 1971), Cmnd. 4595, para. 130.
6. Society of Labour Lawyers: Memorandum to the Pearce Committee, paras. 5, 7.
7. *Ibid*. para. 7.
8. Coldstream Report (see note 3, *supra*), para. 2.
9. Senate submission no. 5 to the Royal Commission, on behalf of the Bar Students Working Party (December 1976), p. 30. Only half the respondents had arranged pupillage at the time of the survey, and it is possible that those with private contacts make arrangements earlier, in which case the overall proportion of those who go through their Inn Pupillage Committees would be higher. The use of the scheme varies greatly from Inn to Inn: *ibid*. p. 32.
10. In 1975 a Senate Planning Subcommittee appointed to consider the admission, organization, conditions and needs of pupils (Chairman John Wilmers Q.C.) reported that '... by October 1974 all those who wanted a pupillage and who were reasonably suitable had found a pupil-master for the first six months of the ensuing year' (para. 15).
11. 'The Report of the Bar Council and the Four Under/Sub-Treasurers recommended the setting-up of a central register of all Bar Students, to be kept by the Bar Council, and indicating those students who will or will not require pupillage when they have passed their Bar Finals. While the Report recommended that standing Pupillage Committees should be established in each Inn, to advise students about pupillage and to direct them to potential pupilmasters, it was contemplated that the Bar Council would continue to afford help to students whose Inns had been unable to place them. The Report further recommended that the Bar Council should communicate with all practising barristers over five years' Call, inviting them to say whether they are able and willing to take pupils': Coldstream Report, para. 3. The Bar Council and the Under-Treasurers therefore also recommended a central register of pupils and pupilmasters, and the only significant difference is that under their scheme the Inns would perform the role of putting pupils in touch with pupilmasters, with the Bar Council providing a link-up service of last resort.
12. Ormrod Report, para. 158.
13. *Ibid*.
14. Ormrod Report, Appendix D, para. 98.
15. *Ibid*. para. 137.
16. The Ormrod Committee was divided on the issue of how the vocational courses should be organized and financed. The majority

thought the courses should be provided within the university and higher education structure, in which case they would be financed by central government; the minority wanted the profession to retain control, with courses being financed by student fees and a professional levy.
17. *Ibid.* para. 158.
18. Final Report (1913), para. 336, quoted in the Ormrod Report at para. 30.
19. Senate Submission no. 5 to the Royal Commission (December 1976). Appendix III, Tables III and IV.
20. *Supplementary Memorandum to the Monopolies Commission,* (February 1969), p. 17.
21. Ormrod Report, para. 160.
22. *Note on Pupillage and Tenancies*: Evidence to the Coldstream Committee, para. 1.
23. Senate submission no. 5 to the Royal Commission (December 1976), pp. 30, 31.
24. *Ibid.* p. 8.
25. *Low Pay Unit Bulletin* (December 1976), p. 1. A survey of articled clerks (80% from London, 20% from the provinces) found their average wage in August 1976 was £38 per week; the most common wage was between £25 and £30 a week. Articled clerks with top firms in the City are paid £75 a week.
26. 'We would also propose that the Bar Council should provide all pupils with an interest-free loan . . . of £500 to £750 . . . collected by means of a levy on each set of chambers . . . These loans should be repayable over the 5 years after pupillage finishes': *Note on Pupillage and Tenancies* (1972), paras. 11 and 12.
27. Ormrod Report, para. 130(5).
28. In 1975 there were roughly 750 pupils at the Bar and 3500 barristers, divided into chambers with an average size of 14 barristers and three pupils. If the marginal (not average) rate of tax on those barristers' earnings is 50% then the total net cost to chambers of paying each pupil £2000 *p.a.* is £3000; split up equally among the 14 barristers this would cost them £215 *p.a.* each. They would probably also have to pay National Insurance contributions.
29. *Supplementary Memorandum to the Monopolies Commission* (1969), p. 49.
30. The top rate for articled clerks with big City firms was £4000 in 1976.
31. Bar Council: *Annual Statement* 1971–2, p. 60.
32. The Under-Treasurer of one of the Inns told me that four vacancies had been reported to him in 1975, but they were not in the kind of chambers he felt he could recommend.
33. See the Coldstream Report, para. 1.
34. *Note on Pupillage and Tenancies* (1972), paras. 13 and 14.
35. *Ibid.* para. 15.

5: *Clerks and Fees*
1. *Inland Revenue Statistics* 1975 Table 9, *Inland Revenue Statistics* 1976 Table 10. These figures relate only to assessments under Case II of Schedule D (the profits from the practice of a profession or vocation); they exclude salaries and fees chargeable under Schedule E, but these form an insignificant element in the earnings of most professional people in private practice. The figures are after deduction of expenses but not of personal allowances.

    Michael Zander's similar table in the *New Law Journal* of 26 August 1976 is highly misleading because his figures for average earnings are derived only from the data on solo practitioners. Thus his figure for the average earnings of solicitors in 1971 of £3466 is based on those 5126 solicitors who practised on their own rather than in partnership. The 17,322 solicitors practising in partnership (three-quarters of the profession) had an average income of £5825 in 1971.
2. This figure may overstate the earnings of solicitors because it appears to exclude assistant solicitors who were not partners in their firms. However the Inland Revenue statistics are based on the Schedule D returns of 22,450 solicitors, all of whom must have been in private practice. In 1970–71 the Law Society issued 24,407 practising certificates, of which 21,200 were to solicitors in private practice. However one reconciles these figures, it would appear that the vast majority of solicitors in private practice were included in the Inland Revenue statistics.
3. But even in earlier years because of the uneven distribution of earnings at the Bar the median is considerably below the mean: in 1969 average earnings were £3390, while median income was about £2500 (*Inland Revenue Statistics* 1973 Table 28).
4. Bar Council: *Survey of Income at the Bar* 1974–5 (Inbucon, March 1977) Tables 5 and 6.
5. *Review Body on Doctors' and Dentists' Remuneration* Fifth Report 1975 para. 53.
6. *Costs in Crown Courts* 1976 Crim LR 5, Table 15. For a critique of Zander's sampling for this study see the memorandum by Michael Hill summarized in *Law Society's Gazette* 30 March 1977.
7. Source: Bar Council *Survey of Income at the Bar 1974–75* Tables 10, 11 and 17. The figures are inevitably highly approximate (for the reasons given on pp. 2, 7 of the Survey) and so are rounded to the nearest £1000. Figures for London silks are unfortunately not available, because there was an insufficient number of returns to yield a statistically useful result (Table 16). They are likely to be high: Table 17D shows that of the 21 senior juniors specializing in criminal work in London the upper decile received prosecution fees from public funds of £32,310, and the upper quartile £26,674. The same group of barristers earned far less from defence work: average earnings from criminal legal aid were only £4308.

8. The average conceals a wide variety of practice: 90% of Q.C.s but only 35% of juniors were making provision for a pension, and sickness cover was very low, probably because it is not considered a legitimate professional expense and so has to be paid out of taxed income.
9. Report no. 6 of the Review Body on Top Salaries (Cmnd 5846, 1974) p. 151.
10. *Hansard* HC deb. 20 May 1976 col. 658.
11. It is extremely difficult to work out exactly what the chances are. The problem is perhaps best approached by dividing the Bar into three cohorts, each corresponding to a 15-year intake (with judges – and some practitioners – not retiring until 70 or 75 the assumption of a 45-year working life is not unreasonable). In a 15-year period we can expect there to be a single complete turnover in the holders of judicial office (some will serve less, some more; but with 15 years' service as the qualifying condition for a full pension 15 years is likely to be the average). The top two cohorts at the Bar contain the pool from which judicial appointees are selected, but because of the 15-year turnover each of these cohorts will have to man all the judicial posts once in its lifetime. Until the mid-1960s the size of the Bar remained relatively stable, with about 2000 barristers in practice and about 250 judicial appointments. Each cohort thus contained 750 barristers, who had a one-in-three chance when their turn came of receiving a judicial appointment. On this analysis one would expect the top two cohorts (including those in judicial office) to number roughly 1500; in fact in 1976 they numbered 750 juniors + 370 Q.C.s + 495 office-holders = 1615. Each of these two cohorts will have to man all the judicial posts once, so that the 1615 barristers who composed the top two cohorts in 1976 will have to fill 990 judicial posts (495×2) before the end of their working lives: i.e. their chances of receiving a judicial appointment are about 60%.
12. Megarry: *Lawyer and Litigant in England* (Stevens, 1962) pp. 55 and 59. For a useful (but very traditional) description of the functions of the clerk see pp. 55–69; and for a critical analysis see Zander: *Lawyers and the Public Interest* (Weidenfeld, 1968), pp. 83–95.
13. *Ibid.* p. 68.
14. *Ibid.* p. 60.
15. There are grounds for suspecting, for example, that fees in Ireland, North and South, where barristers negotiate their own fees, are on a lower scale than in England. But this may simply be a reflection of the fact that professional earnings in general are lower in Ireland than in England.
16. *Law Society's Gazette*, 26 March 1975, p. 351.
17. Bar Council: *Supplementary Memorandum of Evidence to the Monopolies Commission* (February 1969). The Bar Council's original Submission contained only 35 pages; the Supplementary

Memorandum, which consisted wholly of comments on Michael Zander's book, *Lawyers and the Public Interest*, covered 53 pages!
18. See Megarry, *op. cit.* p. 60.
19. Crown Court fees have not been increased since 1971. As a result they are now nearer to being a fair reward for the work done; but few would deny (except perhaps at the criminal Bar, which has lobbied vigorously for an increase) that in the early 1970s Crown Court work offered rewards totally out of proportion to the skill, experience and industry of the counsel involved.
20. *Law Society's Gazette*, 25 June 1975, p. 679. The quotation which follows is to be found on p. 681.
21. For a detailed breakdown see McLaren in *New Law Journal*, 2 December 1976, p. 1180.
22. In the Queen's Bench Division of the High Court $1\frac{1}{4}\%$ of the actions commenced actually get to trial; in the County Courts the proportion is 2%: *Civil Judicial Statistics* 1974 (Cmnd 5756), summarized in the *Law Society's Gazette*, 30 July 1975, at p. 799.
23. Contested cases and cases that settled at the door of the court involved slightly more interlocutory work (average total fees of £45 and £62 respectively). Refreshers were paid in 40 out of the 124 cases in Zander's sample which involved a contest; but in 25 of those cases the total bill for refreshers was under £100: *Law Society's Gazette*, 25 June 1975, p. 682.
24. Law Society, *Assessment and Marking of Counsel's Fees and Related Matters*, 1964 (unpublished), para. 17. The origins of this document are set out in Zander: *Lawyers and the Public Interest* at pp. 88–9. The Memorandum is a highly critical account of the quality, cost and availability of the services provided by the Bar, written from the consumer's point of view. It was actually printed as part of the Law Society's 1965 Annual Report, but was withdrawn at the last moment after strenuous lobbying by the Bar Council, which agreed to set up a Joint Committee with the Law Society to consider the complaints made in the Memorandum. The Report of the Joint Committee was published in April 1967.
25. The modification of the rule was proposed in the 1967 Joint Committee Report of the Bar Council and the Law Society, para. 9. The modified rule now appears in Boulton: *Conduct and Etiquette at the Bar* (6th Edn), p. 49, r. 13.
26. In 31 cases (one-third of the 46%) the case was settled before any hearing, and the average brief fee was £91. In the remaining two-thirds (72 cases) in which the settlement took place at the door of the court the average brief fees were £230.
27. Bar Council, *Annual Statement*, 1963, p. 30.
28. Bar Council, *Annual Statement*, 1974, p. 29.
29. Paras. 24 and 22. For details of the Memorandum see note 24, *supra*.
30. Senate, *Annual Statement*, 1975–6, p. 35.

31. See note 17, *supra*.
32. Cmnd. 8878 (1953), para. 819.
33. Bar Council, *First Submission to the Monopolies Commission*, (1968), p. 29. Interestingly when a referendum was held in 1971 to decide whether separate clerks' fees should be retained, 1230 barristers voted for abolition and only 50 against.
34. Final Report, Cmnd 8878 (1953), para. 819.
35. *Sunday Times* 19 March 1978, 7 May 1978.
36. It requires some courage also on the part of the clerk, who may be regarded as a blackleg by the other barristers' clerks. Celia Hart, a former secretary who accepted a salaried post as a clerk, had to go before the Barristers' Clerks' Association to explain herself: *New Statesman*, 5 March 1976, p. 287.
37. In 1976 the Barristers' Clerks' Association and the Senate were discussing the possibility of day-release courses for junior clerks at the Kingsway College of Further Education.
38. 10 December 1959.
39. See note 28, *supra*.
40. At the Bar A.G.M. in 1973 a barrister who had been called for nine years said he was owed £10,000: Bar Council *Annual Statement* 1974 p. 16. He was seconding a resolution that 'Barristers' fees which remain unpaid after the expiry of three calendar months after completion of a case should henceforth attract interest at the rate of 1% over base rate'. Despite opposition from the Bar Council, which requested that the motion be withdrawn, the resolution was carried by a substantial majority. At the A.G.M. the following year the Chairman announced that the Bar Council 'had found the Law Society, the clerks and many members of the Bar solidly against the resolution. The proposals involved many complications and the Council's firm view was that it could not be implemented': Senate *Annual Statement*, 1975, p. 23. This statement passed unchallenged and since then no more has been heard of the idea.
41. Senate *Annual Statement*, 1975, p. 59.
42. See e.g. 3 Halsbury's Laws (3rd Edn 1953), p. 46: 'If a barrister acts honestly in the discharge of his duty, he is not liable to an action by his client for negligence, or for want of skill, discretion or diligence in respect of any act done in the conduct of a cause, or in settling drafts, or in advising.'
43. *Rondel v. Worsley* (1969) 1 A.C. 191; *Saif Ali v. Sydney Mitchell & Co., Times* Law Report 13 May 1977.
44. The Evershed Committee in its Final Report rejected creating a contractual relationship because: (i) a barrister's advocacy is conducted in public, (ii) it was uncertain whether the contract would be with the solicitor or the client, (iii) it would tend to destroy the cab-rank principle, and (iv) under the present system a barrister can advise boldly and with no fear of the consequences. Cmnd 8878, paras. 778–9.

45. Boulton: *Conduct and Etiquette at the Bar* (6th Edn), p. 24.
46. Megarry (*op. cit.* p. 80), is an honourable exception: 'But I think it matters, and matters greatly. There is a failure of the machinery of justice if a litigant is needlessly deprived of the advocate in whom he has put his trust.'
47. Boulton, *op. cit.* p. 24.
48. Law Society's 1964 Memorandum (see note 24, *supra*) paras. 28, 31 and 33.
49. *Ibid.* para. 32.
50. *Supplementary Memorandum to the Monopolies Commission* (1969), p. 47.
51. Report of the Joint Committee of the Bar Council and the Law Society (April 1967), para. 14.
52. For a fuller discussion of the issues involved see Zander: *Lawyers and the Public Interest*, ch. 11, and the Bar Council's (very detailed) reply in its *Supplementary Memorandum to the Monopolies Commission* (1969), at pp. 43–53.
53. The Bar Council stated that under the present system 'Many young men are accepted into chambers on an informal recommendation and with little knowledge of their potential ability. If the partnership was to pay the young man a salary, then far greater assurance would be required of his abilities and potentialities' (*Supplementary Memorandum*, p. 49). It used this, however, as an argument that partnerships would *not* lead to wider recruitment: whereas it appears directly to support my proposition that chambers would select recruits according to ability rather than their connections.
54. Report of the Royal Commission on Doctors' and Dentists' Remuneration Cmnd 939 (1960); the relevant statistical information is set out in Megarry *op. cit.* at pp. 183–6. For more recent figures see the Table of professional earnings in the annual Inland Revenue Statistics (H.M.S.O.).
55. *Ibid.* It is fair to add that a career at the Bar offers many judicial and other appointments which provide comfortable incomes and a pension on retirement. If the earnings of these barristers in salaried appointments were included the statistics might not show such a marked decline in the years before retirement.
56. A note in the *Observer* on 4 April 1965 said that 'with well planned, carefully managed retirements, very successful barristers have been known to escape with more than £100,000'.
57. *The Times*, 11 November 1958, p. 7.
58. Cmnd 8878 (1953): para. 12 of the Addendum by Sir Thomas Barnes, Geoffrey Crowther, Eric Fletcher and Professor T. H. Marshall.
59. *Law Guardian*, July 1968, p. 31.
60. Bar Council *Annual Statement*, 1961, p. 40.
61. Bar Council *Annual Statement*, 1969, p. 48.
62. *Ibid.*

6: The criminal Bar

1. *Supply Estimates* 1976–7, Class IX, HC 276, pp. 8, 16; *Hansard* 24 March 1977, col. 600.
2. 26th Legal Aid Annual Reports (1975–6) p. 39.
3. *The Times* 6 February 1976.
4. *The Speeches of the Hon. Thomas Erskine; when at the Bar*, vol. II (1810). Erskine was dismissed from his position as Attorney-General to the Prince of Wales.
5. Bar Council *Annual Statement* 1969–70 p. 19.
6. *The Times* 22 May 1972.
7. *R v. Puddick* (1865) 4 F & F 497 *per* Crompton J.
8. *R v. Lattimore* 62 Cr App Rep 53, and the Fisher Report (1978, HC 90).
9. *Law Society's Gazette* 30 September 1975.
10. 'The prosecution process', transcript of a conference held at the University of Birmingham: April 1975. From a paper delivered by Stephen Brown Q.C.
11. American Bar Association: *Project on Standards for Criminal Justice* (1974): Standards relating to the Administration of Criminal Justice.
12. Dimbleby Lecture 1973.
13. Michael Zander: 'Legal Advice and Criminal Appeals' (1972) Crim LR 155.
14. Bottoms and McClean: *Defendants in the Criminal Process* (1976).
15. Devlin Report to the Home Secretary on Evidence of Identification in Criminal Cases (April 1976), ch. 2.
16. *Listener* 2 September 1976.
17. Defendants themselves are aware of the difference: 'As I saw neither the solicitors or barrister before the case except for a very brief moment I have a pretty dim view of legal advice on legal aid.' 'He wanted the case over as quickly as possible. My case was trivial to him. He had only been briefed twenty minutes on full case which was inadequate. The whole legal service in my opinion was very poor.' (See notes 13 and 14.)
18. *R v. Turner* (1970) 2 QB 321 *per* Lord Parker CJ.
19. *R v. Cain* (1976) Crim LR 464, and subsequent Practice Direction.
20. Details of a number of cases in which it is alleged that barristers improperly persuaded their clients to plead guilty are published in Baldwin and McConville: *Negotiated Justice*. A leak of their findings provoked a sharp reaction from the Bar: *The Times* 10 May 1977, and correspondence on 12 May and 17 May 1977.
21. Bar Council *Annual Statement* 1933 p. 9.
22. Bar Council *Annual Statement* 1971–2 p. 33.
23. The general belief is that Kenealy suffered these penalties because of his behaviour during the second Tichborne trial; but in fact it was his behaviour after the trial, as journalist and newspaper editor, that brought his career at the Bar so dramatically to an end: 90 LQR 463.
24. *The Times* 27 September 1957.

25. *R v. McFadden:* judgment of Court of Appeal (unreported) delivered on 10 December 1975.
26. *The Times* 20 March 1975.
27. Bar Council *Annual Statement* 1935 p. 6.
28. 'Evidence in Criminal Cases' (1973): Memorandum of the Criminal Bar Association to the Bar Council on the C.L.R.C.'s Eleventh Report (Cmnd 4991).

7: Women at the Bar
1. Lincoln's Inn *The Black Books* 175–8.
2. *Pension Book of Gray's Inn* (ed. R. J. Fletcher), 1903.
3. Source: Bar Council *Annual Statements.*
4. Source: 1976 *Law List.*
5. The statutory qualification before a barrister is eligible for appointment as a High Court judge, Circuit judge or Recorder is 10 years' standing; but in practice almost no one of less than 15 years' call is ever considered for such an appointment.
6. These figures should not be confused with success rates. The proportions of men and women who hold *or will hold* judicial office during their careers are considerably greater than the figures given in the text: see the first section of chapter 5, and footnote 11 to that chapter (which considers only full-time appointments and thus excludes Recorders). The proportions of men and women of over 15 years' call who held full-time judicial appointments in 1976 were 29% and $12\frac{1}{2}$% respectively. These percentages and those in the text are based on the fact that in 1976 there were 370 Q.C.s and 750 juniors (of both sexes) of over 15 years' call, among whom four of the Q.C.s and 66 of the juniors were women.
7. Source: Senate *Annual Statement* 1975–6; Inns of Court records.
8. The total number of those who started in practice each year is shown in column 6; separate figures for men and women are not available. The ratio between col. 6 and col. 5 indicates the extent to which the figures in cols 3 and 4 should be grossed up in order to obtain some idea of the actual numbers of each sex who started in practice each year. This technique understates the success rate of men, because the proportion of men to women who cease practice each year is almost certainly greater than the proportion who start.
9. Senate submission no. 5 to the Royal Commission, on behalf of the Bar Students Working Party (December 1976) p. 27.
10. Bar Council Special Committee on Women's Careers: unpublished survey results.
11. Source: *Law List* 1967, 1972 and 1975.
12. 28 July 1976 p. 635.
13. The 1972 survey of women barristers showed that 50% of the respondents were single or divorced. Of those who were married two-thirds had had children, but one-third had not come to the Bar until after raising a family.

14. See note 10, *supra*. The percentages add up to more than 100% because respondents with mixed practices were permitted to tick more than one item.
15. *Supplementary Memorandum to the Monopolies Commission*, February 1969.
16. Abel-Smith & Stevens: *Lawyers and the Courts* p. 432.
17. *Times* Law Report 21 November 1975, commented on in a letter from Ms Katherine Gieve and others, *The Times* 29 November 1975.
18. *Supplementary Memorandum* (February 1969) p. 4.
19. Before barristers indignantly protest they would do well to consider the survey of divorce petitioners reported in 38 *Modern Law Review* 609. A typical comment was: 'I suppose it's nice for the solicitors [i.e. barristers] because they like to strut about and look cocky, don't they? Like peacocks they were – with their wigs and gowns – all strutting about' (p. 613). They might also pay heed to the words of the late Sir Morris Finer: 'The lawyer's consciousness of his inner rectitude – a phenomenon which afflicts the Bar more peculiarly than it does the solicitor's branch – is no substitute. It is apt, indeed, to communicate itself to the lay public as an aloofness, or worse still, a pomposity, which they find hard to bear.'
20. *Supplementary Memorandum* (Feb. 1969) p. 15.
21. The committee is mentioned as a subcommittee of the Bar Committee in the first *Annual Statement* of the Senate, for 1974–5 (p. 17), and receives no mention in the *Annual Statement* 1975–6.
22. *Notes for Guidance on Dress in Court*, published by the Bar Council in its *Annual Statement* 1973–4 p. 52.
23. *Supplementary Memorandum* (Feb. 1969) pp. 15–16.
24. 28 July 1976 p. 635.

8: Independence and Fusion

1. 26th Legal Aid Annual Reports (1975–6) Appendix 13. This figure exceeds the number of barristers then in practice because some of the fees were paid to barristers who had retired.
2. *Ibid*. Total payments for civil work and for criminal legally aided work in the magistrates' court where separate counsel was authorized amounted to £3 million. Mr Cyril Glasser of the Lord Chancellor's Advisory Committee kindly confirmed that the value of the latter item was £470,000 (Appendix 12), so that civil legal aid alone yielded £2·525 million to the Bar in 1975–6.
3. 367 barristers (10% of the Bar) earned more than £2000; while 75% of the Bar (2888 barristers) received less than £1000 from civil legal aid.
4. Bar Council *Annual Statement* 1971–2 p. 15.
5. Bar Council *Survey of Income at the Bar* (Inbucon, 1977) Tables 5 and 6.

6. *Judicial Statistics* 1975 (Cmnd 6634) Table G 6.
7. 26th Legal Aid Annual Reports (1975–6) Appendices 4 and 11. Appendix 11 shows the average cost of legal aid bills paid in High Court and County Court matrimonial proceedings in 1975–6 was £182.
8. *Hansard* HL deb. 15 June 1976 cols 1225–7.
9. 26th Legal Aid Annual Reports (1975–6) Appendix 13.
10. 'Judicial Hearings of Undefended Divorce Petitions' 38 Modn LR 609 (Nov. 1975).
11. The brief fee in legal aid undefended cases in 1976 was £12, and the fixed fee for drafting a petition £4.50; in 1975–6 96,000 petitioners were granted legal aid for High Court and County Court matrimonial proceedings. If half this number were represented by counsel at the hearing and one-quarter had their petitions drafted by counsel then the Bar would have received £615,000 from this source in 1975–6.
12. In 1975–6 the cost to public funds of lawyers' fees for proceedings in the Crown Court was £29 million (£17½ million for defence legal aid and £11½ million prosecution costs): *Supply Estimates* 1976–7 (HC 276) Class IX pp. 8, 16; reproduced by Michael Zander in *New Law Journal* 26 August 1976 p. 871. The only study of these costs showed that barristers and solicitors take roughly half the total each: Michael Zander, 'Costs in Crown Courts' 1976 Crim LR 5 at p. 34. As for work in the magistrates' courts, criminal legal aid in 1975–6 was estimated to amount to £14½ million, and prosecution costs paid out of central funds £2½ million. Solicitors tend to appear before magistrates more often than barristers, and separate legal aid certificates for counsel are seldom issued; so that of the £17 million available it is unlikely that the Bar received more than £5 million, and quite possibly less.
13. 1976 *Criminal Statistics*.
14. The Legal Aid in Criminal Proceedings (Fees and Expenses) Regulations 1968 (SI 1968 no. 1230).
15. The Taxation of Costs in the Crown Court (BM 72). Although issued in 1972, the Tables in BM 72 are based on the scales in operation at the Old Bailey in 1971.
16. Michael Zander 1976 Crim LR 5 at pp. 21–2. The average brief fee for the prosecution in contested cases in first- and second-tier courts was £83 and for the defence £71.
17. *The Times* 22 January 1977. In June 1977 the Regulations were amended to make it clear that inflation on its own cannot constitute an 'exceptional circumstance'.
18. This section draws heavily on Michael Zander's article 'Independence of the Legal Profession – What does it mean?' in the *Law Society's Gazette* 22 September 1976 p. 758.
19. Señate *Annual Statement* 1974–5 pp. 41–2.
20. Boulton: *Conduct and Etiquette at the Bar* (6th edn.) p. 69.
21. Quoted by Michael Zander: see note 18.

22. For an extremely thorough and interesting history of the fusion debate in the nineteenth century, see J. R. Forbes 'Division of the Profession: Ancient or Scientific?' in the *Law Society's Gazette* 26 January 1977. His conclusion is that: 'Division, then, is chiefly a 19th-century creation which enabled solicitors, with the acquiescence of the Bar, to become a second legal profession – upon condition that judgeships, advocacy and the historic status of the Bar should remain inviolate. Division is not a division within one legal profession, but a line of demarcation between the old legal profession and the new. It is a delicate balance of the interests of two professions.'
23. *Sunday Times* 17 November 1974 p. 13.
24. *Law Society's Gazette* 24 November 1976 p. 979.
25. For an account of the Bar's side of these negotiations, see Bar Council *Annual Statements* 1971–2 p. 18, 1972–3 pp. 15–16.
26. See Abel-Smith & Stevens: *Lawyers and the Courts* pp. 33–7, 48, 82–3, 92, 234.
27. *Ibid.* p. 222.
28. Bar Council *Bulletin* no. 19 (June 1965) p. 2.
29. The terms of the settlement are contained in the report of the Joint Committee of the Bar Council and the Law Society on Counsel's Fees and Related Subjects (April 1967).
30. Boulton *op. cit.* (6th edn.) pp. 11–13.
31. *Ibid* pp. 12–14.
32. Bar Council *Annual Statement* 1971–2 pp. 25–7.
33. See note 23.
34. *New Law Journal* 7 November 1974 p. 1033.
35. *Report to the Victorian Bar Council on the Case for the Continuance of a separate Bar* (8 November 1973). It is interesting to note also that 'The Circuit system and the chambers and clerk system as practised in England have no counterpart in Victoria' (para. 5).
36. *Ibid.* para. 11. See also unpublished report on *The Bar in Western Australia* (1961) p. 1.
37. Letter by Brian Reid to *Law Society's Gazette* 31 March 1976.

9: *A Look into the Future*
1. *Royal Commission on Civil Liability and Compensation for Personal Injury*, Cmnd 7054 (March 1978).
2. See also T. G. Ison, *The Forensic Lottery* (1967); P. S. Atiyah, *Accidents, Compensation and the Law*; Society of Labour lawyers, *Accidents at work: compensation for all* (1974); JUSTICE report, *No Fault on the Roads* (1974).
3. *Report of the Interdepartmental Committee on the Distribution of Criminal Business between the Crown Court and Magistrates' Courts*, Cmnd 6323 (November 1975).
4. *Supply Estimates* 1976–7 (HC 276) Class IX pp. 8, 16; reproduced by Michael Zander in *New Law Journal* 26 August 1976 p. 871.

5. *Judicial Statistics* 1975 (Cmnd 6634) p. 98. The amount of time spent by barristers on civil work is of course much greater because a higher proportion of civil work is advisory or is devoted to cases which never come to trial.
6. *The Times* 26 January 1976.
7. White Paper on Public Expenditure to 1979/80 (Cmnd 6393) p. 79.

BIBLIOGRAPHY

Books
Abel-Smith, B. & Stevens, R. *Lawyers and the Courts* (Heinemann, 1967)
  In Search of Justice (Allen Lane, 1968)
Abel-Smith, B., Zander, M. & Brooke, R. *Legal Problems and the Citizen* (Heinemann, 1975)
Aubert, V. (ed). *The Sociology of Law* (Penguin, 1969)
B.B.C. *What's Wrong with the Law?* (1970)
Bankowski, Z. & Mungham, G. *Images of Law* (Routledge & Kegan Paul, 1976)
Baldwin & McConville. *Negotiated Justice* (1977)
Barber, D. & Gordon, G. *Members of the Jury* (Wildwood House, 1976)
Bottoms, A. E. & McClean, J. D. *Defendants in the Criminal Process* (1976)
Boulton, W. W. *Conduct and Etiquette at the Bar* (Butterworths, 1975)
Bridges, Suffrin, Whetton & White. *Legal Services in Birmingham* (1975)
Carr-Saunders & Wilson. *The Professions* (Oxford, 1933)
Cecil, H. *Tipping the Scales* (Hutchinson, 1964)
  Brief to Counsel (Michael Joseph, 1972)
Disney, J., Basten, J., Redmond, P. & Ross, S. *Lawyers* (Law Book Co. of Australia, 1977)
Goodman, Lord. *Not for the Record* (Deutsch, 1972)
Harvey, C. P. *The Advocate's Devil* (Stevens, 1958)
Holdsworth. *A History of English Law* (Methuen, 1930s)
Jackson, R. M. *The Machinery of Justice in England* (Cambridge, 1972)
Johnstone, Q. & Hopson, D. *Lawyers and their Work* (Bobbs-Merrill, 1967)
Joseph, M. *The Conveyancing Fraud* (Michael Joseph, 1976)
The Law List (Stevens)
Lincoln, G. *No Moaning of the Bar* (Geoffrey Bles, 1957)
Marjoribanks. *The Life of Sir Edward Marshall Hall* (Gollancz, 1929)
Megarry, R. E. *Lawyer and Litigant in England* (Stevens, 1962)
Parris, J. *Under my Wig* (London, 1961)
Prest, W. R. *The Inns of Court 1590-1640* (Longmans, 1972)
Scarman, Sir L. *English Law – The New Dimension* (Stevens, 1974)
Shetreet, S. *Judges on Trial* (O.U.P., 1976)
Zander, M. *Lawyers and the Public Interest* (Weidenfeld & Nicolson, 1968)

Reports and Pamphlets
Bar Council Reports
Annual Statements 1894-1974
Bulletins nos. 1-41
A Career at the Bar (1972, revised 1974)
The Machinery of Fee Collection (1974)
Report of the Joint Committee with the Law Society on Counsel's Fees and Related Subjects (April 1967)
Report of the Special Committee on Partnerships (1969)
Report and Minority Report of the Special Committee on the Silk System (1970)
Submission to the Monopolies Commission (1968)
Supplementary Memorandum of Evidence to the Monopolies Commission (1969)
Survey of Income at the Bar (Inbucon, 1977)
Young Barristers' Committee. *Note on Pupillage and Tenancies* (1972)
   Report on the financial viability of young members of the Bar during the first three years of practice (1976)
Beeching Report on Assizes and Quarter Sessions (Cmnd 4153, 1969)
Bell, K. *Research Study on Supplementary Benefit Appeal Tribunals* (H.M.S.O., 1975)
Criminal Statistics 1975, 1976
Criminal Law Revision Committee. *Eleventh Report on Evidence* (Cmnd 4991, 1972)
Consumer Council. *Justice out of Reach* (1970)
Denning Report on Legal Education for Students from Africa (Cmnd 1255, 1961)
Devlin Report on Evidence of Identification in Criminal Cases (H.C. 338, 1976)
Evershed Report on Supreme Court Practice and Procedure (Cmnd 8878, 1953)
Home Office. *Consultative Working Paper on Judicial Training* (1976)
James Report on the Distribution of Criminal Business between the Crown Court and Magistrates' Courts (Cmnd 6323, 1975)
Judicial Statistics 1975 (Cmnd 6634)
JUSTICE. *Complaints against Lawyers* (Charles Knight, 1970)
  Going to Law – A Critique of English Civil Procedure (Stevens, 1974)
  Report on the Prosecution Process in England and Wales (1970)
  Report on Subcommittee on the Judiciary (Stevens, 1972)
Legal Action Group. *Legal Services for the Future* (1973)
  Representation before Tribunals (1974)
Megarry, R. E. *Inns Ancient and Modern* (Selden Society, 1972)
Monopolies Commission Report on Professional Services (Cmnd 4463, 1970)
Monopolies Commission. *Barristers' Services* – report on the two counsel rule (H.C. 512, July 1976)
Ormrod Report on Legal Education (Cmnd 4595, 1971)
Prices and Incomes Board. *Remuneration of Solicitors* (Cmnd 3529, 1968) (subsequent reports: Cmnd 4217, 1969; Cmnd 4624, 1971)
Lord Salmon. *Some Thoughts on the Traditions of the English Bar* (Middle Temple, 1964)

Reports of the Senate of the Four Inns of Court
Annual Statements 1966-1974

Coldstream Report on a Scheme for Coordinating the activities of the four Inns in assisting pupils to find places (April 1973)
Pearce Committee. First Interim Report on the Organisation of our Profession (1972)
  Second Interim Report – Amended Scheme for the Organisation of our Profession (May 1973)

Reports of the Senate of the Inns of Court and the Bar
Annual Statements 1974-1976
Submission to the Monopolies Commission on the Two Counsel Rule (December 1974)
Supplementary Submission to the Monopolies Commission (January 1975)
Submissions to the Royal Commission on Legal Services (1976-1977)
Wilmers Report on the admission, organisation, conditions and needs of pupils (1975)
Society of Conservative Lawyers. *Rough Justice* (1968)
Society of Labour Lawyers. *Justice for All* (Fabian Research Series, 1968)
  Legal Education (Fabian Research Series 276, 1969)
  Accidents at Work – Compensation for All (1974)
Review Body on Top Salaries. Report no 6 (Cmnd 5846, 1974)
Streatfield Report on the Business of the Criminal Courts (Cmnd 1289, 1961)
Victorian Bar Council. *Report on the case for the continuance of a separate Bar* (1973)

Articles
Arthurs, H. W. 'Authority, Accountability and Democracy in the Government of the Ontario Legal Profession' (1971) 49 *Canadian Bar Review* 1
'Barrister's Diary'. *Guardian Gazette, passim*
Cheeld, D. 'The Rise of an Angry Young Woman' *Law Society's Gazette* 28 July 1976 p. 635
Clarkson, G., Q.C. 'The Bar in Western Australia' (unpublished, 1966)
Cowper, F. 'Dining in Hall' (1964) 235 *Law Times* 135
Elston, E., Fuller, J., Murch, M.,'Judicial Hearings of Undefended Divorce Petitions' (1975) 38 *Modern Law Review* 609
Forbes, J. R., 'Division of the Profession: Ancient or Scientific?' *Law Society's Gazette* 26 January 1977 p. 67
Gardiner, Lord. 'The Mystery of Silk' (unpublished, April 1969)
  'Two Lawyers or One' 23 *Current Legal Problems* 1
Gower, L. C. B. review of Megarry's *Lawyer and Litigant in England* in 12 *International and Comparative Law Quarterly* 1079 (July 1963)
Knightley, P. 'How the Lawyers' Inns keep competition out' *Sunday Times* 1 Feb. 1976
Leggatt, A., Q.C. 'Why Fusion is a consummation not to be wished' *Law Society's Gazette* 24 November 1976 p. 978
McLaren, I., 'Barristers' Fees' *New Law Journal* 2 December 1976 p. 1180
O'Higgins, P. & Partington, M. 'Industrial Conflict: Judicial Attitudes' (1969) 32 *Modern Law Review* 53
Partington, M. 'Putting Law into Perspective' *The Times Higher Educational Supplement* 25 February 1977
Page, B. & Knightley, P. 'The Huge Cost of Going to Law' *Sunday Times* 10 Nov. 1974
Podium. 'The Bar 30 Years On' *Law Society's Gazette* 27 April 1977
Purpoole, P. 'The Federated Inns' *New Law Journal* 20 June 1974

Rees, W. 'A Critique of the Finals Course given by the CLE' *LAG Bulletin* (November 1973 p. 242)
Reynolds, B. 'Note on Devilling' (unpublished)
'Senate and Bar News'. *Guardian Gazette, passim*
Webster, P.,Q.C. 'Lawyers and Social Welfare Law' *Law Society's Gazette* 31 March 1976 p. 278
Weightman, G. 'Up against the Law' *New Society* 10 June 1976
Williams, R. 'Fusion – An Outsider's View' *Law Society's Gazette* 30 March 1977 p. 278
Wilson, J. F. 'A Survey of Legal Education in the United Kingdom' (June 1966) *Journal of the Society of Public Teachers of Law* p. 1
  'A Second Survey of legal education in the United Kingdom' (July 1975) JSPTL p. 239
Young, H. 'The Bench – Too Quiet for Too Long' *Sunday Times* 5 October 1975
Zander, M. 'The Eating of Dinners – Can the Inns of Court afford Reform?' (1965) 8 *The Lawyer* 21
  'Democracy and the Legal Profession' (Sept. 1966) *Law Guardian* 17
  'The unused Rent Acts' *New Society* 12 September 1968
  'Legal Advice and Criminal Appeals' (1972) *Criminal Law Review* 155
  'Unrepresented Defendants in Magistrates' Courts' (1972) 122 *New Law Journal* 1040
  'Costs of Litigation – A study in the Queen's Bench Division' *Law Society's Gazette* 25 June 1975 p. 679
  'Costs in Crown Courts – A study of Lawyers' Fees paid out of public funds' (January 1976) Crim LR 5
  'New Challenges for Lawyers' *The Listener* 4 March 1976
  'Whatever happened to the Law Society's 1964 criticisms of the Bar?' (1976) 120 *Solicitor's Journal* 642, 654
  'State of Knowledge about the Legal Profession I-XI' *New Law Journal* 12 August – 21 October 1976
  'Independence of the Legal Profession – What does it mean?'*Law Society's Gazette* 22 September 1976 p. 758
  'Why the Royal Commission is likely to recommend reform of the divided profession' *Law Society's Gazette* 27 October 1976 p. 882

INDEX

Abel-Smith, Professor Brian, 49
Accommodation Committee of the Senate, 58
  of Barristers, 35-6, 56-9
Accounts, Inns of Court, 45, 53
Acts of Parliament, 67; Amalgamation Act (1891), 176; Civil Evidence Act (1968), 31; Courts Act (1971), 192, 183, 187; Divorce Reform Act (1919) 149; (1969), 164, 180; Judicature Act (1873), 43; Landlord and Tenant Act (1954), 46; Rent Act (1974) 58, 181; Sex Discrimination Act (1975), 151; Sex Disqualification (Removal) Act (1919), 149
Admiralty Bar, 28; Law, 128
Advertising, restrictions on, 34
Advisory Committee on Legal Education, 77
Advocacy, 18-19
Advocates, 19
  see also Barristers
Africa, 74
Amalgamation Act (1891), 176
American Bar Association, 78, 138, 146, 177
Angry Brigade trial, 134
Annual Statement of the Bar Council, 159
Apprenticeship, 20, 82-98
Articled clerks, 92, 94
Articles, 83
Ashley, Jack, 35
Assizes and Quarter Sessions 186
Atkin, Lord, 22
Attorney-General, 25, 34-5, 41-2, 64, 115, 135-6
Audience rights, 171-2
Australia, 89, 108, 123, 129, 175-7
Awards Committee, 151

Bail, Counsel standing as surety for, 142
Bar, the, Called to, 10, 20, 37; Committee, 19, 32-3; Council, 19, 32-3; Division, 136-8; Fusion, 169-78; Income, 18, 100, 163; Legal education, attitude to, 69, 80;
  Protection of barristers, 19, 118-9; Pupillage, 82-98; Recruitment, 36-7; Separation from Inns, 61-7; Size of, 187; Students, 47-52, 73-5, see also American bar, Criminal bar
Bar Council, 63, 83, 86, 92, 95-6, 98-100, 110, 11-14, 120, 122, 129, 134, 143-4, 153, 155, 158-9 163, 167, 172-3, 186
Bar Council's Special Committee on Women's Careers, 152, 158-61
Bar Exam, 20, 36-7, 48-9, 70-1
Barristers, Accommodation, 35-7; Attitude of detachment, 142-3; Background, 73-4; Careers, 17, 20-7; Criminal cases, 131, 139; Divorce, 165; Fees to Inns, 48-9; Functions, 17-19; Fusion with solicitors, 169-78; Governors of Inns, 66; Incomes, 18, 27, 35, 99-104; Law Courses, 78-81; Membership Inns, 18, 38-9, 45; Pupillage, 69, 83-98; Recruitment, 35; Rent, 54-6; Salary, 167-9; Space, 58; Women, 150-3, 157
Barristers' Clerks' Association, 116-17, 134
Barrister's Diary, 136
Bar Students Working Party, 72-3, 75-6, 91
Beeching, Lord, 183, 187
Belfast, 122
Bench, the, 40, 60, 62, 77, 137, 186, 189-90

Benchers, 20, 33, 38, 40-5, 47-8, 52, 54-5, 59-65, 148
Berkshire, 157
Bills, reform of Inns, 41-2
Birmingham, 5
Bethell, Sir Richard, 41
Black Books, 39-40
Black students, 75, 153, 160
Book-keeping, 107, 116-17
Boyle Review Body on Doctors' and Dentists' Remuneration, 100
Brady, Ian, 133
Briefs, 21-3, 119-22, 172-3

Cab rank rule, 133, 166
Cairns, Lord, 42, 64-5
Cambridge, 50, 53, 65-7 71, 73, 78-9, 91-2
Canada, 129, 170, 177
Capital Transfer Tax, 181
Cardiff University, 79
Caulfield, Mr Justice, 157
Cave, Bertha, 149
Chairmen of Tribunals, 103
Chambers, Accommodation in, 187; Efficiency, 116; Organization of, 26; Reputation of, 22; Seat in, 20-1; Specialization, 27
Chancery Lane, 43
Chancery Law, 23, 27-8, 101, 131, 154, 181
Chancery Motions Court, 182-3
Chancery Registrars, 24
Charity Commissioners, 45-7
Charity status, 63
Cheeld, Diana, 161
Chief Taxing Master, 166
Circuit Bench, 25, 184, 188
Circuit Judges, 23-5, 89, 103, 172, 185
Circuits, 101, 134-5, 142, 157
City, the, 28, 57-8, 94
City of London Court, 45
Civil Evidence Act (1968), 31
Civil Law, 131, 163-5, 189
Civil Service, 25, 82-3, 103
Clarke Q.C., Judge, 132
Clerks, 21-2, 26, 99, 104-29, 139, 154-6, 161, 174
Client, lay, access to, 18, 155
Professional, 172-4
Clifford's Inn Case, 45, 47
Clifford, Lord, 45
Coldstream, Sir George, 84
College of Law, 75
Colleges of Further Education, 69
Committee of Young Barristers, 63
Commissioner of Metropolitan Police 136

Committee on Legal Education for African students, 48
Commission of Inquiry into Inns of Court, 41, 44
Common Law Commissioners, 42, 67
Commonwealth countries, legal systems, 17
Companies Court, 182
Company law, 27, 128
Confait, Maxwell, case, 136
Contract cases, 27
Conveyancing, 18-19
Cost of pupillage, 21, 26-7, 37, 90-5
Council of Legal Education, 20, 41, 49, 69, 71-3, 75-7, 81
County Courts, 18, 71, 78, 87, 89, 129, 157, 163, 165, 171, 180-3, 188
County Court Registrars, 25
Court of Appeal, 24, 46, 69, 144, 171
see also City of London Court, County Court, Crown Court, High Court, Mayor's Court, Superior Court
Courts Act (1971), 172, 183, 187
Crime, 21, 27, 102, 153-4, 164, 184-6, 189
Criminal Bar, 131-47, 163, 167-8
Criminal Law Bill, 183
Criminal Law Revision Committee's Eleventh Report, 146
Criminal trial, 133
Criminology, 79
Cross, Lord, 77
Crown Court, 19, 34, 101, 109, 110, 113, 129, 131, 136; 165-7, 171-2, 183, 185, 188
Custody of children, 164
Customs and Excise, 137

Defendants, attitudes to representation, 139-41
Defending counsel, 137-47
Denning, Lord, 48; Report, 50
Devereux Chambers, 54
Devilling, 89, 92
Dining in Hall, 20, 49-52
Diplock, Lord, 31
Director of Public Prosecutions, 135
Discrimination, against minorities, 160; against students, 86; against women, 149-61
Divorce, 27, 109, 154, 163-4, 167
see also Matrimonial work
Divorce Reform Act (1969), 164, 180
Donaldson, Sir John, 66
Dougherty, Luke, 140-1
Drake, Sir Francis, 40
Dress, 159-60
see also Gowns, Wigs

INDEX

Dublin, 122
Durham Crown Court, 140

Economy, effect of, 184-5
Education, legal, 69-81
Erskine, John, 133
Estate Duty, 181
Europe, 20, 77, 94, 129, 174
European Economic Community, 70, 174
European Law, 79
Evershed Committee, 114-15
Exams, bar, 20, 36-7, 48-9, 70
Expenses, law student's, 76

Family Division of the High Court, 180, 183; Settlements, 27
Fees, Admission and Call, 48-9; Brief, 110-14; for pupillage, 21, 26-7, 37, 90-5; Inn, 20, 48-9; Public funds, 163-7; Q.C.'s, 24; Suing for, 29-30; *see also* Barristers, Solicitors
Fee-note, 107
Finance for students, 75-6
Finer, Sir Morris, 31
Foreign Office, 25
France, 94
Frobisher, Sir Martin, 40
Fusion of the professions, 169-78, 190

General Fund of Inns, 49
General School of Law, 42
Golden Hind, 40
Goodman, Lord, 31-2, 170
Government posts, 25
Gray's Inn, 18, 38-9, 44-5, 47, 53, 55-7, 59, 63-4, 149, 157
'Groups', 122
Guilds, medieval, 38-9

Hailsham, Lord, 184
Haldane Commission, 90
Hall of Inns of Court, 20, 49-52
Halsbury's Laws, 46, 59
Harmsworth Scholarship fund, 53
Havers, Sir Michael, Q.C., 115
Hawkins, Sir Richard, 40
Head of Chambers, 96, 151-3, 155, 161
Heald, Sir Lionel, Q.C., 63
Herbert, A. P., 158
High Court, 19, 24, 29, 34, 59, 71, 87, 132, 141, 149, 163, 165, 171-2, 180, 183
High Court Judges, 23-4, 34, 89, 103, 184
Hindley, Myra, 133
Holdsworth, 58
Home Office, 166
Home Secretary, 136, 143, 166

House of Commons, 41-2; Library, 53, 64
House of Lords, 19, 24, 42, 171
Hull University, 91-2
Human nature, understanding of, 132
Independence of the Bar, 167
Inland Revenue, 46, 137
Inland Revenue Statistics, 99-100
Inner Temple, 38-9, 45-7, 59, 63-4, 149
Inn Pupillage Committees, 84-6
Inns of Court, 17; Admission, 20; Barristers, 20; Block reforms, 31; Constitution, 20; Finances, 53-6; Future of, 65-7; Government of, 59-65; History of, 39-44; Importance of, 38-9; Landlords, 56-60, 65; Members, relationship with, 44-7; Origins, 18; Overcrowded, 35; Pupillage, 86; Space, 33-4; Students, 47-52; Women, 148-50; *see also* Gray's Inn, Inner Temple, Lincoln's Inn, Middle Temple
Inns of Court Property Company, 62-3
Inns of Court School of Law, 69
In Search of Justice, 49
Ireland, 108, 122, 143
Irish Republican Army trials, 134, 143-4

Jackson, Professor R. M., 71
James I, 47
James Committee, 183
Judicature Act (1873), 43
Judges, 19, 34, 38, 40-4, 59, 66-7, 86, 89, 121, 143-4, 149-50, 154, 167, 183-4; *see also* High Court Judges
Judges Advocate General, 25
Juniors, 23-4; *see also* Barristers
Jury trial, 130-2
JUSTICE, 140, 146

Keeping terms, 41, 49-52
Kenealy, Dr Q. C., 143
Kenya, 50
King's Counsel, 42

Labour law, 70
Lady Chatterley case, 29
Landlord and Tenant Act (1954), 46
Landlord and tenant law, 27, 181
Land law, 27
Latin, legal pronunciation, 29
Law Centres, 138
Law Commission, 146
Law Courts, 28, 109, 116
Law List, 61
Law reform, 179-83
Law Society, 62, 77, 113, 120-2, 153, 166, 170, 172-3, 175-6

Law Society's Gazette, 136, 152, 161
Lawton, Lord Justice, 77
Leader, 23; see also Barristers
Legal Advisers Department, 25
Legal Aid, 35, 109, 131, 153, 163-9, 182, 184
Legal Aid Fund, 131-2, 142, 184
Legal education, 69-81; see also Bar exam, Council of Legal Education
Legal system, changes in, 183-4
Leggatt, Andrew, Q.C., 170-1
Levin, Mr Bernard, 144
Libel law, 28, 177
Libraries of Inns of Court, 65
Litigation, increase in, 35
Lincoln Crown Court, 141
Lincoln's Inn, 18, 27-8, 38-9, 44, 53-5, 59, 61, 63, 148
Lindley, Lord, 43
London, 20, 33
London Borough of Camden, 57
London University, 50, 71
Lord Chancellor, 19, 25-6, 42, 59, 69, 134, 164-6, 184
Lord Chief Justice, 29
Lords Justices, 24
Lords of Appeal, 24
Lyon, 94

Madame Tussaud's, 143
Magistrates' courts, 18, 21, 71, 78, 87, 89, 110, 131-2, 138, 163, 171, 183
Maintenance, 164
Manchester, 50
Mark, Sir Robert, 138
Marshal to High Court Judge, 89
Masters of the Bench, 38; see also Benchers
Masters of the Supreme Court, 25, 88
Matrimonial work, 27, 180
Mayor's Court, 45
Megarry, Sir Robert, 52, 105-6
Meehan, Patrick, 145
Metropolitan police, 138
Middle Temple, 38-40, 45, 47, 53-7, 60-1, 63, 65
Midland Circuit, 157
Miscarriages of Justice, 145
Monopolies Commission, 34, 158, 169, 180
Moots, 39-40

Napier, J., Q.C., 41
Napley, Sir David, 170, 175
National Council for Civil Liberties, 146.
National Insurance Commissioners, 25
National Legal Service, 167
Neill, Patrick, Q.C., 170-1, 174

New Zealand, 170, 181
Nigeria, 50
No-fault liability, 181-2
Northern Circuit, 156
Northern Ireland, 50
Notes of Guidance (1972), 131

Obscenity trials, 138
Office managers, 21, 106-8; see also Clerks
Office of Manpower Economics, 103
Old Bailey, 136-7
Ormrod, (Sir Roger), Report, 50-2, 69-73, 76-7, 81, 87-93
Overseas practice rules, 174; Students, 74-5, 83
Oxford, 53, 65-7, 71, 73, 78-9, 92

Paine, Tom, 133
Palmer, Sir Roundell, 64-5
Pankhurst, Christabel, 149
Parker, Roger, Q.C., 46
Parliament, 67, 145, 149; see also Acts of Parliament
Parliamentary Counsel's office, 25
Partnership, 18, 21, 26, 124-9, 173-4
Patent law, 28, 154
Payment for pupils, 92-5
Pearce Committee, 33, 44-5, 47, 53, 55, 58, 61-4, 66
Pearson, Lord, 181-2
Pensions, 24, 103-4, 166
Personal appearance by litigants, 19
Personal injury claims, 27, 109, 110
Personal injuries law, 181-2, 185
'Pink Form' Scheme, 113
Planning law, 154, 176
Plea bargaining, 141-2
Pleaders, 17
Police, metropolitan, 138
Pollock, Sir Frederick, 20
Prejudice, effect of, 157-8
Probate, 18
Procedural changes in the law, 182-3
Professional Conduct Committee, 142
Profits, 21
Prosecuting counsel, 134-6
Pupillage, 20-3, 36, 41, 69, 74-5, 82-98, 151, 186

Queen's Bench Division, 110, 181
Queen's Bench Masters, 24
Queen's Counsel, 23, 26, 29, 61, 99-101, 103, 105-6, 110-12, 131-2, 134, 151, 166

Rawlinson, Sir Peter, 163, 167
Recorder, 25, 184-5, 188
Recruitment of barristers, 35-6

INDEX

Refreshers, 101, 110
Registrars of the Supreme Court, 25, 89
Register, central pupillage, 86, 98
Regulations (1968), 165-6
Release, 146
Rents, from Inns of Court property, 53-6, 62
Revenue law, 79, 128
Robes, 30-1
Roman law, 79
Royal Commission of the Inns of Court (1855), 45, 53
Royal Commission on Legal Service, (1976), 34-5, 73, 99, 102-3, 169-70, 172, 174, 177, 181-3, 189-90
Royal Courts, 38
Royal family, 61

Salary for barristers, 167-9
Sachs, Lord Justice, 46
Scholarships, 82
Scotland, 50, 89, 92
Scotland Yard, 137
Scottish Faculty of Advocates, 89
Scriveners, 17
Seat in chambers, 20
Selborne, Lord, 42, 64-5
Senate of the Inns of Court and the Bar, 33-4, 39, 58, 61, 63, 65, 69, 86, 116, 159, 162, 166, 170
Serjeants, 17, 42-4, 66
Sex Discrimination Act (1975), 151
Sex Disqualification (Removal) Act (1919), 149
Shakespeare, William, 40
Shawcross, Lord, 22, 37
Shipping law, 28
Silk, 23-4, 26, 43, 101, 134, 180
Social Security law, and Labour, 70
Society of Labour Lawyers, 83
Solicitor-General, 25
Solicitors, 17, 26, 30, 105, 138, 155, 157, 188-9; Access to barristers, 18; As advocates, 18; Briefs, 21-4; Circuit Court judgeships, 25; Competition of, 172; Divorce, 165; Fees, 107, 113, 118; Function, 18-19; Fusion with barristers, 169-78; High Court judgeships, 24; Incomes, 18; Member Inns of Court, 18; Recorders, 25; Separate from barristers, 18; Specialization, 18; System of legal education, 64, 77-8, 80-1, 88-9; Women, 153-4
Solicitors Acts, 34

South Africa, 89, 108, 122, 175
Specialization, 174-5, 177, 190
Standing Pupillage Committee, 84-5
Stevenson, Mr Justice Melford, 143-4
Stevens, Professor Robert, 49
Steward, 44
Stipendiary Magistrates, 25, 103
Subscriptions to the Inns, 56
Sullivan, Serjeant, 43
Superior Courts, 18-19
Supreme Court, 77-146

Tax, Law, 27-8, 154, 177, 181; Paid by Inns, 46-7
Temple Bar, 18, 27-8, 57, 134, 153, 160
Tenancy, in chambers, 21-2, 95-8, 151
Tenant, 21-2, 95-8
Terrell, Stephen, Q.C., 45
Tichborne trial, 143
The Times, 60, 63, 117, 134, 157, 170, 186
Treasury Counsel, 136
Treasurers of Inns of Court, 60, 62-3
Trial by jury, 130-2; *see also* Irish Republican Army trial, Obscenity trial
Trust of Benchers, 62
Tudor period, 40-1, 49, 59

United States, 77-9, 94, 145-6, 170, 177; *see also* American Bar Association
Universities, Content of courses, 78-9; Role of, 76-7
University of Kent at Canterbury, 79

Value Added Tax, 107
Vocational course, 89

Warwick University, 78-80
Widgery, Lord Chief Justice, 143
Wigoder Q.C., Lord, 164
Wigs, 17, 30, 159
Williams, Ivy, 149
Women, Admission to the Bar, 149-50; Barriers to entry, 150; Childbearing, 156, 160-1; Dress, 159-60; Matrimonial work, 105, 153-6; Prejudice, 156; Representation in Inn, 61; Special Committee, 158-9

Young Barristers Committee of the Bar Council 85, 91-2, 96

Zander, Michael, 101-2, 110-12, 167